Applying Communication Theory *for* Professional Life

Applying Communication Theory *for* Professional Life

A Practical Introduction

Marianne Dainton
Elaine D. Zelley
La Salle University

SAGE Publications
Thousand Oaks ▪ London ▪ New Delhi

For information:

Sage Publications, Inc.
2455 Teller Road
Thousand Oaks, California 91320
E-mail: order@sagepub.com

Sage Publications Ltd.
1 Oliver's Yard
55 City Road
London EC1Y 1SP
United Kingdom

Sage Publications India Pvt. Ltd.
B-42, Panchsheel Enclave
Post Box 4109
New Delhi 110 017 India

Printed in the United States of America

Library of Congress Cataloging-in-Publication Data

Dainton, Marianne.
Applying communication theory for professional life: A practical introduction / Marianne Dainton, Elaine D. Zelley.
p. cm.
Includes bibliographical references and index.
ISBN 0-7619-2914-2 (pbk.)
1. Communication—Philosophy. I. Zelley, Elaine D. II. Title.
P90.D245 2005
302.2'01—dc22 2004010475

06 07 10 9 8 7 6 5 4 3 2

Acquisitions Editor: Todd R. Armstrong
Editorial Assistant: Deya Saoud
Production Editor: Melanie Birdsall
Copy Editor: Elizabeth Budd
Typesetter: C&M Digitals (P) Ltd.
Proofreader: Tricia Lawrence
Cover Designer: Ravi Balasuriya

Contents

Preface

This book is designed to serve as a communication theory textbook for upper-level undergraduate and master's degree students. Although it is intended for upper-level students, we make no presumption that the students have previous knowledge or background in communication or communication theory. Rather, the text is meant to serve as a practical introduction to the topic for students who are pursuing (or are currently working in) careers in communication-related industries.

We have found that the primary challenge of instructors teaching communication theory to career-oriented students is the abstract nature of the topic; many students have difficulty seeing the relevance of communication theory in their professional lives. Accordingly, our goal for this text is to make communication theory tangible to students by explaining the theories in practical ways and by assisting students in seeing how theory can be used in professional life.

Because of these goals, the theories selected are those that have strong pragmatic value. That is, this textbook is not meant to provide a comprehensive survey of all communication theory, nor is it meant to focus only on particular contexts of communication. Instead, we have selected representative theories that have clear applicability to communication practitioners. Finally, we did not limit ourselves only to theories developed in the communication discipline because we believe that all theories that address communication—whether developed within the field are not—are important tools for communication professionals.

A central pedagogical feature of this text is the inclusion of a case study after each group of theories. As Littlejohn, Rogers, and Gray

(1996) acknowledged, case studies are an effective way of assisting career-oriented students to see the practicality and value of theory (see also Barnes, Christensen, & Hansen, 1994). Popularized by the Harvard Business School, case studies are associated with greater student engagement, more effective application of course content, and increased instructor satisfaction with the quality of classroom interaction (Wulff & Nyquist, 1999). The use of case studies is one of the most common ways to teach organizational communication (Putnam & Conrad, 1999). To our knowledge, this is the first book using case studies to teach communication theory.

Acknowledgments

We began this project with the intent of assuaging the frustrations of our students at La Salle University (and others who might have had similar frustrations). We are grateful to all of those students who have assisted us in understanding what professionals need in their higher education, and especially to Allison Burke, Laura Kanzler, Scott Mangini, Jonathan Myers, and Palmer Forbes, who allowed us to use their experiences as a loose foundation for some of the case studies. (All names and organizations listed in the case studies are pseudonyms.) In addition, we thank G. L. Forward from Point Loma University, Steven Rolston from the University of Michigan at Flint, and Wallace V. Schmidt from Rollins College for their considerable advice and wisdom for how to make the text stand out. Lastly, we acknowledge Rebecca Strawbridge Jones for editing an earlier version of the book and Olga McHugh, who assisted us with the references.

We also would like to thank La Salle University, who provided both Marianne and Elaine with summer research grants to assist with the writing of this book. In addition to the financial support, we are indebted to our colleagues in the Department of Communication, who not only serve as outstanding instructor role models, but who continue to greet our work with enthusiasm and provide us with much needed social support. In particular, both Brooks Aylor and Patrice Oppliger gave us numerous suggestions for improving the text.

Next, we thank our friends and family members for putting up with the frenzy associated with writing of this book. Both Marianne and Elaine are especially grateful to their husbands, Scott and Bryan, for serving as sounding boards and providing shoulders to cry on (figuratively, of course).

Finally, the folks at Sage have helped to make this a (relatively!) smooth process, and we particularly appreciate the assistance of Todd Armstrong and Deya Saoud.

About the Authors

Marianne Dainton (MA, PhD, The Ohio State University; BA, Villanova University) is an associate professor of communication at La Salle University in Philadelphia, where she also serves as assistant chair. She teaches communication theory, interpersonal communication, group communication, and organizational communication. Marianne's research focuses on the symbolic exchanges that facilitate relationship maintenance. She has published in *Communication Monographs,* the *Journal of Social and Personal Relationships, Family Relations,* and *Communication Quarterly,* among other places. She has also published numerous book chapters, and is the coeditor (with Daniel Canary) of the Erlbaum book *Maintaining Relationships Through Communication.*

Elaine D. Zelley (MA, PhD, The Pennsylvania State University; BA, Ursinus College) is an assistant professor of communication at La Salle University in Philadelphia. She teaches communication theory, interpersonal communication, group communication, sex and gender in communication, and communication ethics. Elaine's research also focuses broadly on the communication of relationship maintenance. She is particularly interested in women's friendships and the messages used to sustain such relationships. She has recently published in *Communication Yearbook* and has also coauthored several book chapters dealing with the topics of relationship maintenance and friendship.

1

Introduction to Communication Theory

A recent advertisement for the AT&T cellular service has a bold headline that asserts, "If only communication plans were as simple as communicating." We respectfully disagree with their assessment. Cellular communication plans may indeed be intricate, but the process of communicating is infinitely more so. Unfortunately, much of popular culture tends to minimize the challenges associated with the communication process. We all do it, all of the time. Yet one need only peruse the content of talk shows, classified ads, advice columns, and organizational performance reviews to recognize that communication skill can make or break an individual's personal and professional lives. Companies want to hire and promote people with excellent communication skills. Divorces occur because spouses believe that they "no longer communicate." Communication is perceived as a magical elixir, one that can ensure a happy long-term relationship and can guarantee organizational success. Clearly, popular culture holds paradoxical views about communication: It is easy to do yet powerful in its effects, simultaneously simple and magical.

The reality is even more complex. "Good" communication means different things to different people in different situations. Accordingly, simply adopting a set of particular skills is not going to guarantee success. Those who are genuinely good communicators are those who understand the underlying principles behind communication and are able to enact, appropriately and effectively, particular communication skills as the situation warrants. This book seeks to provide the foundation for those sorts of decisions. We focus on communication theories that can be applied in your personal and professional lives. Understanding these theories, including their underlying assumptions and the predictions that they make, can make you a more competent communicator.

❖ WHAT IS COMMUNICATION?

This text is concerned with communication theory, so it is important to be clear about the term *communication.* The everyday view of communication is quite different from the view of communication taken by communication scholars. In the business world, for example, a popular view is that communication is synonymous to information. Thus, the communication process is the flow of information from one person to another (Axley, 1984). Communication is viewed as simply one activity among many others, such as planning, controlling, and managing (Deetz, 1994). It is *what* we do in organizations.

Communication scholars, on the other hand, define communication as ***the process by which people interactively create, sustain, and manage meaning*** (Conrad & Poole, 1998). As such, communication both reflects the world and simultaneously helps to create it. Communication is not simply one more thing that happens in personal and professional life; it is the very means by which we produce our personal relationships and professional experiences—it is *how* we plan, control, manage, persuade, understand, lead, love, and so on. All of the theories presented in this book relate to the various ways in which human interaction is developed, experienced, and understood.

❖ WHAT IS THEORY?

The term *theory* is often intimidating to students. We hope that by the time you finish reading this book, you will find working with theory to be less daunting than you might have expected. The reality is that you have been working with theories of communication all of your life, even if they haven't been labeled as such. Theories simply provide an abstract understanding of the communication process (Miller, 2002). As an abstract understanding, they move beyond describing a single event by providing a means by which all such events can be understood. To illustrate, a theory of customer service can help you to understand not only the bad customer service you received from your credit card company this morning, it can also help you to understand a good customer service encounter you might have had at a restaurant last week. Moreover, it can assist your organization in training and developing customer service personnel.

At their most basic level, theories provide us with a lens by which to view the world. Think of theories as a pair of glasses. Corrective lenses allow wearers to observe more clearly, but they also impact vision in unforeseen ways. For example, they can limit the span of what you see, especially when you try to look peripherally outside the range of the frames. Similarly, lenses can also distort the things you see, making objects appear larger or smaller than they really are. You can also try on lots of pairs of glasses until you finally pick one pair that works the best for your lifestyle. Theories operate in a similar fashion. A theory can illuminate an aspect of your communication so that you understand the process much more clearly; theory also can hide things from your understanding or distort the relative importance of things.

We consider a communication theory to be ***any systematic summary about the nature of the communication process.*** Certainly, theories can do more than summarize. Other functions of theories are to focus attention on particular concepts, clarify our observations, predict communication behavior, and generate personal and social change (Littlejohn, 1999). We do not believe, however, that all of these functions are *necessary* for a systematic summary of communication processes to be considered a theory.

What does this definition mean for people in communication, business, and other professions? It means that any time you say that a communication strategy *usually* works this way at your workplace, or that a specific approach is *generally* effective with your boss, or that certain types of communication are *typical* for particular media organizations, you are in essence providing a theoretical explanation. Most of us make

Table 1.1 Three Types of Theory

Type of Theory	*Example*
Commonsense theory	• Never date someone you work with—it always ends up badly. • The squeaky wheel gets the grease. • The more incompetent you are, the higher you get promoted.
Working theory	• Audience analysis should be done prior to presenting a speech. • To get a press release published, it should be newsworthy and written in journalistic style.
Scholarly theory	• Effects of violations of expectations depend on the reward value of the violator (expectancy violations theory). • The media do not tell us what to think, but what to think about (agenda-setting theory).

these types of summary statements on a regular basis. The difference between this sort of theorizing and the theories provided in this book centers on the term *systematic* in the definition. Table 1.1 presents an overview of three types of theory.

First, the summary statements described in the table are what are known as **commonsense theories**, or theories-in-use. This type of theory often is created by an individual's own personal experiences, or such theories might reflect helpful hints that are passed on from family members, friends, or colleagues. They are useful to us and are often the basis for our decisions about how to communicate. Sometimes, however, our commonsense backfires. For example, think about common knowledge regarding deception. Most people believe that liars don't look the person they are deceiving in the eyes, yet research indicates that this is not the case (DePaulo, Stone, & Lassiter, 1985). Let's face it: If we engage in deception, we will work very hard at maintaining eye contact simply *because* we believe that liars don't make eye contact! In this case, commonsense theory is not supported by research into the phenomenon.

A second type of theory is known as **working theory.** These are generalizations made in particular professions about the best techniques for doing something. Journalists work using the "inverted pyramid" of story construction (most important information to least important information). Filmmakers operate using particular shots to invoke particular effects in the audience, so close-ups are used when a filmmaker wants the audience to place particular emphasis on the object in the close-up. Giannetti (1982), for example, describes a scene in Hitchcock's *Notorious* in which the heroine realizes she is being poisoned by her coffee, and the audience "sees" this realization through a close-up of the coffee cup. Working theories are more systematic than are commonsense theories, because they represent agreed-on ways of doing things for a particular profession. In fact, they may very well be based on scholarly theories. Such theories more closely represent guidelines for behavior rather than systematic representations. These types of theories are typically taught in content-specific courses (such as public relations, media production, or public speaking).

The type of theory we will be focusing on in this book is known as **scholarly theory.** Students often assume (incorrectly!) that because a theory is labeled as *scholarly,* it is not useful for people in business and the professions. Instead, the term scholarly indicates that the theory has undergone systematic research. Accordingly, scholarly theories provide more thorough, accurate, and abstract explanations for communication than do commonsense or working theories. The down side is that scholarly theories are typically more complex and difficult to understand than commonsense or working theories. If you are genuinely committed to improving your understanding of the communication process, however, scholarly theory will provide a strong foundation for doing so.

❖ THE THEORY–RESEARCH LINK

Although theory and research are related, we have not yet articulated the exact nature of this link, in part because there is some debate about the theory–research relationship that is akin to the classic question, which came first, the chicken or the egg? In this case, scholars disagree as to what starts the process, theory or research.

Some scholars say that research comes before theory. This approach is known as **inductive theory development.** Also known as *grounded theory,* scholars using inductive theory development believe that the best theories emerge from the results of systematic study

(Glaser & Strauss, 1967). That is, these scholars study a particular topic, and, based on the results of their research, they develop a theory; the research comes *before* the theory. If someone wanted to develop a theory about how management style affects employee performance, then that person would study management style and employee performance in great depth before proposing a theory. Preliminary theories may be proposed, but the data continue to be collected and analyzed until adding new data brings little to the researcher's understanding of the phenomenon or situation.

On the other hand, some scholars believe in **deductive theory development.** Deductive theory is generally associated with the scientific method (Reynolds, 1971). The deductive approach requires that a hypothesis, or a working theory, be developed before any research is conducted. Once the theory has been developed, the theorist then collects data to test or refine the theory (i.e., to support or reject the hypothesis). What follows is a constant set of adjustments to the theory with additional research conducted until evidence in support of the theory is overwhelming. The resulting theory is known as a **law** (Reynolds, 1971). In short, deductive theory development starts with the theory and then looks at data. As an example, a researcher might start with the idea that supportive management styles lead to increased employee performances. The researcher would then seek to support his or her theory by collecting data about those variables.

As indicated earlier, these two approaches represent different starting points to what is in essence a "chicken or the egg" type of argument. The reality is that neither approach advocates a single cycle of theorizing or research. Instead, both approaches suggest that theories are dynamic—they are modified as the data suggest, and data are reviewed to adjust the theory. Accordingly, the model in Figure 1 is the most accurate illustration of the link between theory and research. In this model, the starting points are different, but the reality of a repetitive loop between theory and research is identified.

❖ WHAT IS RESEARCH?

Thus far, we have talked about the nature of communication and the nature of theory. Next we turn our attention to the question of what

Figure 1.1 The Theory–Research Link

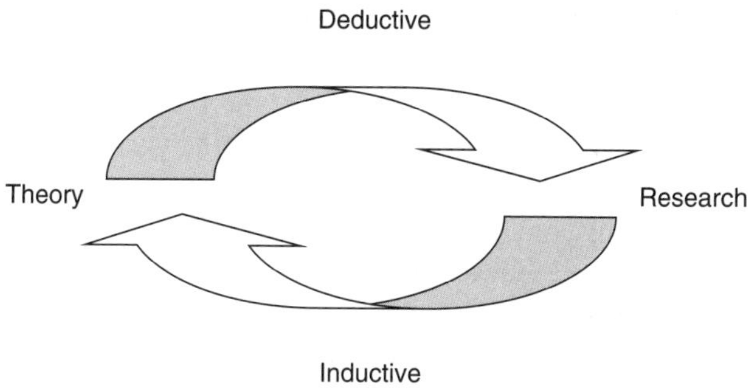

counts as research. Frey, Botan, and Kreps (2002) described research as "disciplined inquiry that involves studying something in a planned manner and reporting it so that other inquirers can potentially replicate the process if they choose" (p. 13). Accordingly, we do not mean informal types of research, such as reflections on personal experience, off-the-cuff interviews with acquaintances, or casual viewing of communication media. When we refer to **research,** we mean the methodical gathering of data as well as the careful reporting of the results of the data analysis.

Note that *how* the research is reported differentiates two categories of research. **Primary research** is research reported by the person who conducted it. It is typically published in academic journals. **Secondary research** is research reported by someone other than the person who conducted it. This is research reported in newspapers, popular or trade magazines, handbooks, and textbooks. Certainly, there is value to the dissemination of research through these media. Textbooks, for example, can summarize hundreds of pages of research in a compact and understandable fashion. Newspaper articles or news broadcasts can reach thousands of people. Trade magazines can pinpoint the readers who may benefit most from the results of the research. Regardless of whether the source is popular or academic, however, primary research is typically valued more than secondary research as a source of information; with secondary research, readers risk the chance that the writers have misunderstood or distorted the results of the research.

❖ RESEARCH METHODS IN COMMUNICATION

"The sheer volume of research we are exposed to in our daily lives is formidable and growing" (Crossen, 1994, p. 17). Even if you aren't an academic, even if your job doesn't require you to conduct research, we are all inundated with research "facts," both at work and at home. Politicians cite polls and surveys to bolster their platforms. Advertisers cite research studies that indicate their product is superior. Organizations use research to make decisions for strategic planning. Even if you never conduct a research study in your life, understanding how research is performed will help you make more informed personal and professional decisions. This section focuses on the four research methods commonly used in the development of communication theory. When reading about these methods, pay particular attention to the types of information revealed and concealed by each method. This approach will allow you to be a better consumer of research.

Experiments

When people think of "experiments," they often have flashbacks to high school chemistry classes. People are often surprised that communication scholars also use experiments, even though there isn't a Bunsen burner or beaker in sight. What makes something an experiment has nothing to do with the specific equipment involved; rather, experimentation is ultimately concerned with **causation** and **control.** It is important to emphasize that an experiment is the *only* research method that allows researchers to conclude that one thing causes another. For example, if you are interested in determining whether friendly customer service causes greater customer satisfaction, whether advertisers' use of bright colors produces higher sales, or whether sexuality in film leads to a more promiscuous society, the only way to determine these things is through experimental research.

Experimental research allows researchers to determine causality because experiments are so controlled. In experimental research, the researcher is concerned with two variables. A **variable** is simply any concept that has two or more values (Frey et al., 2002). Sex is a variable, because we have men and women. Note that just looking at maleness is not a variable because there is only one value associated with it; it doesn't *vary*, so it isn't a *variable*. Masculinity is considered a variable, however, because you can be highly masculine, moderately masculine, nonmasculine, and so on.

Returning to our discussion of experimental research, then, the research is concerned with two variables. One of the variables is the presumed cause. This is known as the **independent variable.** The other is the presumed effect. This is known as the **dependent variable.** If you are interested in knowing whether bright colors in advertisements cause increased sales, your independent variable is the color (bright vs. dull) and the dependent variable is the amount of sales dollars (more, the same, or less). The way the researcher determines causality is by carefully controlling the study participants' exposure to the independent variable. This control is known as **manipulation,** a term which has a negative connotation but is not meant in a negative fashion in the research world. In the study of advertisements just described, the researcher would expose some people to an advertisement that used bright colors and others to an advertisement that used dull colors, and she or he would observe the effects on sales based on these manipulations.

Experiments take place in two settings. **Laboratory experiments** take place in a controlled setting, so that the researcher might better control his or her efforts at manipulation. In the communication field, laboratories are often rooms that simulate living rooms or conference rooms. Typically, however, they have two-way mirrors and cameras mounted on the walls to record what happens. For example, John Gottman has a mini "apartment" at the University of Washington. He has married couples "move in" to the apartment during the course of a weekend, and he observes all of their interaction during that weekend.

Some experiments don't take place in the laboratory, and these are called **field experiments** because they take place in participants' natural surroundings. These sorts of experiments often take place in public places, such as shopping malls, libraries, or schools, but they might take place in private areas as well. In all cases, participants must agree to be a part of the experiment to comply with ethical standards set by educational and research institutions.

Survey Research

The most common means of studying communication is through the use of surveys. Market research, audience analysis, and organizational audits all make use of surveys. Unlike experiments, the use of surveys does not allow researchers to make claims that one thing causes another. The strength of survey research is that it is the *only* way to find out how someone thinks, feels, or intends to behave. If you want to know what people think about your organization, how they feel about a social issue, or whether they intend to buy a product after viewing an advertising spot you created, you need to conduct a survey.

In general, there are two types of survey research. **Interviews** ask participants to respond orally. They might take place face-to-face or over the phone. One special type of interview is a focus group, which is when the interviewer (called a facilitator) leads a small group of people in a discussion about a specific product or program (Frey et al., 2002). **Questionnaires** ask participants to respond in writing. They can be distributed by mail or administered with the researcher present. Particular types of research are more suited for interviews rather than questionnaires. Interviews, for example, allow the researcher to ask more complex questions because he or she can clarify misunderstandings through probing questions. Questionnaires, however, might be more appropriate for the collection of sensitive information because they provide more anonymity to the respondent (Salant & Dillman, 1994).

The key concepts associated with either type of survey research are **questioning** and **sampling.** First, the purpose of a survey is quite simple; surveys provide a means to ask questions of a group of people to understand their thoughts, feelings, and behaviors. Questionnaires might take two forms. **Open-ended questions** allow respondents to answer in their own words, taking as long (or short) as they would like. For example, a market researcher might ask study participants to describe what they like about a particular product. Or an interviewer might ask someone to respond to a hypothetical situation. **Closed-ended questions** require respondents to respond using set types of answers. In this case, a market researcher might say something like, "Respond to the following statement: product X is a useful product. Would you say you strongly agree, agree, neither agree nor disagree, disagree, or strongly disagree?" Neither method is better than the other; the two types of questions simply provide different kinds of data that are analyzed using different means.

The second key concept associated with survey research is **sampling.** Researchers are typically concerned with large groups of people when they conduct surveys. These groups are known as a **population,** which means all people who possess a particular characteristic (Frey et al., 2002). For example, marketing firms want to study all possible consumers of a product. Newspaper publishers want to gather information from all readers. Pharmaceutical industries want to study everyone with a particular ailment. The size of these groups makes it difficult simply to study everyone of interest. Even if every member of the population can be identified, which isn't always the case, studying all of them can be extremely expensive.

Instead, survey researchers study a **sample,** or a small number of people in the population of interest. If the sample is well selected and of sufficient size, the results of the survey are likely also to hold true for the entire group. **Random samples,** in which every member of the target group has an equal chance of being selected, are better than **nonrandom samples,** such as volunteers, convenience samples (people who visit a particular physician), or purposive samples (people who meet a particular requirement, such as age, sex, race, etc.). Essentially, a random sample of consumers is more likely to give representative information about brand preferences than a convenience sample, such as stopping people at the mall on a particular day to answer a few questions.

Textual Analysis

The third method used frequently by communication scholars is textual analysis. A **text** is any written or recorded message (Frey et al., 2002). A television show, a transcript of a medical encounter, and an employee bulletin can all be considered texts. Textual analysis is used to uncover the **content, nature,** or **structure** of messages. It can also be used to **evaluate** messages, focusing on their strengths, weaknesses, effectiveness, or even ethicality. So textual analysis can be used to study the amount of violence on television, how power dynamics play out during doctor–patient intake evaluations, or even the strategies used to communicate a corporate mission statement.

There are three distinct forms that textual analyses take in the communication discipline. **Rhetorical criticism** refers to "a systematic method for describing, analyzing, interpreting, and evaluating the persuasive force of messages" (Frey et al., 2002, p. 229). There are numerous specific types of rhetorical criticism, including historical criticism (how history shapes messages), genre criticism (evaluating particular types of messages, such as political speeches, or corporate image restoration practices), and feminist criticism (how beliefs about gender are produced and reproduced in messages).

Content analysis seeks to identify, classify, and analyze the occurrence of particular types of messages (Frey et al., 2002). It was developed primarily to study mass mediated messages, although it is also used in numerous other areas of the discipline. For example, public relations professionals often seek to assess the type of coverage given to a client. Typically, content analysis involves four steps: the selection of a particular text (e.g., newspaper articles), the development of content categories (e.g., "favorable organizational coverage," "neutral organizational coverage," "negative organizational coverage"), placing the content into categories, and an analysis of the results. In our example, the results of this study would be able to identify whether a particular newspaper has a pronounced slant when covering the organization.

The third type of textual analysis typically conducted by communication scholars is **interaction analysis** (also known as **conversation analysis**). These approaches typically focus on interpersonal or group communication interactions that have been recorded, with a specific emphasis on the nature or structure of interaction. The strength of this type of research is that it captures the natural give-and-take that is part of most communication experiences. The weakness of interaction analysis, content analysis, and rhetorical criticism is that *actual* effects on the audience can't be determined solely by focusing on texts.

Ethnography

Ethnography is the final research method used by scholars of communication. First used by anthropologists, ethnography typically involves the researcher immersing him- or herself into a particular **culture** or **context** to understand communication rules and meanings for that culture or context. For example, an ethnographer might study an organizational culture, such as Johnson & Johnson's corporate culture, or a particular context, such as communication in hospital emergency rooms. The key to this type of research is that it is naturalistic and emergent, which means that it must take place in the natural environment for the group under study and that the particular methods used will be adjusted on the basis of what is occurring in that environment.

Typically, those conducting ethnographies need to decide on the role they will play in the research. **Complete participants** are fully involved in the social setting, and the participants do not know that the researcher is studying them (Frey et al., 2002). This approach, of course, requires that the researcher knows enough about the environment to be able to fit in. Moreover, there are numerous ethical hurdles that the researcher must overcome. Combined, these two challenges prevent much research from being conducted in this fashion. Instead, **participant–observer** roles are more frequently chosen. In this case, the researcher becomes fully involved with the culture or context, but she or her has admitted his or her research agenda before entering the environment. In this way, knowledge is gained firsthand by the researcher, but extensive knowledge about the culture is not necessarily a prerequisite (Frey et al., 2002). Researchers choosing this strategy may also elect which to emphasize more, participation or observation. Finally, researchers may choose to be **complete observers.** Complete observers do not interact with the members of the culture or context, which means they do not interview any of the members of the group under study. As such, this method allows for the greatest objectivity in recording data, while simultaneously limiting insight into participants' own meanings of the observed communication.

In sum, communication scholars use four primary research methods. These methods include experiments, which focus on causation and control; surveys, which focus on questioning and sampling; textual analyses, which focus on the content, nature, or structure of messages; and ethnography, which focuses on the communication rules and meanings in a particular culture or context. A summary of the strengths and weaknesses of each of the four methods is summarized in Table 1.2.

❖ SOCIAL SCIENCE AND THE HUMANITIES

Communication has been described as both an art and a science (Dervin, 1993). On one hand, we respect the power of a beautifully crafted and creatively designed advertisement. On the other hand, we look to hard numbers to support decisions about the campaign featuring that advertisement. Although art and science are integrally related in the everyday practice of communication, in the more abstract realm of theory the two are often considered distinct pursuits. This concept

Table 1.2 Four Methods of Communication Research

Research Method	*What It Reveals*	*What It Conceals*
Experiment	Cause and effect	Whether the cause–effect relationship holds true in less controlled environments
Survey	Respondents' thoughts, feelings, and intentions	Cannot establish causality; cannot determine what people actually do
Textual analysis	The content, nature, and structure of messages	The effect of the message on receivers
Ethnography	Rules and meanings of communication in a culture or context	May provide a highly subjective (and therefore biased) view of the culture or context

can be traced to distinctions between the academic traditions of the humanities (which includes the arts) and the social sciences.

You might have some ideas about the terms *humanistic* and *social scientific,* because most college students are required to take some courses in each of these areas. The distinctions between the humanities and social science are based on more than just tradition, however; they are based on very different philosophical beliefs. With regard to the humanities, the interpretation of meaning is of central concern (Littlejohn, 2002). Meaning is presumed to be something that is subjective and unique to the individual, even though meanings are likely influenced by social processes. For individuals trained in the humanistic tradition, **subjectivity** is a hallmark; one's own **interpretation** is of interest. Think about the study of English literature, a discipline at the heart of the humanities. English scholars study the interpretation of texts in an effort to understand the meaning of the object of study.

On the other hand, **objectivity** is a central feature of social science. Social scientists believe that through careful standardization (i.e., objectivity), researchers can observe patterns of communication that can hold true for all (or most) people, all (or most) of the time. These patterns that

Table 1.3 Differences Between Social Scientific and Humanistic Approaches to Communication

Issue	*Social Science*	*Humanities*
Belief about human nature	Determinism	Pragmatism
Goal of theory	Understand and predict	Understand only
Process of theory development	Deductive	Inductive
Focus of research	Particularism	Holism
Research methods	Experiments; quantitative survey and textual analysis	Ethnography; qualitative survey and textual analysis

hold true across groups, time, and place are known as **generalizations.** To illustrate, psychology is a discipline rooted in the social sciences. As such, psychology scholars seek to explain general principles of how the human mind functions. These principles are intended to explain all people, all over the world, throughout history.

Because the humanities and social sciences have different areas of interest, they treat theory and research differently. Table 1.3 seeks to identify some of those distinctions. The first area of difference is the philosophical commitment to understanding the **nature of human beings** and the extent of their free will. Certainly, no one believes that human beings are mere puppets that have no choice in how they behave. Communication theorists vary, however, in the extent to which they believe people *act* versus *react* to communication situations. For example, social scientists tend to take a **deterministic** stance, which means that they believe that past experience, personality predispositions, and a number of other antecedent conditions *cause* people to behave in certain ways. Accordingly, deterministic approaches to human interaction propose that people in general tend to react to situations. Social scientists tend to look at the causes and effects of communication, such as what causes a marriage to fail or the effects of a particular marketing campaign.

Conversely, most humanists believe that people have control over their behavior; they believe that people make *conscious choices* to communicate to meet their goals. Theorists taking this stance are called

pragmatists because they believe that people are practical and that they plan their behavior. In short, pragmatists believe that human beings are not passive reactors to situations, but dynamic actors. Humanists, then, tend to focus on the choices that people make, such as the communication strategies a company such as Exxon chose to enact in the face of a corporate crisis.

A second way to differentiate between humanistic and social scientific scholarship is through a focus on *why* theories are developed. For example, the **goal** of social scientific theory is both to **understand and predict** communication processes. Because social science is interested in generalizations, the ability to predict is paramount; if a theorist understands the general pattern that is at the heart of a social scientific theory, then she or he should be able to predict how any one individual might communicate. Those in the humanities, however, believe that interpretations are always subjective; they are unique to the individual. Accordingly, humanists believe that theorists can never actually predict how a person will behave; all that can be done is to try to **understand** human communication.

Although not directly related to the distinction between social science and the humanities, we note that some theories strive to do more than simply predict or understand. A special group of theories, called **critical approaches,** seeks to improve the world through social change. The goal of critical theory is to empower people in their professional and personal lives. For more information about critical communication theory, see Craig (1999).

The third difference between social science and the humanities is the process of **theory development.** Recall our discussion of the theory–research link discussed earlier in the chapter. Deductive theory is based on the scientific method, so it should be no surprise to you that the social scientific approach to theory development is **deductive.** Those in the humanities, however, tend to start with data and subsequently develop theory. For example, scholars of English literature would start with reading Shakespeare's plays before developing a theory about them. Thus, those in the humanities tend to use **inductive** theory development.

Finally, the focus and methods of research also vary in the social scientific and humanistic approaches. Regarding the focus of research, the social scientific method requires standardization and control. Because of these objectives, social scientists incrementally study narrowly defined areas at a time, believing that the whole picture will be uncovered eventually. This approach is known as **particularism.** Humanists, on the other hand, believe in looking at the big picture; they propose that all pieces of the puzzle contribute to an understanding of the problem. Accordingly, they utilize **holism,** looking at the situation in its entirety, as the focal point of research.

Given the different areas of focus, it's not a surprise that the final difference between social scientists and humanists are the research methods they use. Earlier in this chapter, we discussed the four research methods used by communication scholars. Of the four, one is clearly social scientific, and one is clearly humanistic. **Experimental methods,** with their concern for causation and control, are uniquely suited for the social sciences. Remember that social science seeks to make predictions, and the best way to do that is to have research that supports particular causes and effects. Similarly, ethnography is uniquely suited for humanistic research. **Ethnography** leans to the understanding of communication in contexts and cultures, which is appropriate for theory that uses holism in its quest for interpretation of communicative events.

The uses of survey research and textual analysis cannot be easily classified. Instead of the methods themselves being associated with either social science or the humanities, the specific way data are analyzed determines whether the method is social scientific or humanistic. The two methods of data analysis are quantitative and qualitative. Quantitative methods are adapted from those used in the hard sciences, such as chemistry and biology. Accordingly, quantitative methods are associated with social science. Qualitative methods are those that have historically been used by the humanities.

Quantitative methods typically rely on numbers or *statistics* as the source of data (Reinard, 1998). These data and statistics are generally explanatory and comprehensive in nature; they seek to predict what will happen for large groups of people. To accomplish this, researchers control the study by identifying the variables of interest before data collection takes place and trying to prevent extraneous influences from affecting the data. As described earlier, these commitments allow social scientists to make generalizations.

Qualitative methods reject the limitations on individual interpretation that control requires. Moreover, qualitative research eschews the use of numbers and uses verbal descriptions of communicative phenomena. Typically, the data are in the form of extended quotes or transcripts of communication. Finally, qualitative research typically centers on a description or critique of communication rather than on generalizations (Reinard, 1998).

In summary, then, social scientists tend to use quantitative surveys or textual analyses. For example, they'll collect data about how many people prefer a new formulation of a product versus a previous formulation of a product or how frequently a manager uses a particular communication strategy in interaction. Humanists tend to use qualitative surveys and textual analyses. They ask participants to respond at length to questions in their own words about a particular product or they identify various communication themes evident in a corporate brochure.

A final note should be made about the distinctions between social science and the humanities. The purpose of talking about these two academic traditions is because communication is *both* social scientific and humanistic. As such, you shouldn't view these distinctions as dichotomies, but as continua. Individual theories may be more or less social scientific or humanistic (not either–or), with elements borrowed from both traditions.

❖ EVALUATING THEORY

The final topic of this chapter is evaluating theory. Earlier we suggested that all theories have strengths and weaknesses; they reveal certain aspects of reality and conceal others. An important task that students and scholars face is to evaluate the theories that are available to them. We are not talking about evaluation in terms of "good" versus "bad," but evaluating the *usefulness* of the theory. Each of you is likely to find some of the theories presented in this text more useful than others. Such a determination is likely due at least in part to your own background and experiences, as well as your profession. We would like to challenge you to broaden your scope and consider not just the usefulness of each theory to you personally, but the usefulness of the theory for people's personal and professional lives in general.

A number of published standards can be used to evaluate theories (e.g., Griffin, 2003; Littlejohn, 2002; West & Turner, 2000). All are appropriate and effective tools for comparing the relative usefulness of a

Table 1.4 Criteria for Evaluating Theory

Area of Evaluation	*What to Look For*
Accuracy	Has research supported that the theory works the way it says it does?
Practicality	Have real-world applications been found for the theory?
Simplicity	Has the theory been formulated with the appropriate number (fewest possible) concepts or steps?
Consistency	Does the theory demonstrate consistency within its own premises and with other theories?
Acuity	To what extent does the theory make clear an otherwise complex experience?

given theory. Because this text is geared toward working professionals, however (or those who wish to soon be working in the profession of their choice), we believe that the following five criteria best capture the way to assess the relative usefulness of communication theories in the communication, business, and related the professions. Note that we are talking about the *relative* usefulness of the theory. We are not talking about either–ors—good or bad, weak or strong. Instead, we hope you look at these distinctions as *continua* that range from very useful at one end to not particularly useful at the other end. A description of these criteria are in Table 1.4.

The first area of focus is **accuracy.** Simply put, the best theories correctly summarize the way communication actually works. Recall, however, that we are referring to scholarly theories. As such, we do not mean accuracy in terms of whether the theory accurately reflects your own personal experience (although we would hope that it does!). Instead, when we use the term *accuracy* we are suggesting that systematic research supports the explanations provided by the theory. Thus, in assessing this quality, you should look at research studies that have used the theory and see whether the research supports the theory or fails to find support for it.

A second way to evaluate theories is **practicality.** The best theories can be used to address real-world communication problems; in fact,

Lewin (1951) said "there is nothing so practical as a good theory" (p. 169). Clearly, there are some profound theories that have changed the way we understand the world that aren't actually *used* by most people on a daily basis (Einstein's theory of relativity, or Darwin's theory of evolution, for example). In terms of *communication* theories, however, theories that are accurate but can't be used in everyday life are not as good as theories that have great practical utility. For example, a theory that can help a person make better communicative decisions in his or her interactions with coworkers is better than a theory so abstract that it cannot be used by an individual in daily communication. Thus, a theory with more applications is better than a theory without practical uses. In assessing this criterion, you should look for how the theory has been used in the research literature, as well as whether the theory has made the leap to professional practice.

Simplicity is the third way to evaluate a good business or professional communication theory. This does not mean that the theory is easy to understand; because the world is complex, theories trying to explain the world are often fairly complex as well. What we mean by simplicity is that the theory is formulated as simply as possible. The "three bears" analogy works here. Theories that have extra steps or include variables that don't help us to understand real-world experiences would be considered overly complex. Theories that do not have enough steps, that don't delve beneath the surface, or that don't have enough variables to understand real-world problems are too simple. Theories that include no more nor no less than necessary to understand a phenomena thoroughly are just right; they have a useful amount of simplicity. The best way to think of simplicity is to compare how much of communication is explained by the theory versus how many concepts are being used to explain it.

The fourth way to evaluate a theory is to consider its **consistency.** The most useful theories have both internal and external consistency. By **internal consistency,** we mean that the ideas of the theory are logically built on one another. A theory that proposes at one point that cooperation among team members guarantees success and at a different point proposes that competition is more effective than cooperation has a logical flaw. Similarly, theories that "skip" steps do not have much internal consistency. A theory predicting that age is related to the experience of jealousy and that one's expression of jealousy affects the future of the relationship, but then fails to tell us how the experience of jealousy is related to the expression of jealousy, has a logical gap. As such, it does not have strong internal consistency.

External consistency, on the other hand, refers to the theory's consistency with other widely held theories. If we presume that the widely held theories are true, then the theory under evaluation that disagrees with those believed supported theories also presents a logical problem. As such, the notion of consistency, whether internal or external, is concerned with the logic of the theory. The most useful theories are those that have a strong logical structure.

The final area for evaluation is **acuity.** Acuity refers to the ability of a theory to provide insight into an otherwise intricate issue. Earlier we said that theories that are simple are not necessarily easy to understand, because the real world is often complex. A theory that explains a difficult problem, however, is better than a theory that explains something less complex. For example, a theory that explains a complex problem such as how organizational cultures can influence employee retention is a more useful theory than a theory that explains a relatively straightforward problem such as how to gain attention in a speech. Those theories that explain difficult problems show acuity; those that focus on fairly obvious problems demonstrate superficiality.

❖ CHAPTER SUMMARY

In this chapter, we discussed the popular perception of communication, which suggests that the communication process is paradoxically simple yet powerful. We defined communication as **the process by which people interactively create, sustain, and manage meaning.** Next, we discussed the nature of theory. The distinctions between commonsense theories, working theories, and scholarly theories were addressed. Because scholarly theory must be researched, regardless of whether the research precedes or follows the initial formulation of a theory, we then turned our attention to the nature of research. We differentiated between primary and secondary research. We also identified the four primary research methods used by communication scholars: experiment, survey, textual analysis, and ethnography. In addition to describing the key elements of each of these methods, the chapter focused on what each reveals and conceals about communication. Next we turned our attention to the differences between social scientific and humanistic approaches to theory and research, centering our discussion on beliefs about human nature, the goal of theory, the development of theory, the focus of research, and the research methods used. Finally, we provided a means by which scholarly theories of communication can be evaluated, including accuracy, practicality, simplicity, consistency, and acuity.

Case Study 1 Theory and Research in Communication Consulting

Community General Hospital was facing a crisis. As a small, urban hospital, it was having difficulty balancing its budget. The Balanced Budget Act (BBA) of 1997 reduced Medicare and Medicaid reimbursements, which typically make up nearly two-thirds of billed hospital charges (Jones, 2001). Accordingly, revenues are down. The Balanced Budget Refinement Act (BBRA) of 1999 has restored some of the budget cuts, but small rural hospitals have benefited over urban hospitals (Freeman, 2002). Moreover, the nationwide hospital workforce shortage has caused high turnover and vacancy rates, which costs the hospital money; inpatient and outpatient care capacity is reduced, surgeries are delayed, and laboratory and X-ray work has to be sent off-site (American Hospital Association, 2001).

Bruce Norris, the chief administrator of the hospital, has recognized the crisis and is committed to doing something about it. He has sought the advice of two consultants, one of whom was trained in the social sciences and one of whom was trained in the humanities. Here is their advice.

Consultant A

"I believe that reducing costs is not feasible, so the hospital needs to work on increasing demand. A possibility is to create a niche specialty so that Community General is the first place people consider when they need that type of medical care. Hospital marketing staff members should conduct a marketing survey and gather statistics about the particular health needs of people in the community. Then they should look at the services provided by their competitors and determine which niche Community General is not filling sufficiently. By creating a niche in the saturated health care market, Community General can develop a communication campaign that emphasizes how it stands out from the crowd; increased demand will mean increased revenues."

Consultant B

"This problem is complex and needs to be understood in the context of the entire health care industry in the United States, which is undergoing a major transition. Before assuming what the problem is, we need to understand thoroughly the challenges and motivations of all of the hospital's stakeholders: members of the local community, the hospital's staff and administration, suppliers, government agencies, and current and past patients. In so doing, the unique strengths and weaknesses of Community General should emerge. Once we uncover these qualities, we can develop a campaign that shares this vision with the necessary stakeholders."

Questions for Consideration

1. Both Consultant A and Consultant B are operating on generalizations about how to market the hospital. These generalizations could be considered commonsense theories. Look at the advice each provides and develop a description of the commonsense theory each is using (i.e., create a name and prediction for the theories). Then recall the metaphor of theories as glasses (p. 3). What concepts do these commonsense theories highlight? What might be hidden or distorted because of the theory being used?

2. One of these consultants is demonstrating social scientific assumptions, and the other is demonstrating humanistic assumptions. Which is which? Which specific elements of their advice have led you to these conclusions? (*Hint:* See Table 1.3 for the key distinctions between these approaches.)

2

Explaining Theories of Intrapersonal Communication

As we emphasize throughout this book, communication is, at minimum, a two-way process. Certainly, the transactional nature of communication has been widely established and is viewed as self-evident. However, messages have no meaning without an individual's interpretation. Everyone has to process every message internally while considering how best to interpret these messages. In other words, meaning is derived only after an individual perceives a message and gives it meaning; meanings reside in people's interpretations, not in the words or behaviors themselves. Consequently, communication is also an *intra*personal process.

❖ INTRAPERSONAL COMMUNICATION DEFINED

Intrapersonal communication is defined simply as "communication with oneself" (DeVito, 2003). That is, individuals analyze others' behavior, attitudes, and messages to assign meaning to a given event. Here, we explain four theories that examine the intrapersonal aspects of communication. First, message design logics accounts for individual differences in both message construction and interpretation based on divergent beliefs about communication. The second theory presented in this chapter, attribution theory, explains how and why individuals assign causation or motivation to their own and others' behavior. Third, uncertainty reduction theory aims to explain initial encounters with people. In other words, what drives you to initiate a relationship? The fourth theory presented, expectancy violations theory, strives to predict and explain people's behavior when their expectations are violated. Together these theories emphasize the internal processes that serve as antecedents to the highly personalized creation of meaning, and each perspective applies to numerous communication contexts. From making judgments about why a coworker always seems to miss deadlines (attribution theory) to determining how best to reduce one's uncertainty during a job transfer (e.g., uncertainty reduction theory), each of the theories presented illustrates the internally driven process necessary to bring individual meaning to various messages.

❖ MESSAGE DESIGN LOGICS

Everyone has been faced with the challenge of having to confront a coworker or subordinate who isn't pulling his or her weight. The dilemmas that communicators confront when dealing with these sorts of situations can be understood by the theory of message design logics. According to O'Keefe (1988, 1997), because people *think* about communication differently, they will also *construct* very different types of messages. A **message design logic** (MDL), then, is your belief about communication that, in turn, links thoughts to the construction of messages. Stated differently, people who have different views about the nature and function of communication will construct different types of messages. This difference in message type is particularly evident when a person is faced with communication challenges such as dealing with a difficult coworker. According to O'Keefe (1997), there are three types of design logics from which to choose.

Three Message Design Logics

Using an inductive approach to theory building, O'Keefe (1988) developed her theory after studying the techniques people used to try to persuade others. Despite a plethora of strategies that might be used, she found that people tended to use "fairly uniform" techniques (1997, p. 87). Through this work O'Keefe uncovered three distinct message design logics: expressive, conventional, and rhetorical.

The **expressive message design logic** is a sender-focused pattern (O'Keefe, 1988). That is, a person using this pattern is concerned primarily with self-expression. Communication is viewed as a means for conveying the sender's thoughts and feelings. People who use the expressive message design logic have a very difficult time holding back their thoughts; if it's in their head, it's out their mouth. They value openness, honesty, and clarity in communication and are mistrustful of anyone who seems overly strategic in his or her communication. Such communicators pay little attention to context and what may be appropriate behavior for a particular context. They can't help themselves—they feel a genuine pressure to say what is on their mind right here and right now. When the situation calls for them to protect someone else's self-esteem, they typically accomplish this by editing their comments (e.g., replacing profanity with a euphemism) rather than through genuine efforts at politeness (see Chapter 3 for a discussion of politeness theory). For example, when faced with potential sexual harassment, a person using an expressive MDL might respond:

> You are the most rude and disgusting man I have ever met. You're nothing but a dirty old man. Where do you get off thinking you could force me to have an affair with you? You make me sick! (Bingham & Burleson, 1989, p. 162)

Note that the content of this message is focused entirely on what the sender is feeling at the time. The sender might have made an effort to temper his or her anger by editing his or her language, but other than that, little effort is made to modify the expression of thoughts and feelings.

Second, a person who uses the **conventional message design logic** views communication as a game that is played cooperatively

(O'Keefe, 1988). As such, those using a conventional MDL are primarily concerned with appropriateness; these individuals view communication contexts, roles, and relationships as having particular guidelines for behavior (O'Keefe, 1997). They are concerned about saying and doing the "right" thing in any given situation. To do the "right" thing, they follow the rules of politeness (see Chapter 3 for more on politeness theory). Keeping our example of dealing with potential sexual harassment, a person using a conventional message design logic might respond:

> There's absolutely no chance I will have an affair with you, and if you try to fire me over this I won't keep quiet about it. That kind of behavior is not appropriate in the workplace. Besides that, you're married. Don't approach me again. (Bingham & Burleson, 1989, p. 162)

In this case, the message sender makes several allusions to communication rules; not only does she or he point out that this behavior is "not appropriate in the workplace," the speaker also refers to an implicit rule by saying "you're married," which is a social relationship that is constrained by certain behavioral guidelines.

The third MDL is the **rhetorical message design logic.** Individuals using a rhetorical MDL view communication as the means to create situations and negotiate multiple goals (O'Keefe, 1988). This approach is noted for flexibility, as well as for its sophistication and depth of communication skill. Those using a rhetorical design logic pay close attention to other peoples' communication in an effort to figure out others' points of view. They try to anticipate and prevent problems by redefining situations to benefit all parties involved in the interaction. Unlike the expressive MDL, which is reactive, the rhetorical MDL is proactive (O'Keefe, 1988). An example of a rhetorical MDL in the potential sexual harassment situation is as follows:

> We've got a great working relationship now, and I'd like us to work well together in the future. So I think it's important for us to talk this out. You're a smart and clear-thinking guy and I consider you to be my friend as well as my boss. That's why I have to think you must be under a lot of unusual stress lately to have said something like this. I know what it's like to be under pressure. Too much stress can really make you crazy. You probably just need a break. (Bingham & Burleson, 1989, p. 163)

In this case, the sender seeks to balance his or her own goal of stopping the harassment with the target's goal of protecting against embarrassment. At the same time, the sender strives to maintain a good working relationship with the person in the future. This is accomplished by redefining the situation from one of sexual harassment to one of excessive stress. By reframing the message, the rhetorical communicator has found "a common drama in which to play" (O'Keefe, 1988, p. 88).

Message Design Logics Preferences

Reading the three examples presented might give you insight into the message design logic under which you tend to operate. More than likely, one of those messages is similar to something you might say in a situation you perceive as harassing, and the other message types might reflect something that you would never say in a million years. Indeed, one of the challenges highlighted by this theory is the difficulty that individuals have when dealing with others who use a different MDL. O'Keefe, Lambert, and Lambert (1997) argued that when two people use the same message design logic, these individuals recognize that the problems are communication problems. When two parties use different MDLs, however, these individuals often do not realize they have communication problems; instead, they blame the difficulties on perceived bad intentions, mistaken beliefs, or undesirable personality characteristics (see attribution theory presented later in this chapter). For example, a person who uses an expressive MDL tends to view those using a rhetorical MDL as dishonest because they "manipulate" their perception of the situation. Table 2.1 presents some forms of miscommunication that occur due to differing message design logics.

Although individuals tend to prefer using one MDL to another, O'Keefe and colleagues have cautioned that message design logics are not the same as personality traits. Unlike personality traits, MDLs are not stable, but can change and develop over an individual's lifespan. In fact, O'Keefe and Delia (1988) found that the three MDLs reflect a developmental process, with the expressive MDL the least developed and the rhetorical MDL the most developed pattern. However, O'Keefe et al. (1997) cautioned that this developmental trajectory should not imply that the rhetorical strategy is superior to others; "Every design logic provides a logically consistent and potentially satisfactory way for an individual to use language" (p. 49). They believe that all communicators should recognize and accommodate diversity in MDLs. Knowing the variation is half the battle.

Table 2.1 Forms of Miscommunication Due to Message Design Logics (MDL)

	Message Recipient		
Message Producer	*Expressive MDL*	*Conventional MDL*	*Rhetorical MDL*
Expressive MDL	Genuine differences in opinion prevent communicators from achieving any connection.	Expressive remarks perceived as embarrassing or crude due to inappropriateness.	Expressive person perceived as inconsiderate and uncooperative.
Conventional MDL	Ritualistic messages are taken literally by the expressive person (such as "Let's get together soon").	Differing views of appropriateness of the situation lead to perceived inappropriate behavior.	Conformity to appropriateness viewed as rigidity, overly conservative approach to interaction.
Rhetorical MDL	Messages viewed as unnecessarily elaborate and indirect; sender viewed as dishonest.	Failure to see coherence of complex messages because of focus on "correct" context.	Incompatible assumptions about goals can lead to misunderstanding of others' intent.

SOURCE: O'Keefe, B. J., Lambert, B. L., & Lambert, C. A. (1997). Conflict and communication in a research and development unit. In B. D. Sypher (Ed.), *Case Studies in organizational communication* 2. New York: Guilford Press. Reprinted by permission of Guilford Press.

Again, O'Keefe's (1988, 1997) theory suggests that individuals tend to operate using one of three message design logics. Users of expressive design logics view communication primarily as a means of sharing their unique feelings, beliefs, and ideas. Those who rely on conventional design logics perceive communication as a rules-based game; to play the "game" one must operate using social conventions for appropriateness. Last, a rhetorical design logic emphasizes a highly flexible approach to communication in which the speaker adapts to the situation, using self-expression or relying on social conventions as appropriate.

❖ ATTRIBUTION THEORY

According to attribution theorists, human beings often work like naïve detectives, continually trying to understand and make sense of what inspired various events, personal mannerisms, and individuals' conduct. Just as a crime scene investigator pieces together clues in an effort to determine a suspect's motive, you, too, go through life picking up clues and making judgments about what you believe influenced your own and other's behavior. These judgments and conclusions that provide reasons for behavior are called attributions. Attribution theory, then, explains the cognitive process one uses when trying to make causal explanations for behavior.

Attributions as Naïve Psychology

Attribution theory is not a new concept; researchers have long studied the ways in which people process events and then derive explanations for them. In the mid-1950s, however, Heider (1958) focused his attention on the process of drawing inferences—the assumptions individuals make regarding the causes of behavior as well as the judgments made about who is responsible for that behavior. According to Heider, individuals act as "naïve psychologists." When you see a person act, you immediately make judgments about the causal nature of the conduct. Specifically, Heider found that individuals try to determine whether a behavior in question was caused by dispositional or situational factors. **Dispositional factors** refer to internal or personal features, such as one's personality, character, or biological traits. These factors are relatively stable and unique to each individual. Conversely, **situational factors** refer to external dynamics that are relatively uncontrollable and determined by the environment or circumstance at hand. External factors obviously vary to a much greater extent than do internal factors because they are inherently based on the context of a given situation, not on more stable personality traits.

For example, if, at your monthly staff meeting, Ronald's presentation of current sales figures appears disjointed and jumbled, you might attribute his awkwardness to the fact that his PowerPoint slides failed to upload properly onto the laptop. Here, the inference made suggests that because of the situation (i.e., defective software), Ronald was forced to give the presentation from memory and without visual aids. Thus, you might attribute Ronald's bumbled speech to a technological glitch, thereby making a situational attribution for his behavior. On the other hand, you might attribute Ronald's poor presentation to his lack of preparation (i.e., character flaw). Surely by now everyone knows not to rely solely on PowerPoint; Ronald should have come prepared with a backup plan ready in case of technical difficulties. Looking at the presentation this way, you might blame Ronald's failed presentation on his lazy preparation—something within his personal control, thereby making an internal attribution.

Correspondent Inference Theory

Expanding Heider's work, Jones and Davis (1965) were concerned with the **intentionality** of dispositional (internally driven) behavior. They argued that when a perceiver attributes the cause of a behavior to dispositional factors, the perceiver also makes judgments about the actor's intentions. Jones and Davis referred to these judgments of intention as **correspondent inferences**.

As Texter (1995) noted, "before we can draw correspondent inferences from observing a person's behavior, we must make a determination about the person's intention: Did the person intentionally act in a certain way, knowing the effects the behavior would have?" (p. 55). When a dispositional inference mirrors an action and the perceiver labels the disposition and the action similarly (e.g., lazy), it is said that these inferences "correspond." For instance, you might infer the disposition of laziness or apathy from Ronald's seemingly lazy preparation for the meeting.

Determining the intentionality of an act is not easy; however, there are several factors that one can consider when determining the purpose of another's behavior: choice, assumed desirability, social role, prior expectations, hedonic relevance, and personalism (Jones & Davis, 1965). Beginning with **choice,** individuals can assess an actor's intention by examining whether the actor in question had any alternatives. If you perceive alternative courses of action, then you are also likely to assume that the "selected" behavior was deliberate. Second, you can assess intentions by focusing on the **assumed social desirability** of the actor's actions. That is, if a person behaves in a manner contrary to social conventions, you are more likely to infer that the behavior reflects the person's true character and not merely an attempt at social correctness. Similarly, an actor's **social role,** or public position, can help determine the intentionality of a behavior, particularly when this person behaves in a manner contrary to the prescribed role.

Just as one's position affects expectations and assumptions of intentionality, so do **prior expectations** of that individual. Thus, your previous encounters with an actor, or knowledge about the person's background, may influence your assessments about the actor's intentions. **Hedonic relevance,** or the degree to which you believe an actor's behavior directly affects you (either positively through rewards or negatively through punishment), also shapes your assessment of the actor's intentions. The greater you perceive the hedonic relevance, the more likely you are to view the actor's behavior as deliberate. Last, **personalism** refers to the belief that an actor specifically and intentionally behaves in ways to hurt or help you. Thus, if you assume that a person's behavior changes when you are not present, you may imagine that the actions are intentional. Notably, although each of these six factors can aid in assessing an actor's intentions, relying on any of these reasons may lead to biased judgments of an actor's disposition.

Kelley's Covariation Model

Perhaps a more holistic approach to attribution theory, Kelley's (1967, 1973) **covariation model** explains the causal nature of the complete attribution process. Specifically, this model has a greater scope than does Jones and Davis's correspondent inference theory because Kelley seeks to explain attributions overall, whereas Jones and Davis focused only on the intentionality of dispositional inferences.

According to Kelley (1967, 1973), individuals judge the causality of another's behavior by examining four factors: consensus, consistency, distinctiveness, and controllability. When the first three of these features are combined (i.e., consensus, consistency, distinctiveness), a perceiver can judge whether the actions were internally controlled (i.e., disposition) or externally controlled (i.e., situational). That is, you assign meaning based on perceived controllability—how much command an individual had over the behavior.

First, the perceiver determines if an actor's behavior demonstrates **consensus,** that is, would other people react similarly if placed in the same situation? The more people whom you observe behaving similarly increases the perception of consensus. If Rebecca storms out of the quarterly sales meeting in a huff and snarls at everyone in her path while the other members of the sales team leave the meeting with smiles and small talk, low consensus has occurred. Here, you might conclude that something unique to Rebecca has caused her ill temper. If, however, everyone on the sales team heads out of the meeting sporting a grimace and a foul mood, then you have observed high consensus. In this case, you would probably conclude that the situation (the meeting) caused the employees' crankiness.

Second, the perceiver must determine whether the actor's behavior demonstrates consistency. **Consistency** refers to whether the person in question engages in similar behaviors over time. Comparable to consensus, the more often you observe an actor engaging in the same behavior, the more your perception of consistency will increase. If Rebecca always seems to be angry and rude to colleagues, then you would say that her ill-tempered behavior after the sales meeting is highly consistent with her previous behavior. Here, you would likely conclude that Rebecca is simply an obnoxious person. Conversely, if you typically view Rebecca as pleasant and enthusiastic, you would conclude that her sudden change of behavior has low consistency. In this case, you would attribute her mood to the situation; perhaps a superior provided some negative feedback at the meeting, for example.

Third, a perceiver judges an actor's **distinctiveness**, that is, whether the person acts differently in one situation than in others. Unlike consensus and consistency, which increase with others' conformity and number of observances over time, distinctiveness decreases when the actor behaves similarly across many different situations. That is, a behavior is only labeled distinctive if it is "markedly different in one situation or task from others" (Texter, 1995, p. 60). Continuing with our example, if Rebecca speaks rudely and demonstrates hostility toward everyone in the company, to her friends, to her children, and to her neighbors, then Rebecca's offensive mannerisms have low distinctiveness. Moreover, you will likely make an internal attribution and assume that Rebecca is simply a rude person. On the other hand, if Rebecca's anger and disrespectful tone occurred only after this one meeting and in no other meetings or situations, then you would conclude this behavior is highly distinctive because it appears contrary to the other circumstances in her life. In this case, you would attribute Rebecca's unfriendly means of communication as situational; something happened at the meeting that really troubled her.

As mentioned earlier, by combining one's judgments of consensus, consistency, and distinctiveness, the perceiver can determine the controllability of the actor's behavior. For example, you suppose an **interior locus of control** when you believe the actor could have controlled the behavior. Alternatively, you assume an **exterior locus of control** when the behavior appears to have been unavoidable.

According to Kelley and others' research, three possible sequences result when you combine your judgments of consensus, consistency, and distinctiveness. First, an external (or situational) attribution is made when your judgment of the actor yields high consensus, high consistency, and high distinctiveness. In other words, if nearly everyone leaves the sales meeting feeling irritable (high consensus), this petulance happens each time there is a sales meeting (high consistency), and yet most days go by with pleasant employees who are not typically grouchy in other circumstances (high distinctiveness), then you would attribute the crabby mood to an uncontrollable situation. That is, something happens during these meetings that creates palpable unhappiness in people.

Similarly, the behavior is judged as an external situation if the observer perceives the event to be one of high consensus, low consistency, and high distinctiveness. The only difference in this case is that the behavior has not been observed over time (low consistency). Nonetheless, if employees leave the meeting feeling disgruntled, this has not happened before, and employees are typically quite satisfied at work, you would still attribute this frustration as a consequence of the environment—the meeting. The same prediction is made for low consensus, low consistency, and highly distinctive behavior because the actions are so out of character for the actor and others around that you simply conclude the situation is to blame.

Conversely, when the behavior is judged as low consensus, high consistency, and low distinctiveness, you are likely to make an internal attribution. For example, if Rebecca is the only person who storms out of the meeting (low consensus), Rebecca usually leaves the sales meeting feeling irritable (high consistency), and Rebecca exhibits crankiness in most other situations (low distinctiveness), then you would attribute her irritability to her personality. That is, Rebecca chooses to be an unpleasant person. A summary of the predictions of Kelley's covariation model are in Table 2.2.

Table 2.2 Types of Attributions Based on Kelley's Predictions

Consensus	"Do other people act this way?" If **yes,** an external attribution is likely. If **no,** an internal attribution is likely.
Consistency	"Has this person behaved in a similar fashion in **this** sort of situation before?" If **yes,** an internal attribution is likely. If **no,** an external attribution is likely.
Distinctiveness	"Has this person behaved in a similar fashion in **other** types of situations before?" If **yes,** an internal attribution is likely. If **no,** an external attribution is likely.

To review, attribution theorists have emphasized various explanations for the attributions you make about assigning the causes and motivations of your own and others' behavior. Whereas Heider examined the causal location of dispositional and situational sources of behavior, Jones and Davis focused more narrowly on determining the perceived intent that drives dispositional behavior. Kelley broadened the scope of attribution theory by examining the interplay of consensus, consistency, and distinctiveness.

❖ UNCERTAINTY REDUCTION THEORY

The third theory we discuss here is uncertainty reduction theory. Berger and Calabrese's (1975) uncertainty reduction theory (URT) holds that social life is filled with ambiguities. Not knowing what to wear on the first day at a new job (*Should I wear a suit or go with business casual?*), unsure as to how to greet a new boss (*Should I call her Megan? Ms. Smith? Mrs. Smith? Dr. Smith?*), and wondering whether you will get along with the new officemate who just transferred from another location (*Will she bother me with questions? Will he gossip about team members?*) are just a few typical concerns during an average workday. Guided by several assumptions and axioms of human behavior, URT seeks to explain and predict when, why, and how individuals use communication to minimize their doubts when interacting with others.

Three assumptions guide the uncertainty reduction framework. First, Berger and Calabrese (1975) maintained that the primary goal of communication is to minimize uncertainties that humans have about the world and the people therein. Second, they proposed that individuals experience uncertainty on a regular basis and that the experience of uncertainty is an unpleasant one. Third, Berger and Calabrese assumed that communication is the primary vehicle for reducing uncertainty. Importantly, with so many uncertainties presented to you within a given 24-hour period, Berger (1979) admitted that individuals couldn't possibly reduce uncertainty about all of these new people or situations. Instead, he argued that there are three possible preceding conditions that influence whether people have the motivation necessary to reduce their uncertainty.

Reducing Uncertainty

Antecedent Conditions. Berger (1979) argued that individuals are motivated to reduce uncertainty only under one of three specific antecedent conditions. First, **anticipation of future interaction** suggests that you are more motivated to reduce uncertainty about someone who you are likely to see again. Thus, you are more inclined to use uncertainty reduction behaviors when a new office mate joins the team because you know that you will be working with this person on a daily basis. The second condition, **incentive value,** includes the notion that you are prompted to learn more about someone when the individual in question has the potential to provide you with rewards or even punishments. In other words, what can this person do for you or to you? The third antecedent condition is **deviance.** If a person is odd, eccentric, bizarre, or unusual in some way that counters your expectations, URT suggests that individuals will be more likely to reduce their uncertainty about the individual.

Types of Uncertainty. Beyond the antecedent conditions that prompt people to want to reduce uncertainty, Berger and Bradac (1982) argued that there are two distinct variations, or types, of uncertainty. The first type, **behavioral uncertainty,** takes into account your insecurity about which actions are appropriate in a given situation. For example, when starting a job at a new company, there is often some ambiguity about the hours "required." *Do employees of my position begin at 9:00 a.m. and* *leave at 5:00 p.m.? Or, am I expected to arrive early and stay late? Should I work through lunch, eating at my desk, or do colleagues expect me go out to lunch with them and socialize?* These are all examples of typical behavioral uncertainty for a new employee who is not yet sure as to how to act within the new corporation.

The second type of uncertainty is **cognitive uncertainty.** Whereas individuals experiencing behavioral uncertainty question how they should *act* in a given situation, those who experience cognitive uncertainty are unsure as to *what to think* about someone or something. In other words, cognitive uncertainty emphasizes the doubts in your ability to pinpoint the attitudes and beliefs of others. When a colleague makes a comment about how "comfortable" you look on a casual Friday, you may wonder, *Was this a compliment? Or was the remark a subtle hint that you maybe dressed in a manner that is too casual for the office? Should you even care what the person thinks of your attire?* All of these questions emphasize cognitive uncertainty.

Axioms Explaining the Uncertainty Reduction Process

URT seeks to explain and predict the ways in which individuals use communication to reduce ambiguity. Specifically, the process of reducing uncertainty is predicated on eight axioms, or self-evident truths, that have been established and supported in previous research (Berger & Calabrese, 1975). These axioms are summarized in Table 2.3.

As is plainly evident, these axioms make sense; they are, after all "self-evident truths." Unlike a commonsense theory, however, URT's axioms have been classified, paired together to create theorems, and tested systematically over time, thereby providing URT with scholarly credence. Moreover, the axioms presented in Table 2.3 supply only the backbone of the theory. In other words, to say that using friendly nonverbal behaviors reduces uncertainty is not enough to warrant a scholarly theory. Discussed next, communication strategies to reduce uncertainty provide additional substance to URT's axioms.

Uncertainty Reduction Strategies

When examining communication strategies for reducing uncertainty, it is important to remember Berger and Calabrese's (1975) original premise: uncertainty reduction is central to all social relations.

Table 2.3 Axioms of Uncertainty Reduction Theory

Axiom 1	As your verbal communication with a communication partner increases, your level of uncertainty about that person decreases; as a result, verbal communication continues to increase.
Axiom 2	As welcoming nonverbal expressions increase, uncertainty decreases and vice versa.
Axiom 3	The greater your uncertainty, the more information-seeking behaviors you use. Conversely, as your uncertainty lessens, you seek less information.
Axiom 4	When uncertainty in a relationship is high, the intimacy level of communication content will be low. On the other hand, the reduction of uncertainty leads to greater intimacy.
Axiom 5	The more uncertain you are, the more you will use reciprocal communication strategies and vice versa.
Axiom 6	The more similarities you perceive to share with the target person(s), the more your uncertainty is reduced. Alternatively, perceiving dissimilarities leads to increased uncertainty.
Axiom 7	As uncertainty decreases, liking increases. Conversely, if your uncertainty rises, your liking of the person will decrease.
Axiom 8	Shared communication networks, or shared ties, lessen your uncertainty. On the other hand, if you share no common relations, your uncertainty intensifies.

SOURCE: Axioms 1 through 7 adapted from Berger and Calabrese, 1975. Axiom 8 adapted from Parks and Adelman, 1983.

Likewise, Berger (1995, 1997) noted that much of social interaction is goal driven. In other words, you communicate for a reason, and you create cognitive plans that guide individuals' social interaction.

URT is related to Berger's (1995, 1997) notion of plan-based messages. Specifically, when seeking information about social realities, individuals create and use plans that vary in complexity. Individuals may vary widely in their relational goals and have a range of specific tactics available to cope with uncertainty. Three overarching strategies typify most uncertainty reduction communication, however: passive, active, and interactive.

Indicative of the **passive strategy,** individuals observe their surroundings and surreptitiously gather clues about which behaviors are appropriate as well as which attitudes and beliefs others hold. The passive approach is much like playing detective. The **active strategy** to uncertainty reduction involves seeking information from a third party. Rather than playing detective yourself, you go to someone else who may know more about the person or situation in question. Last, the **interactive strategy** is when you go straight to the source in question and ask for as much information as possible.

For example, imagine yourself in a new position at a new company. As the December holiday season approaches, you begin to wonder whether you should give a gift to your boss. You could wait to see if others give gifts (passive strategy), you could ask several peers what they do for their supervisors (active strategy), or you could directly ask your boss what the company culture is like and what he or she expects (interactive strategy). Clearly, there are many possible goals that would influence which plan to enact. If the overarching goal is to appear appropriate, effective, and appreciative, the active strategy is probably the best choice. By asking others in your position what they do, you can get a good sense of what your supervisor expects without offending or embarrassing him or her.

Beyond Initial Interactions

Uncertainty reduction theory was originally concerned with explaining and predicting the ambiguity associated with initial interactions (Berger & Calabrese, 1975; Berger, 1979). That is, research using URT emphasized when, why, and how individuals minimize doubt when in new situations or when meeting new people. Berger (1997) has since expanded his position on URT, however, noting that uncertainty exists in new and developing relationships as well as in long-term, ongoing relationships. For example, individuals in ongoing interpersonal relationships also experience uncertainty, in part because relationships themselves are characterized by change and growth—both of which promote the rise of uncertainty. Furthermore, as discussed later in Chapter 3, some researchers believe that a little bit of uncertainty is actually necessary for maintaining a healthy relationship.

To review, URT focuses on when and why individuals use communication to reduce uncertainty about others. Uncertainty predictably decreases when nonverbal immediacy, verbal messages, self-disclosure, shared similarities, and shared social networks increase. People routinely use passive, active, and interactive information-seeking strategies to reduce their uncertainty when encountering others.

❖ EXPECTANCY VIOLATIONS THEORY

Developed by Judee Burgoon (1978, 1994), expectancy violations theory (EVT) explains the various meanings that people attribute to the violation, or infringement, of their personal space. Importantly, whereas much of Burgoon's work emphasizes nonverbal violations of physical space (known as the study of proxemics), personal space can also refer to psychological or emotional space. Similar to URT, EVT is derived from a series of assumptions and axioms.

Assumptions

EVT builds on a number of communication axioms; most central to the understanding of EVT, however, is the assumption that humans have competing needs for **personal space** and for **affiliation** (Burgoon, 1978). Specifically, humans all need a certain amount of personal space, also thought of as distance or privacy; people also desire a certain amount of closeness with others, or affiliation. When you perceive that one of your needs has been compromised, EVT predicts that you will try to do something about it. Thus, Burgoon's initial work focused on the realm of physical space—what happens when someone violates your expectations for appropriate physical distance or closeness.

Beyond explaining individuals' physical space and privacy needs, EVT also makes specific predictions as to how individuals will react to a given violation. Will you **reciprocate,** or match, someone's unexpected behavior, perhaps moving closer or turning toward the individual? Or will you **compensate,** or counteract, by doing the opposite of your partner's behavior? Before making a prediction about reciprocation or compensation, however, you must evaluate EVT's three core concepts: expectancy, violation valence, and communicator reward valence.

Core Concepts of Expectancy Violations Theory

First, **expectancy** refers to what an individual anticipates will happen in a given situation. Expectancy is similar to the idea of social norms and is based on three primary factors. First, the *context* of the behavior is important. In a formal business meeting, for example, hugging a colleague to show support may be inappropriate and may raise some eyebrows. If, however, you hug the same colleague while attending his mother's funeral, the gesture may be perfectly acceptable. Second, the *relationship* one has with the person in question must be examined. If attending the funeral of your boss's mother, a hug may be still be perceived as inappropriate, whereas if the funeral is for the mother of a colleague who is also a personal friend, a hug would likely be more suitable. Third, the *communicator's characteristics* also fuel your expectations; you have expectations for the way people of both sexes and of certain ages, ethnicities, and the like will communicate.

By examining the context, relationship, and communicator's characteristics, individuals arrive at a certain expectation for how a given person should and will likely behave. Changing even one of these expectancy variables might lead to a different expectation. Once you have determined, however, that someone's behavior was, in fact, a breach of expectation, you then judge the behavior in question. This breach is known as the **violation valence**—the positive or negative evaluation you make about a behavior that you did not anticipate. Importantly, not all violations are evaluated negatively. Very often, a person behaves in a way that you might not have expected, but this surprising behavior is viewed positively. For example, a normally cantankerous colleague brings coffee and bagels to the Monday morning staff meeting or the habitually shy intern actually makes eye contact with you and asks for your opinion on a new project.

The third element that must be addressed before predicting reciprocation or compensation involves assessing the person whose behavior is in question. Similar to the violation valence, the **communicator reward valence** is an evaluation you make about the person who committed the violation. Specifically, does this person have the ability to reward (or punish) you in the future? If so, then the person has a positive reward valence. Rewards simply refer to this person's ability to provide you with something you want or need. Similarly, punishment refers to the person's ability to thwart your desires. A boss, a spouse, or a client might also be examples of someone whom you perceive to have such reward–punishment power. Again, however, it is possible for someone with a positive reward valence to engage in a negative violation.

Figure 2.1 Predictions of Expectancy Violations Theory

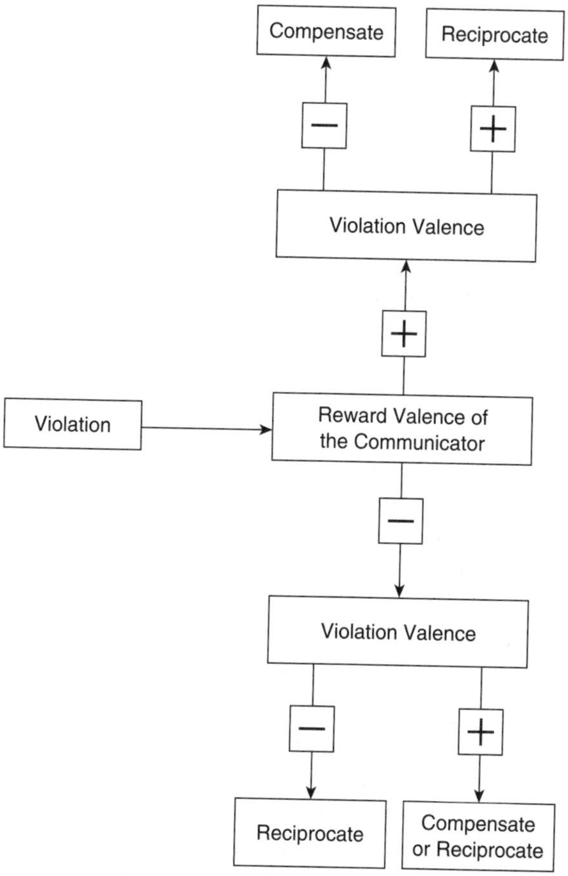

Predicting Reactions When Expectations Are Violated

After assessing expectancy, violation valence, and communicator reward valence of a given situation, it becomes possible to make rather specific predictions about whether the individual who perceived the violation will reciprocate or compensate the behavior in question. These predications are described in Figure 2.1.

Guerrero and Burgoon (1996; Guerrero, Jones, & Burgoon, 2000) noticed that predictable patterns develop when considering reward valence and violation valence together. Specifically, if the violation valence is perceived as positive and the communicator reward valence is also perceived as positive, the theory predicts you will reciprocate the positive behavior. For example, your boss gives you a big smile after you've given a presentation. Guerrero and Burgoon would predict that you smile in return. Similarly, if you perceive the violation valence as negative and perceive the communicator reward valence as negative, the theory again predicts you reciprocate the negative behavior. Thus, if a disliked coworker is grouchy and unpleasant to you, you will likely reciprocate the negative expression and also be unpleasant.

Conversely, if you perceive a negative violation valence but view the communicator reward valence as positive, it is likely that you will compensate for your partner's negative behavior. For example, one day your boss appears sullen and throws a stack of papers in front of you. Rather than grunt back, EVT predicts that you will compensate for your boss' negativity, perhaps by asking if everything is okay (Guererro & Burgoon, 1996). More difficult to predict, however, is the situation in which someone you view as having a negative reward valence violates you with a positive behavior. In this situation, you may reciprocate, giving the person the "benefit of the doubt." Alternatively, you may view the communicator as having suspicious motives, thereby compensating. For example, if the disliked coworker comes in one day and is very pleasant to you, you might be pleasant in return, but you also might treat the person with suspicion.

In summary, EVT focuses broadly on the infringement of one's expectations for "normal" behavior. Burgoon's research has chiefly emphasized the violation of nonverbal space; however, other expectations, such as behavioral norms, can be also violated. Notably, violations are not necessarily negative. One must evaluate the anticipated behavior, the communicator's characteristics, and the violation itself.

❖ CHAPTER SUMMARY

This chapter focused on intrapersonal communication, which refers to the way that individuals assess others' behavior, attitudes, and messages to assign meaning. We discussed four theories. The first, **message design logics,** is concerned with the different beliefs that people have about communication and the way that communication varies because of these beliefs. Second, **attribution theory** focuses on how and why individuals assign causes to other peoples' behavior. Third, **uncertainty reduction theory** states that when individuals encounter someone or something new, they experience uncertainty; uncertainty is uncomfortable, so people use communication strategies to reduce it. Finally, **expectancy violations theory** predicts whether people will reciprocate or compensate when their conversational partner violates their expectations.

Case Study 2 Military Misunderstanding

Much like a large corporation that divides its employees into departments based on task and expertise, the U.S. Air Force organizes its tasks and personnel into divisions called squadrons. Each squadron has a specific job to do; for example, the 705th AGS performs air ground support, and the 714th handles maintenance. Although ultimately all working for the Air Force, each squadron operates relatively independently from the others; as a result, there is a high degree of loyalty to one's squad. Despite intrasquad allegiance, however, a person's rank supercedes this loyalty. For example, if a major were to approach an enlisted or lower ranking individual from a different squadron, let's say a sergeant, the sergeant would always have to defer to the major. Obviously, then, one's squad and rank mean a great deal, particularly when sending and receiving messages.

A civilian employee, Suzanne Miller, worked as administrative assistant at a nearby Air Force base. Although she worked for the 714th MXS squadron that handles maintenance, her unit was required to share half of its hangar with another squadron—and for reasons unknown to Suzanne, the two units didn't get along to say the least. Sure, she knew that intrasquad loyalty was important; however, the constant bickering between members of the two squadrons seemed adolescent.

As a civilian, Suzanne wasn't required to defer to anyone other than her direct supervisors—Master Sergeant (MSGT) Rabby and Staff Sergeant (SSGT) Lakey. Even if a high-ranking officer from another squadron asked her to make some copies or run an errand, Suzanne couldn't comply; only MSGT Rabby and SSGT Lakey had the authority to make requests or require specific duties.

Usually Suzanne's days consisted of filing paperwork, answering phones, and helping to manage the squadron's snack bar. Conveniently located in the main hall of the hangar, the snack bar was common ground for members of both squadrons to mill around. For a civilian just out of college, Suzanne found her job to be an interesting experience, if a bit mundane.

Last month, however, her military experience became a bit more remarkable. Suzanne had recently discovered that an old friend, Michelle Strawbridge, was working as a civilian for the other squadron occupying the hangar. On this particular day, Suzanne decided to use her mandatory midmorning break to catch up with Michelle. She walked over to Michelle's work area, and the two women began chatting. A few minutes into their conversation, an unfamiliar man stormed over. Standing directly in front of Suzanne with his hands on his hips, he angrily fired off questions, demanding, "Who are you? What are you doing here? You're causing a commotion!"

Shocked, Suzanne stared blankly at him. Usually she could distinguish rank and squadron immediately by looking at a person's uniform, complete with pins of rank and commendation, as well as a nametag. This man was not wearing his uniform or a nametag, however. Not recognizing him from her own squadron, Suzanne was unsure of who he was or why he was there barking at her. Irritated, she retorted: "Who are you? I'm allowed to be here chatting with my friend because we are civilians taking our required morning break." The strange man took another step closer; with his face leaning into Suzanne's, he shot back: "Get out of here! I have work to do!" He abruptly turned and marched away.

Suzanne's face turned red; she was shocked and irate. What was going on? Rather than stay and cause any difficulties for her friend, however, Suzanne quickly left Michelle's work space and went back to her squadron's office, trying to forget the incident.

Unfortunately, the episode didn't go away. Later that afternoon, SSGT Lakey called Suzanne into her office. The sergeant explained that the enraged man who had confronted Suzanne was actually Lieutenant Meyers. Suzanne's face went white because she realized that the lieutenant was an officer—and thus higher ranking than any sergeant. Moreover, Suzanne had heard rumors that Lt. Meyers made trouble for those he didn't like.

SSGT Lakey told Suzanne that the lieutenant had approached Suzanne's chief supervisor, MGST Rabby, and had filed a formal complaint against her. Apparently, the Lieutenant had a radically different perception of his encounter with Suzanne, thus casting her in a poor light. His complaint indicated that Suzanne was disruptive, unprofessional, and noncompliant. He wanted her disciplined for incompetence and insubordination. His report concluded by saying, "The Air Force can't afford to have sloppy and defiant employees, even if they are civilians!"

Hearing the report, Suzanne protested, "But that's not what happened!" She gave her account of the situation to SSGT Lakey. Familiar with Lt. Meyers's hotheaded temper and "jump-the-gun" conclusions, SSGT Lakey was inclined to believe Suzanne. After conferring with MSGT Rabby, however, the two sergeants agreed that they didn't want to approach the lieutenant to clarify the situation.

The next day, Suzanne was still bothered by the incident. She wanted to protect her reputation and her record. She asked to meet with MSGT Rabby and explained to him that she was still concerned. In fact, Suzanne thought that the lieutenant could be accused of defamation of character for some of the things he had claimed in the report against her. She wanted the report dismissed from her records. MSGT Rabby replied, "Well, I think that both sides have been explained and now we can all move on. Just try to stay away from the lieutenant. I'm sure he's just been having a rough week or something. But he's no concern to you, really."

MSGT Rabby thought he had diffused the situation until Lt. Meyers approached him, demanding to know what actions had been taken against Suzanne. Suzanne overheard MSGT Rabby saying, "I think everything's fine. I spoke with her and there's no need for everyone to be upset. Why don't we just forget this whole thing?"

Questions for Consideration

1. What message design logic does Lt. Meyers appear to rely on? What about Suzanne? Could this exchange have been more effective if different MDLs were used?

2. What attributions did Lt. Meyers make about Suzanne? What attributions did Suzanne and SSGT Lakey make

about the lieutenant? How might these attributions have exacerbated the problem?

3. What strategies does Suzanne use to reduce her uncertainty during her initial encounter with the "unusual man?" Immediately after the encounter, Suzanne wants to forget about it; why wasn't she initially motivated to find out more about this stranger? Which antecedent condition(s) makes her more motivated to reduce uncertainty?

4. Give examples for each of EVT's core components: expectancy, communicator reward valence, and violation valence. What does EVT explain about Suzanne's reaction to the lieutenant?

5. Which theory seems to explain the situation "better" than the others? Why do you believe this to be the case? What situations might surface that would make a different theory or theories better at explaining the situation? What theories could you combine to make for an even "better" explanation of the encounter?

3

Explaining Theories of Interpersonal Communication

It's difficult to imagine a profession that doesn't require you to interact with other people. You likely use interpersonal communication every day—to handle complaints from a demanding client, to persuade your boss to give you some time off, or to comfort a friend dealing with a difficult relationship. This chapter explains a variety of interpersonal communication theories, including those that explain how relationships are initiated and developed, theories of how relationships are maintained over time, and theories that explain why and what to do when people behave in ways that are unexpected.

❖ INTERPERSONAL COMMUNICATION DEFINED

Interpersonal communication (IPC) has been defined many ways. Some scholars define IPC based on the situation and number of participants involved (e.g., Miller, 1978). Using Miller's definition, IPC occurs between two individuals when they are close in proximity, able to provide immediate feedback and utilize multiple senses. Others define IPC based on the degree of "personalness," or perceived quality, of a given interaction (e.g., Peters, 1974). In Peters's view, IPC includes communication that is personal and occurring between people who are more than acquaintances. Another view of IPC is a goals approach; that is, IPC includes communication used to define or achieve personal goals through interaction with others (e.g., Canary, Cody, & Manusov, 2003).

For the purpose of examining interpersonal communication theory, we argue that IPC encompasses a number of these definitions. Interpersonal communication includes those messages that occur between two, interdependent persons; IPC messages are offered to initiate, define, maintain, or further a relationship. Interpersonal communication is more than just saying a polite hello to the salesclerk in our favorite department store and then scurrying away never to be seen again. Instead, it refers both to the *content* and *quality* of messages relayed and the possibility of further relationship development. We present four theories in this chapter that are critical to current understandings of interpersonal communication and the relationships that develop from these communications. First, the systems perspective takes an interactional view of relationship maintenance by focusing on repeated and interdependent dealings. The second theory, politeness theory, clarifies the strategies individuals use to maintain their "face" or sense of desired public image. Third, social exchange theory evaluates relationships on the basis of rewards and costs; this ratio of benefits to drawbacks explains whether a relationship will continue as well as whether partners will feel satisfied. Fourth, the dialectical perspective describes the contradictions individuals inevitably face within their personal relationships and explains how management of these contradictions can predict a relationship's success or failure.

❖ SYSTEMS PERSPECTIVE

Rather than one specific theory, systems approaches are a constellation of theories that share common assumptions and concepts. Although we have classified this approach as an interpersonal communication theory, in reality systems theories are used to explain nearly all communication contexts, including small group and organizational communication.

The core of all systems approaches is a focus on the interdependence that develops whenever people interact with each other. In this chapter, we focus on some common assumptions of systems perspectives and then the axioms of one specific approach, the work of the Palo Alto Group.

Assumptions of the Systems Perspective

A central assumption of systems approaches is that communication is the means by which systems are created and sustained (Monge, 1973). In addition, systems approaches provide both macro and micro approaches to studying the communication that takes place in relationships. As a macro approach, systems approaches allow for a recognition of how larger social institutions (such as a company or, larger still, a national culture) might influence smaller groups of people such as work groups or families. As a micro approach, systems theories provide a way to understand how individuals and interpersonal relationships between individuals might influence the group as a whole. In short, systems approaches center on the mutual influence between system members, as well as between subsystems, systems, and suprasystems.

First, of course, we have to define what is meant by the term system. A **system** is a group of individuals who interrelate to form a whole (Hall & Fagen, 1968). Examples of systems are a family, a work group, and a sports team. Any time that a group of people has repeated interaction with each other, they represent a system. Systems are embedded in a hierarchy, with systems existing within other systems (Pattee, 1973). Accordingly, a **subsystem** is a smaller part of the group as a whole: the defensive line of a football team or the parents in a family. A **suprasystem** is the larger system within which the system operates: the National Football League is a suprasystem for an individual football team, and the extended kinship network would be a suprasystem for a nuclear family.

More than simply focusing on these sorts of interrelationships, however, there are several assumptions inherent in systems approaches. Systems theories believe in **nonsummativity,** which means that the whole is greater than the sum of its parts (Fisher, 1978). Think of your favorite sports teams. Some sports teams have few superstars, but when they work together, they win a lot of games. On the other hand, some teams have "big-name" athletes, but as systems, these teams are not successful. From a systems perspective, individuals in and of themselves don't make or break the system. Instead, the system as a whole might work together to create more than what might be accomplished by those individuals alone. This ability to achieve more through group effort than individual effort is **positive synergy** (Salazar, 1995). Of course, occasionally **negative synergy** occurs, meaning the group achieves less than the individual parts would suggest (Salazar, 1995). Nevertheless, the point of nonsummativity is that the whole is qualitatively and quantitatively different from the individual components.

A major reason nonsummativity takes place is because of **interdependence** (Rapoport, 1968). Interdependence means that all system members are dependent on all other system members; if one group member drops the ball, literally or figuratively, the group as a whole is unlikely to achieve its goals. Many of you probably have had this experience at work, because there are few professional positions in which an individual operates completely independently. In the example of a newspaper, the failure of an advertising sales rep to meet his or her deadline means the editor can't determine how many pages an issue will have, which means a writer doesn't know whether his or her story will run in that issue and also that the production people can't do preproduction. Every member of a system is dependent on every other member.

Another principle central to systems approaches is **homeostasis** (Ashby, 1962). Homeostasis refers to the natural balance or equilibrium within groups. From a systems perspective, homeostasis is not meant to imply that change doesn't happen. Instead, it is the tendency for a given system to maintain stability in the face of change. This effort at stability can be either functional or dysfunctional for the system. On one hand, a successful system that achieves homeostasis is likely to continue to be successful. However, imagine a system that has a great deal of conflict, which impedes the system's ability to achieve its goals. Homeostasis would suggest that efforts to reduce the conflict might only engender more conflict, because conflict is the "natural" balance of that group. Thus, systems theory recognizes that when a system experiences a novel situation, whether positive or negative, its members will somehow adjust to maintain stability, whether that stability is positive or negative.

A final systems concept of interest in the study of interpersonal communication is **equifinality.** Equifinality suggests that there are multiple ways to achieve the same goal (von Bertalanffy, 1968). Let's say a production group is challenged with the goal of increasing revenues by 10 percent. They can do so by selling more product, increasing the prices of the old product, reducing manufacturing costs of the old product, developing new products, or reducing the workforce needed to make the product, among other things. In short, there are multiple paths the group might take to achieve its goals. In addition, at any given time, there are multiple goals that the group can address. If a group is not only trying to increase revenues but also trying to increase employee morale, it might choose to develop new products, which would simultaneously increase revenues and morale. The group might decide that morale is more important than revenues, however, and focus on that rather than the revenue issue.

In summary, systems approaches focus on the communication that takes place among groups of interacting individuals. It focuses on patterns of communication that exist to sustain homeostasis and achieve systemic goals. The approach also recognizes the influences of larger suprasystems as well as subsystems. As a theoretical approach, it is typically perceived as a description of interpersonal communication, rather than as providing specific testable principles (Fitzpatrick & Ritchie, 1992). One specific systems approach, the Palo Alto Group, has, however, had a profound impact on the study of communication. We turn to this specific systems theory next.

The Palo Alto Group

In 1967, a group of psychiatrists at the Mental Research Institute in Palo Alto, California, published a book called *Pragmatics of Human Communication.* In the book, the three authors, Watzlawick, Bavelas, and Jackson (1967) presented a model for human communication that was grounded in systems thinking. Although the book was intended to focus on interpersonal interaction—and particularly family interaction with behavioral pathologies—these authors provided a foundation for understanding all communication.

According to the Palo Alto Group, there are five axioms of communication (Watzlawick et al., 1967). Summarized in Table 3.1, the first axiom is **on the impossibility of not communicating.** Widely misinterpreted and debated, the axiom suggests that all behavior has the potential to be communicative, regardless of whether the sender intended

Table 3.1 Systems Axioms and Implications for Interpersonal Communication

Axiom	*Implication for Interpersonal Communication*
The impossibility of not communicating	Interactional partners' interpretations of your behavior will affect your relationship, regardless of whether you intended that interpretation.
Content and relationship levels	How you say what you say will affect your partners' interpretations and will also give others clues about the relationships between the interactants.
The problem of punctuation	What you view as the cause and effect is not necessarily how an interactional partner will view it. To resolve the problem, forget about assigning blame.
Digital and analogic communication	Digital communication can express detailed meaning if the interactants share the same set of symbols; analogic communication can express powerful feelings directly.
Complementary and symmetrical communication	Within systems, patterns of interaction develop such that people behave differently or behave similarly. These patterns particularly illustrate power in the relationship.

SOURCE: From Watzlawick, Bavelas, and Jackson, 1967.

the behavior to be interpreted as a message. For example, according to this axiom the "silent treatment" is indeed communicative, because the recipient of the silent treatment is clearly receiving the message: "I'm angry with you." Within a work setting, the person who is chronically tardy might be perceived as communicating his or her disinterest in the work activities. The group member who answers a cell phone in the middle of a meeting might be perceived as sending the message to his or her teammates that "I'm more important than you are." Intentionality is a complex issue in the field of communication, with scholars on both sides of the debate passionate about the role of intent (cf. Andersen, 1991; Motley, 1991). Nevertheless, the Palo Alto group is firmly committed to the belief that communication need not be intentional.

The second axiom is that all communication has both **content and relationship levels** (Watzlawick et al., 1967). When people interact with each other, they are sending particular messages, which are considered the content level. These messages may be verbal or nonverbal. At the same time that they are sending content, they are also sending additional information. The relationship level is characterized as how the content should be understood, particularly in terms of the relationship between the communicators. To illustrate, consider the following statements: "Peter, can you work on getting that brochure copy done?" and "Peter, get the brochure copy done." The content is virtually the same; however, the relationship level gives us quite different information in the two scenarios. The first statement can be understood as a request, whereas the second can be understood as a command. More than that, in the first situation you understand that the two people are on an equal footing and that their relationship is respectful. In the second situation, the speaker either has a legitimate superior status over the listener or the speaker is trying to exert dominance over a status equal. The implications of this information are likely to affect the patterns of communication throughout the entire system.

The third axiom focuses on the tendency of communicators to **punctuate sequences of behavior** (Watzlawick et al., 1967). The grammatical definition of the term *punctuation* refers to the use of marks to separate sentences, clauses, and so forth. For example, the previous sentence has a capital "T" to indicate the beginning of the sentence, two commas to indicate pauses between a series, and a period to indicate the end of the sentence. Watzlawick et al.'s notion of punctuation is similar. They believe that interaction is understood by the people involved in it as a series of beginnings and ends, of causes and effects. For example, in the example used for content and relationship levels, Peter might respond to the command by sarcastically responding, "Why yes, ma'am, right away ma'am, whatever you say, ma'am." Peter would likely view the perceived inappropriate command as the cause of his sarcasm, whereas the person who gave the command might view his flippant attitude as the reason why she had to give a command rather than a request in the first place. The point of this axiom is that although communicators tend to assign causes and effects to interactions, it is likely that interactants will view the same interaction as having different causes and effects; punctuation is always a matter of individual perception, with no perception being wholly correct or incorrect.

Moreover, Watzlawick et al. argued that differences in punctuation frequently lead to conflict among system members.

The fourth axiom is that communication entails both **digital and analogic codes** (Watzlawick et al., 1967). Analogic codes are those in which the symbol actually resembles the object it represents. For example, holding two fingers up to indicate the number 2 is an analogue. Another analogue is crying to represent sadness; the tears are a physical representation of the emotion. Most nonverbals are analogues, although this is not entirely the case. Many emblems, such as giving someone the middle finger or using the okay sign, are not analogues. On the other hand, few verbal messages are analogues, but there are exceptions. Onomatopoeia, in which the word sounds like what it means (words such as *buzz, click,* etc.), can be considered examples of analogic communication.

Digital communication is that in which the symbol and the meaning of the symbol are arbitrarily linked (Watzlawick et al., 1967). For example, there is nothing inherently catlike about the word *cat,* nor is there anything particularly democratic about the word *democracy.* The symbol H_2O does not in any way resemble water. Instead, the meanings of these symbols are culturally determined by the assignment of meaning. Most digital communication is verbal, but as with the exceptions noted here, some nonverbals, particularly emblems, which have dictionary-type definitions, can be considered digital. The OK symbol, wherein you make a circle with your thumb and forefinger, is an example of digital communication (which is why it has different meanings in different cultures).

All in all, this axiom suggests that communication takes place both digitally and analogically, but there are strengths and weaknesses of both means of communication, and communicators have difficulty translating between the two. How does one adequately capture feelings of frustration in words? Conversely, there are tears of sadness and tears of joy; analogic communication alone does not allow you to determine which emotion is being felt.

The fifth and final axiom proposes that **interaction can be symmetrical or complementary** (Watzlawick et al., 1967). When communicators behave in the same manner, they are behaving symmetrically. For example, Mike is sarcastic to you, you are sarcastic to Mike. Mike defers to you, you defer to Mike. When the communicators behave in different ways, they behave in a complementary fashion. For example,

Mike commands, you defer. Mike is sarcastic, you whine. Notice that behaving in a complementary fashion does not mean that interactants are behaving in an *opposite* fashion, just that the patterns of behavior are different. This axiom has most frequently been used to study control behaviors (Millar & Rogers, 1976).

In sum, systems theories recognize the complexities of interaction. They focus on the patterns of relationships that develop between people who interact. The Palo Alto Group's work particularly places emphasis on how communication happens in interpersonal communication systems.

❖ POLITENESS THEORY

Mentioned in the previous chapter, EVT presents an explanation and specific predictions about what individuals do when others behave in ways that contradict their assumptions, particularly assumptions and preferences for personal space. In a somewhat related vein, politeness theory explains how and why individuals try to promote, protect, or "save face," especially when embarrassing or shameful situations arise unexpectedly.

Developed by Brown and Levinson (1978, 1987), politeness theory (PT) clarifies how we manage our own and others' identities through interaction, in particular, through the use of politeness strategies. Building on Goffman's (1967) notion of identity and facework, Brown and Levinson (1978, 1987) determined when, why, and how interpersonal interaction is constructed through (or in the absence of) politeness.

Assumptions of Politeness Theory

Three primary assumptions guide politeness theory. First, PT assumes that all individuals are concerned with maintaining face (Brown & Levinson, 1978, 1987). Simply put, **face** refers to the desired self-image that you wish to present to others; face also includes the recognition that your interactional partners have face needs of their own. There are two dimensions to the concept of face: positive face and negative face. **Positive face** includes a person's need to be liked, appreciated, and admired by select persons. Thus, maintaining positive face includes using behaviors to ensure that these significant others continue to view you in an affirming fashion. **Negative face** assumes a person's desire to act freely, without constraints or imposition from others. Importantly, it is difficult to achieve positive and negative face simultaneously; that is, acting in a way so that you gain others' approval often interferes with autonomous and unrestricted behavior.

Second, politeness theory assumes that human beings are rational and goal oriented, at least with respect to achieving face needs (Brown & Levinson, 1978, 1987). In other words, you have choices and make communicative decisions to achieve your relational and task-oriented goals within the context of maintaining face. Notably, Brown and Levinson posited that face management works best when everyone involved helps to maintain the face of others. In other words, because "everyone's face depends on everyone else's [face] being maintained" (Brown & Levinson, 1987, p. 61), it is in your own best interest to make decisions that uphold this mutual, and rather vulnerable, construction of face.

The final assumption, and despite the understanding of face as mutually constructed and maintained, PT maintains that some behaviors are fundamentally face threatening (Brown & Levinson, 1978, 1987). Inevitably, you will threaten someone else's face, just as another person will, at some point, threaten yours. These **face-threatening acts** (FTAs) include common behaviors such as apologies, compliments, criticisms, requests, and threats (Craig, Tracy, & Spisak, 1993).

Politeness theory, then, ties together these assumptions to explain and predict how, when, and where FTAs occur, as well as what individuals can do to restore face once endangered. Discussed next, we clarify strategies used to uphold and reclaim one's own face and present strategies that pertain to maintaining or threatening the face of others.

Preserving Face

As stated earlier, face is the self-image that individuals desire to present to others as well as the acknowledgment that others have face needs of their own. To create and maintain this desired self-image, individuals must use **facework**—specific messages that thwart or minimize FTAs (Goffman, 1967). **Preventive facework** strategies include communications that a person can use to help oneself or another avert

FTAs (Cupach & Metts, 1994). For example, avoiding certain topics, changing the subject, or pretending not to notice the occurrence of an FTA are all preventive facework strategies.

Similar to preventive facework, **corrective facework** consists of messages that an individual can use to restore one's own face or to help another restore face after an FTA has occurred (Cupach & Metts, 1994). Corrective facework includes the use of strategies such as avoidance, humor, apologies, accounts or explanations of inappropriate actions, and physical remediation wherein one attempts to repair any physical damage that has resulted from the FTA.

Importantly, and as noted earlier, your own face needs may conflict with your partner's face needs. How you manage this discrepancy between self and other's needs may instigate your use of an FTA. As you might imagine, behaving so as to gain others' approval (positive face) can obviously interfere with acting so as to appear self-sufficient and unrestricted (negative face). Sometimes, then, individuals need to choose between positive and negative face needs. Especially when your desire to appear unencumbered outweighs your desire to be liked, you may need to engage in a face-threatening act.

According to PT, individuals can choose one of five suprastrategies when communicating in a manner that could potentially threaten the face of another (Brown & Levinson, 1978). Moving from most polite (and least direct) to least polite (and most direct), these suprastrategies include avoidance, going off record, negative politeness, positive politeness, and bald on record. A speaker who uses **avoidance** simply chooses not to communicate in a way that would create embarrassment or a loss of face for another, whereas when a speaker **goes off record,** he or she subtly hints or indirectly mentions the face-threatening topic. Hinting or making indirect suggestions leave the message open to interpretation, thereby minimizing any face threat. For example, Josephine works as a technician in a veterinary hospital where every fourth weekend, she is expected to be on call for emergencies and to make daily rounds, checking in on the animals. If something comes up and Josephine wants to switch her weekend shift with a colleague, she can hint that "it really stinks that I have to work this weekend; my friends invited me to go to a beach resort for one of those last-minute weekend getaway specials." If Josephine's coworker picks up the hint, he may offer to cover her weekend shift. If the colleague doesn't pick up on her subtlety or doesn't want to work the weekend, he can simply take her disclosure at face value—Josephine wishes she were spending the weekend at a beach resort with friends.

A somewhat more direct approach, **negative politeness,** occurs when the speaker makes an effort to recognize the other's negative face needs, that is, the receiver's need of freedom and lack of restraint. With negative politeness, you appeal to the receiver's negative face needs through apologies and self-effacement to make yourself appear vulnerable to the other, while also acknowledging that the FTA is impolite and inhibits the other's independence. For example, when Josephine attempts to get a coworker to cover her weekend shift, she might say, "I am so sorry to ask, but I need a huge favor. I know this is last minute, and I really hate to be such a pain, but could you cover my shift this weekend? I know this is really inconvenient and I wouldn't ask if it weren't really important." By expressing such regret and making oneself appear self-conscious about committing an FTA, the speaker directly acknowledges the other person's discomfort and potential restriction, while still managing to engage in the face-threatening act for which she claims to be so embarrassed.

An even more direct yet less polite strategy is that of **positive politeness**. Using positive politeness, the speaker emphasizes the receiver's need for positive face, that is, the need to be liked. By ingratiating the receiver with flattery and compliments, you hope to camouflage your face-threatening behavior. For example, Josephine might attempt to "butter up" her colleague with praises before asking him to cover her weekend shift, saying "Bill, you are such a reliable colleague, and so well-respected. I feel like I can really count on you. Would you cover my weekend shift?" Finally, the most direct and least polite strategy is **bald on record.** Using this strategy, the communicator makes no attempt to protect the other's face and simply commits the FTA. Continuing Josephine's predicament, then, she might simply demand that Bill cover for her, saying "Bill, cover my shift this weekend."

According to politeness theory, people choose to engage in FTAs rather tactically. Specifically, there are a number of factors people use to decide how polite to be. These factors are described in Table 3.2. For example, when considering how polite to be, communicators determine whether the person has more or less **prestige** than they do, whether the communicator has **power** over them at the time, and whether what is going to be said runs the **risk** of hurting the other person (Brown & Levinson, 1987).

Table 3.2 Factors Influencing Politeness Strategies

Consideration	*Prediction*
Social distance	If someone has more prestige than you (someone with an impressive title or a great deal of money), you will be more polite; if someone holds little or no prestige over you, you need not be so polite.
Power	If someone has power over you (your boss, or even your auto mechanic if your car is not running), you will be more polite; if it is someone with little power over you, you need not be so polite.
Risk	If what you are going to say has a high chance of hurting someone (you are going to fire them or you are going to report that a spouse is cheating), you will be more polite; if it is not likely to hurt, you need not be so polite.

As well, each of the strategies you can use to engage in an FTA has positive and negative consequences. Going off record to make a request, for example, leaves much room for ambiguity and a high chance that the hint will be ignored. Conversely, using the bald-on-record approach will likely get you what you want but may cost you your own positive face in the process. Furthermore, PT predicts that because humans typically commit FTAs to achieve a desired goal (e.g., to obtain weekend shift coverage), individuals will not use strategies that are more polite than necessary because the cost of ambiguity is too great (Brown & Levinson, 1978).

We should also underscore that the very understanding of face, both positive and negative, varies across cultures, within specific relationships, and even among individuals, to some degree (see face negotiation theory, presented in Chapter 4). Thus, a person must carefully weigh each decision to commit an FTA, considering the anticipated payoff in relation to the context, culture, and individual communicator characteristics of a potential FTA target.

In brief, politeness theory emphasizes the notion of face. Particularly in embarrassing or inappropriate situations, individuals typically try to balance their own positive and negative face while also attending to the other's face needs. When deliberately committing a face-threatening act, individuals can save face using a variety of strategies.

❖ SOCIAL EXCHANGE THEORY

Social exchange theory (SET) is a broad approach used to explain and predict relationship maintenance. Developed by Thibaut and Kelley (1959), SET clarifies when and why individuals continue and develop some personal relationships while ending others. Additionally, the theory takes into account how satisfied you will be with the relationships that you choose to maintain.

As the name of the theory suggests, an exchange approach to social relationships is much like an economic theory based on the comparison of rewards and costs. Thibaut and Kelley's (1959) theory therefore looks at personal relationships in terms of costs versus benefits. What rewards do you receive from a given relationship, and what does it cost you to obtain those rewards? Before making specific predictions, however, certain assumptions must be understood.

Assumptions of Social Exchange Theory

Three assumptions guide SET. First, Thibaut and Kelley (1959) argued that personal relationships are a function of comparing benefits gained versus costs to attain those benefits. Second, and intrinsically tied to the first assumption, people want to make the most of the benefits while lessening the costs. This is known as the **minimax principle.** Last, Thibaut and Kelley maintained that, by nature, humans are selfish. Thus, as a human being, you tend to look out for yourself first and foremost. Although these assumptions are sometimes difficult for students and the general public to accept, they become easier to recognize when explained more clearly within the frame of SET's three core components: outcome, comparison level, and comparison level of alternatives.

Core Components of Social Exchange Theory

Three core components make up social exchange theory. First, and prefaced in the previous paragraphs, to understand SET, we must acknowledge that social relationships bring both rewards and costs. The **outcome** of a relationship, therefore, is the ratio of rewards to costs in a given relationship; this can be represented by a simple mathematical equation: Rewards – Costs = Outcome (Thibaut & Kelley, 1959).

Relational rewards include any benefits that you perceive as enjoyable or that help you to achieve specific aspirations. For example, rewards between spouses might include companionship, affection, and sharing a joint savings account. Relational costs are those drawbacks that we perceive as unpleasant or that prevent us from pursuing or achieving an objective. For example, negotiating holiday visits with the in-laws, loss of social independence, and having to put grad school on hold because of family obligations all could be potential costs for a married couple.

What an individual perceives as a reward or a cost in a given relationship will, of course, vary. The general idea is that people make mental notes of the rewards and costs associated with their relationships. One hopes that the rewards outweigh the costs, resulting in a positive outcome value. If an individual perceives that the relationship yields more drawbacks than benefits, however, a negative outcome value will result. Importantly, the outcome value itself is not enough to predict whether a person will choose to stay in or leave a relationship. Rather, the outcome value becomes a benchmark used to help measure our relational rewards in comparison to our expectations and our alternatives. Once the outcome value of a relationship is determined, individuals can begin to determine satisfaction with and stability of that relationship, as well as the likelihood of its continuing.

The second core element of SET is the **comparison level.** The comparison level (CL) represents what rewards a person *expects* to receive in a particular relationship (Thibaut & Kelley, 1959). Expectations may be based on models for relationships (e.g., parents, friends), one's own experiences with relationships, television and other media representations of relationships, and the like. The importance of understanding what you expect in a relationship is this: SET maintains that individuals compare their current outcome value with their CL. In other words, if you perceive more rewards than costs in your relationship and this matches or exceeds your expectations for the relationship, SET predicts your satisfaction (Outcome > CL). Conversely, if you perceive more rewards than costs in a current relationship, but expected to receive even more rewards than you currently have, a sense of dissatisfaction is predicted (CL > Outcome). Thus, predicting one's satisfaction with a relationship is based on a positive outcome value that also meets or exceeds one's expectations (CL).

The third and final component to SET is the **comparison level of alternatives.** Thibaut and Kelley (1959) recognized that simply determining one's satisfaction, or dissatisfaction, with a relationship is still not enough to predict whether the relationship will continue or end. Everyone knows a handful of individuals who are dissatisfied with any one of their personal relationships—be it a friendship, marriage, or work partnership—and yet, despite their unhappiness, these individuals remain in that relationship. Why?

SET holds that for any relationship to continue or end, individuals must also examine their comparison level of alternatives or CL_{alt} (Thibaut & Kelley, 1959). That is, what are your alternatives to staying in the relationship? Is ending it better or worse than the current situation? Only when you perceive that the alternatives are greater than your outcome and greater than our CL will you end a relationship. Even if satisfied with a current relationship (i.e., Outcome > CL), you may perceive that your alternatives are even better, in which case SET predicts that you will terminate the relationship (represented mathematically by CL_{alt} > Outcome > CL).

It should be obvious, then, that many scenarios are possible, depending on the perceptions of **Outcomes : CL : CL_{alt}.** Only when individuals or researchers have knowledge about all three elements is it possible to make predictions about the state and status of a relationship. An overview of the specific predictions made is in Table 3.3.

To review, SET explains and predicts an individual's decision to maintain or de-escalate a particular relationship. Specifically, people evaluate the rewards and costs associated with remaining in their relationships while also considering their expectations and other alternatives.

Table 3.3 Predictions Made by Social Exchange Theory

Outcomes > CL = Satisfied
Outcomes < CL = Dissatisfied
Outcomes > Cl_{alt} = Stay
Outcomes < Cl_{alt} = Terminate

❖ DIALECTICAL PERSPECTIVE

The dialectical perspective is also useful for explaining and understanding how individuals sustain interpersonal relationships. Specifically, Baxter and Montgomery (1996; Baxter, 1988) argued that relationships are dynamic; these researchers believe that it is impossible for a relationship to maintain a certain level of satisfaction or reach a constant status quo. Much like a spiraling trajectory, Baxter and Montgomery proposed that the relational partners continue to develop their relationships by managing a series of opposing, yet necessary, tensions or contradictions.

Four primary assumptions guide a dialectical approach to relationship maintenance: praxis, change, contradiction, and totality (Baxter & Montgomery, 1996). First, **praxis** suggests that relationship trajectories are neither linear (always moving forward) nor repetitive (cycling through the same things again and again). Instead, a dialectical perspective assumes that relationships can become more intimate or less intimate over time (Canary & Zelley, 2000). Thus, relational partners act and react while their relationship's trajectory spirals—moving forward in time and therefore transforming reality.

Change, or motion, is the second assumption (Baxter, 1988; Baxter & Montgomery, 1996). A dialectical approach presumes that the only guarantee in a relationship is that it will change. Viewed this way, it is virtually impossible to "maintain" a relationship because maintenance implies a steady state. Instead, Montgomery (1993) argued that relationships are "sustained," not maintained.

Third, a dialectic approach assumes that relationships are grounded in interdependent, yet mutually negating **contradictions** (Baxter, 1988; Baxter & Montgomery, 1996). Stated differently, within every relationship, both partners have essential, yet opposing needs. Because these needs counteract each other such that you can't achieve both needs at the same time, ongoing tensions result. For example, spouses need to spend time together to sustain their marriage; on the other hand, both partners need to have some time to themselves, away from their partner and relational obligations. Both togetherness and independence are needed, but you can't have both at the same time. The dialectical perspective maintains that relationships are sustained based on partners' communication used to manage these ever-present contradictions.

The fourth and last assumption, **totality,** emphasizes interdependence between relationship partners (Baxter, 1988; Baxter & Montgomery, 1996). Much like systems perspectives, dialectics recognizes that without interdependence, a relationship cannot exist. Accordingly, a tension that you feel will ultimately affect your relationship partner and vice versa, even if that person didn't initially feel the tension.

When these four assumptions are brought together, we reach a rather complex understanding of relationships. To sustain a relationship, therefore, means that the relationship will constantly fluctuate, spiraling forward in time, while relational partners experience and try to satisfy interdependent yet opposing needs.

Three central tensions are thought to exist between relationship partners: autonomy–connection, openness–closedness, and predictability–novelty (Baxter, 1988). With each pairing of tensions, you can see that both individuals in a given relationship need both elements; yet is impossible to fulfill both needs simultaneously. The **autonomy–connection** dialectic refers to the tension between the desire to feel connected to one's partner versus the desire to maintain a sense of independence. Similarly, the **openness–closedness** dialectic includes the pull between wanting to open up and self-disclose while also wanting to maintain one's privacy. Finally, the **predictability–novelty** dialectic is the tension between wanting stability or steadiness while also wanting opportunities for spontaneity. According to the dialectical perspective, then, relational partners continually vacillate between each of these three poles.

For example, Will and Vanessa have been married for 8 years. Both have demanding careers and are raising twin boys. To feel satisfied within this marriage while balancing two careers and a family, Will and Vanessa must make time to spend together. This might mean hiring a babysitter and going to dinner occasionally or making a point of staying up after the boys go to bed to discuss their day. In each case, however, the couple is trying to feel connected. At the same time, Will and Vanessa need to maintain a certain amount of independence, some time to pursue their own hobbies, or just some quiet time to meditate or read a book.

It should be obvious that it is difficult, if not impossible, to have togetherness and independence simultaneously, hence the dialectical tension. Furthermore, these tensions become magnified when one partner desires connection while the other needs some autonomy. It is this constant struggle and balancing act that propels a relationship forward.

Similarly, three central tensions are thought to exist between the relational partners as a unit and their social world. These tensions parallel the internal dialectical tensions and include inclusion–seclusion, revelation–concealment, and conventionality–uniqueness (Baxter, 1988).

Again, note that it is both necessary and difficult to satisfy both poles of each contradiction simultaneously. The **inclusion–seclusion** dialectic emphasizes the tension partners experience when they want to spend time with friends, family, or coworkers versus wanting to spend their time alone together as a couple. The **revelation–concealment** dialectic involves the tension between relationship partners who want to reveal aspects of their relationship to the outside world while also wanting to keep some aspects of their relationship private. Last, the dialectic of **conventionality–uniqueness** emphasizes the tension partners feel between wanting to behave in ways that are considered normative or traditional versus wanting to emphasize their relationship's uniqueness by doing something differently. Table 3.4 presents an overview of internal and external dialectics.

Returning to Will and Vanessa, they learn that they are pregnant with their third child. Elated but also worried about the complications involved in the early stages of pregnancy, they aren't sure whether they should reveal their good news to their family or if they should wait until the first trimester passes. The struggle between deciding whether to disclose their news to friends and family (revelation) or to keep the pregnancy secret (concealment) until the second trimester is difficult, particularly if one partner wants to reveal and the other wants to conceal.

To manage or sustain a relationship, then, these tensions must be managed. Baxter and Montgomery (1996) identified four primary strategies used to handle the internal and external tensions: selection, cyclic or spiraling alteration, segmentation, and integration. The **selection** strategy involves choosing to favor one pole or need at the expense of the other. For example, a couple that dates over long distance may eventually choose autonomy and break up because the tension between living an independent life versus making time to visit the other partner proves too difficult. Much like children playing on a seesaw, partners who use **cyclic alteration** (sometimes referred to as spiraling alteration) fulfill one pole or need now and will shift to fulfill the other pole at a later time, creating a back-and-forth, back-and-forth strategy of coping.

The third strategy, **segmentation,** compartmentalizes the relationship such that certain issues coincide with one pole or need, and other issues are appropriate for the opposite pole. For example, if two close friends agree on most everything except for their bitter arguments

Table 3.4 Internal and External Dialectics

Internal Dialectics	*Corresponding External Dialectics*
Autonomy–Connection. Desiring some independence but also desiring a union with your partner.	*Inclusion–Seclusion.* Desiring to have strong friendship and family networks but also desiring alone time with your partner.
Openness–Closedness. Desiring to be completely open and honest but also desiring to have some private thoughts and feelings.	*Revelation–Concealment.* Desiring to tell your family and friends relational information but also desiring to have some private information.
Predictability–Novelty. Desiring a stable relationship but also desiring some excitement and spontaneity.	*Conventionality–Uniqueness.* Desiring to have a traditional relationship but also desiring a unique relationship.

about politics, a segmentation strategy would allow the friends to choose the closedness pole for politics but the openness pole for everything else. The fourth strategy, **integration,** includes several variations and is predicated on incorporating aspects of both poles so as to create a more fulfilling experience. For example, a couple who wants to integrate novelty and predictability might agree that Friday is date night—every Friday (predictability) they will get a babysitter and try a new restaurant (novelty). Obviously a more sophisticated way of managing relational tensions, integration implies that relationship partners have an awareness of the tensions and can talk about them so as to find ways to creatively integrate and manage relational tensions.

All told, dialectics presents a rather complicated view of close relationships. This unwieldy depiction is also why it is a "perspective" and not a more precise theory. Nonetheless, dialectics' emphasis of the changing nature of relationships as well as its understanding of the various contradictions and tensions that individuals experience, make it a logical approach to which many can easily relate.

❖ CHAPTER SUMMARY

This chapter provided an overview of four theories of interpersonal communication. **Systems perspectives** suggest that by studying the interrelated patterns of communication of people in a relationship, you can understand the relationship. **Politeness theory** explains and predicts strategies that individuals use to maintain "face" or sense of desired public image. **Social exchange theory** predicts that individuals initiate and maintain relationships so as to maximize personal outcomes; at the same time, however, expectations and alternatives play a role in individuals' ultimate satisfaction and whether they stay in the relationship. Finally, the **dialectical perspective** suggests that sustaining interpersonal relationships requires communication to manage the necessary but contradictory tensions inherent in all relationships.

Case Study 3 Coworker Conflict

Laura Abbott is simultaneously worried about her coworker, John Brown, and irritated that she is wasting her own energy worrying about him. Laura and John had always gotten along well; they had started working at *WEML* roughly at the same time, both doing lowly production assistant duties for the station. After a year, they both had the opportunity to move to the assignment desk. Because they have spent so much time together, they are friends, although Laura wouldn't consider them to be close friends. The two of them are really different from each other; John is desperate to be liked, and he is always doing little favors for people. Laura doesn't much care if people like her. She wants to do her job, and do it well. Of course, it would be nice if people respected her for doing a good job, too, but for the most part, she doesn't want to be bothered. The two also have different career goals. Laura knows that John really wants to be a news writer. She has wanted to be a producer and has been eyeing a field production position.

She started worrying about John because yesterday the station manager called Laura into his office and told her that a news writer position was going to open up, and he wanted Laura to take the job. On one hand, Laura was ambitious, and it would be a step up in the world. On the other hand, she didn't really want to be a news writer, and she knew that John would love the job. So she told her boss that she was interested in the position but wasn't sure if she or John would be the better choice. Her boss' response was "John isn't going anywhere fast. He needs to learn to be more assertive or he'll never make it in this business. You, on the other hand, have got what it takes." She felt torn between telling her boss that she wasn't really interested in writing and John was and just keeping her mouth shut. John was her friend, and she thought she ought to tell her boss so. Instead, she thanked her boss and told him she would let him know the next day.

Almost as soon as she walked out of her boss' office, she ran into John.

"Hey, Laura, what's the matter?" John asked.

"What?" she responded, confused about why he thought something might be wrong. Then the guilt set in, and she quickly threw in "Nothing. Nothing's wrong."

"You don't look like nothing's wrong," John asserted. "You look like you have a lot on your mind."

"Uh, no," she said, and dropped her eye contact. "There's just a lot going on and I'm tired," she said, trying to walk away.

"So much to do that you're blowing off lunch?" John asked.

Laura mentally cursed. It was lunchtime, and the two of them usually grabbed something together. She just didn't want to have to face him right now. "Uh, I'm just not hungry right now. Let's try something new and exciting and skip lunch."

For the rest of the day John kept looking at her with both hurt and concern in his eyes. Over the course of the day, she became increasingly irritated with the "puppy dog thing," and she got more terse and sarcastic when she spoke with him. Unfortunately, this just seemed to make John look at her with more hurt and concern.

That night, Laura tried to look at the situation rationally. She liked John, he was nice and he was someone to hang around with, but realistically they weren't that close, and she wasn't looking to make the relationship any closer. A career opportunity was more important than a casual friendship, wasn't it? It's not like she wouldn't be able to make friends with other people at work once she moved up the ladder. She decided to take the job.

She also decided she wasn't going to tell John because she didn't want to be the person to hurt him. As soon as she saw his look of concern the next morning, however, she lost her patience. She knew she would have to tell him.

"Okay, you want to know what is wrong?" Laura asked. "Well, nothing's wrong, I just got offered a job as a news writer, and I'm going to take it," she said defiantly.

John was stunned. Not only had someone he considered to be a good friend taken a job she knew he wanted, she was rude in the process! Clearly she didn't respect him at all, he thought. At his stricken look, Laura softened.

"I'm sorry, John, I know you wanted the job. I told the manager that you're a great guy, but he wanted me in the job, and

I figured one of us was better than neither of us. I hope we can still be friends."

Questions for Consideration

1. What axioms of communication were present in the friendship system of John and Laura?
2. What face needs do John and Laura have? How did Laura respond to the face-threatening act of telling John that she was taking the job? Is this what politeness theory would predict? Why or why not?
3. Social exchange theory predicts the satisfaction and stability of relationships. Using Laura's perspective and John's perspective, what would the theory predict about the future of their relationship?
4. What internal and external dialectics were present in the coworker conflict?
5. Do any of the theories emerge as "better" than the others? Why do you believe this to be the case? What situations might surface that would make a different theory or theories better at explaining the situation?

4

Explaining Theories of Culture

Understanding the dynamics of cross-cultural and intercultural communication is critical in today's multicultural society and global economy (Ting-Toomey, 1992). Within the United States, multicultural communities continue to expand and flourish. Here and abroad, international travel is both relatively easy and common, and in the corporate sector, global competition and cooperation is no longer the exception but the norm. Although the proliferation of cross-cultural and intercultural communication is probably not new to you, the implications, difficulties with, and strategies for improving the competence of these exchanges is profound, particularly considering the high failure rate of such interaction (Ting-Toomey, 1992).

❖ CULTURE DEFINED

Okay, so you recognize that today's personal and professional landscape is more diverse than ever, but what exactly is culture? We embrace Collier's (1989) notion of **culture** as one's identification with and acceptance into a group that shares symbols, meanings, experiences, and behavior. Similarly, cross-cultural communication and intercultural communication have specific definitions. **Cross-cultural** communication is the comparison of two or more cultural communities (Ting-Toomey, 1991b), for example, comparing conflict styles of U.S. managers with those of Korean managers. Somewhat differently, **intercultural communication** involves the actual interaction between members of different cultures, for instance, examining what happens when a German executive reprimands a Chinese subordinate.

Using these definitions, we have selected four theories that examine broadly defined notions of culture and emphasize how culture shapes and is shaped by communication. First, Hofstede's dimensions of culture provides a typology useful for assessing cultural differences across social contexts. Next, communication accommodation theory explains and predicts speech convergence through the perception of cultural and social identities. Third, face negotiation theory addresses how cultural differences with face concern influence conflict management. Fourth, we look at perspectives that view gender as culture.

❖ HOFSTEDE'S CULTURAL DIMENSIONS

Geert Hofstede is a Dutch management researcher who created an inductive theory of culture. Specifically, he gathered statistical data from 100,000 employees of IBM around the world to determine the values on which cultures vary (Hofstede, 1980). In the process, he surveyed workers from 50 countries and three regions. His analysis concluded that there are five dimensions that can be used to differentiate and rate various cultures (Hofstede, 1980; Hofstede & Bond, 1984). Each of the dimensions is described as a continuum, with distinct cultures classified somewhere along the continuum.

Individualism-Collectivism

The first dimension is **individualism-collectivism.** This dimension addresses how people define themselves and their relationships with others. Discussed first, there are four characteristics of cultures that fall on the individualism side of the continuum (Triandis, 1995). First, such cultures support the belief that the individual is the most important entity in any social setting. Think about some common phrases you have heard in the United States (a highly individualistic culture). When asked to do something beyond one's responsibilities, an American is likely to ask, "What's in it for me?" In explaining why an individual is ending a romantic relationship, the person might say, "I was putting more into it than I was getting out of it." In short, in individualistic cultures the focus is on the self before all other relationships.

Second, individualistic cultures stress independence rather than dependence (Triandis, 1995). Recall the description of positive versus negative face needs in Chapter 3. Positive face is the desire to be appreciated and liked. Negative face need is the desire to be free from impositions. Ting-Toomey (1988) argued that people from individualistic cultures tend to place relatively more emphasis on negative face needs compared with individuals from collectivistic cultures; there is a cultural preference to be free from imposition, which is in essence a desire to be independent.

Third, individualistic cultures reward individual achievement (Triandis, 1995). To illustrate, U.S. organizations frequently use merit pay and employee recognition programs. These programs focus on recognizing particular individuals and their performance, raising them above other employees in the organization. The focus on individual achievement tends to be associated with an increased belief in the value of competition. In individualistic cultures, competition is viewed as a good thing. This is not always the case in collectivistic cultures.

Finally, according to Triandis (1995), individualistic cultures value the uniqueness of each individual. In individualistic cultures, standing out from the crowd is an important value, whereas in collectivistic cultures standing out from others is a source of embarrassment. Consider the variations in two cultural proverbs (Mieder, 1986). An American proverb is "the squeaky wheel gets the grease." This implies that you will receive rewards by distinguishing yourself from others; you ought to speak up and be noticed. A Japanese proverb is "the tallest nail gets hammered down." This implies that punishment is associated with being different—you are better off being the same as others.

Thus far we have talked at length about individualism but have not addressed collectivism in detail. Collectivism refers to a social system that is based on in-groups and out-groups. In collectivistic cultures, groups (relatives, clans, organizations) are the central way of understanding relations between people; identity is understood solely through group membership. There are also four characteristics associated with collectivism (Triandis, 1995).

First, in collectivistic cultures the views, needs, and goals of the group are more important than any individual views, needs, or goals (Triandis, 1995). For many Americans, the idea of kamikaze pilots or suicide bombers makes no sense. Yet in collectivistic cultures, the needs of the group supercede the needs of the individual. In these sorts of systems, dying for the good of a group makes sense.

Second, obligation to the group is the norm in collectivistic cultures; behavior is guided by duty not by individual pleasure or rewards (Triandis, 1995). This focus on duty over pleasure is apparent in mate selection. In individualistic cultures, people are "free" to marry the mate of their choice. In collectivistic cultures, acceptance of the potential mate by the family is of central importance (Dion & Dion, 1993).

Third, in collectivistic cultures, the self is defined in relation to others, not as distinct from others (Triandis, 1995). Jandt (2004) provided an example to illustrate this point. Imagine a person from Colombia (a more collectivistic culture) coming to the United States. In the United States people are likely to ask this visitor what he or she does for a living because Americans are understood by their individual accomplishments. In Colombia, the first question asked of this same person would likely be, "Who are you related to?" Knowing a person's "connections" enables strangers to place that person into particular groups; knowing where a person comes from is the same as knowing who that person is.

Fourth and finally, those from collectivistic cultures focus on cooperation rather than competition (Triandis, 1995). This characteristic manifests in particular communication patterns in collectivistic cultures. Collectivistic cultures tend to use a **high-context communication style** (Hall, 1976). A high-context message is one that privileges relational harmony over clarity or directness; messages tend to be indirect, circular, or unspoken so as not to offend. It is assumed that the receiver will actively seek to understand what is really meant. By contrast, a **low-context communication style,** which is characteristic of individualistic cultures, values the direct, explicit expression of ideas. In low-context communication, the meaning is in the message, and sometimes "the truth hurts."

We have presented a number of details unique to individualism and collectivism, but individualism and collectivism exist together in all cultures—they are, in essence, two sides of the same coin. Certain cultures, however, tend to operate at one end of the continuum or the other. We turn next to the second dimension of culture as described by Hofstede (1980), uncertainty avoidance.

Uncertainty Avoidance

We talked about the concept of *uncertainty* in Chapter 2. As a cultural dimension, uncertainty avoidance refers to the extent to which "people within a culture are made nervous by situations which they perceive as unstructured, unclear, or unpredictable" (Hofstede, 1986, p. 308). Those cultures that seek to avoid ambiguity are known as **high uncertainty avoidance** cultures. Typically, cultures that are high in uncertainty avoidance maintain strict codes of behavior, and support a belief in absolute truths (Hofstede, 1986). For instance, in high uncertainty avoidance cultures, the workplace is typified by rules, precision, and punctuality (Jandt, 2004). The preference for a business meeting would be a structured agenda, which would be rigidly followed (Lewis, 2000).

Cultures that are low in uncertainty avoidance tend to accept ambiguity and lack of structure more easily (Hofstede, 1986). Individuals in **low uncertainty avoidance cultures** are more inclined to take risks, innovate, and value "thinking outside of the box." Clearly, American culture is a low uncertainty avoidance culture. In the workplace, individuals from low uncertainty avoidance cultures tend to work hard only when needed (Jandt, 2004). Rules are often rejected or ignored, and punctuality has to be taught and reinforced.

Power Distance

The third dimension uncovered by Hofstede (1980) is power distance, which refers to the extent to which people with little power in society consider inequity normal and acceptable. Those cultures with a **high power distance** accept power as a scarce resource and power differences as natural and inevitable. In these sorts of cultures there is greater centralization of power, and there is a great importance placed on status and rank. When it comes to the workplace, high power distance cultures tend to have a large number of supervisors, a rigid system that classifies each job along a hierarchy, and decision making only among those at the high end of the hierarchy (Adler, 1997). There tends also to be a wide salary gap between those high and low in the hierarchy (Jandt, 2004).

Cultures that have a **low power distance** value the minimization of power differences (Hofstede, 1980). Although hierarchy might exist, people who are higher in the hierarchy are not assumed to be superior to people lower in the hierarchy; people at all levels reach out to people at all other levels. Moreover, people lower in power believe that through motivation and hard work, they can achieve power (Hofstede, 1980). In the workplace, low power distance cultures view shared decision making with subordinates as empowering (Jandt, 2004).

Despite the fact that the U.S. Declaration of Independence asserts that "all men are created equal," the United States is becoming increasingly higher in power distance. Consider the following statistics. In 1980, the average salary of a CEO was 42 times that of the average worker. In 1990, the figure rose to 85 times as much. In 2000, the average CEO made 531 times as much as the average worker (Jandt, 2004). These figures mirror statistics indicating that the difference between the "haves" and the "have-nots" is growing in the United States; the rich are growing richer, but the poor are not sharing the wealth (Jandt, 2004). To the extent that American citizens believe that this power differential is acceptable and normative they are demonstrating an acceptance of increasingly higher power distance.

Masculinity–Femininity

When we look around the world, the role of women varies dramatically. Hofstede's (1980) fourth dimension focuses on the relationship between biological sex and what is considered sex-appropriate behavior. **Masculine cultures** are those that use the reality of biological sex in the creation of distinct roles for men and women. In masculine cultures, men are expected to be assertive, ambitious, and competitive; women are expected to be supportive, nurturing, and deferent. Translating these values to the workplace, countries with a masculine orientation believe that managers are supposed to be decisive and assertive (Jandt, 2004). More important, women have a difficult time achieving workplace equality; they are given lower wages, less stable work, and few opportunities to advance (Kim, 2001).

The United States is a masculine country. Although women are making inroads in organizational life, there is still a significant wage gap, and the glass ceiling remains a reality (Women Employed Institute, 2002). Moreover, women are often expected to conform to masculine norms if they hope to succeed at work (Ragins, Townsend, & Mattis, 1998).

By contrast, **feminine cultures** are those that have fewer rigid roles for behavior based on biological sex (Hofstede, 1980). Men and women are equally permitted to be assertive or deferent, competitive or nurturing. Instead of rigid sex roles, the focus in feminine cultures tends to be on the facilitation of interpersonal relationships and concern for the weak (Jandt, 2004). In the workplace, feminine cultures manifest consensus seeking and a preference for quality of life over material success. To illustrate, consider Sweden, a highly feminine culture. In Sweden the law allows both men and women to balance parenthood and employment. At the birth of a child, both the mother and the father are eligible for a paid 360-day leave of absence from work ("Child Care in Sweden," 1998).

Long-Term and Short-Term Orientation

Hofstede's (1980) original research stopped after the first four dimensions. After accusations that there was a Western bias to his work, Hofstede collected additional data with the assistance of Chinese scholars and ultimately added a fifth cultural dimension. Grounded in Confucian thinking, Hofstede (2001) called this dimension the orientation toward long-term versus short-term. A **long-term orientation** is associated with thrift, savings, perseverance, and the willingness to subordinate one's self to achieve a goal. In cultures with a long-term orientation, employees typically have a strong work ethic and keep their eyes toward the achievement of distant goals (Hofstede, 2001). A **short-term orientation** centers on a desire for immediate gratification. Individuals in these cultures tend to spend money to "keep up with the Joneses" and prefer quick results to long-term gain (Hofstede, 2001). Employees seek immediate pay and benefits and are less willing to sacrifice in the short run to achieve in the long run.

The Dimensions Combined

Table 4.1 plots eight countries on each of the five dimensions (Hofstede, 2001). Note that just because two countries are similar in

Table 4.1 Rankings of Select Countries on Hofstede's Dimensions

	Individualism–Collectivism	*Uncertainty Avoidance*	*Power Distance*	*Masculinity–Femininity*	*Long–Term, Short–Term*
Arab countries	Both	Moderate	Large	Mod masc	Not available
Italy	High ind	Moderate	Moderate	Extreme masc	Not available
Japan	Both	Extreme high	Moderate	Extreme masc	Long term
Mexico	Mod coll	High	Large	Extreme masc	Not available
South Korea	High coll	High	Moderate	Mod fem	Long term
Sweden	Mod ind	Extreme low	Very small	Extreme fem	Both
United States	Extreme ind	Low	Moderate	High masc	Short term
Venezuela	Extreme coll	Moderate	Large	Extreme masc	Not available

one dimension does not mean they will be similar in another. Moreover, recognize that the rankings described are generalizations about each culture; it should come as no surprise that individual variations exist within each culture. Finally, in many countries, including the United States, different groups in the same culture might rank quite differently within a given dimension. For example, although the dominant U.S. culture is individualistic, researchers believe that African Americans and Hispanics tend more toward collectivism (e.g., Hecht, Collier, & Ribeau, 1993).

In sum, Hofstede collected data and then proposed a theory of culture that allows scholars to understand variations within and across cultures. His dimensions consist of individualism–collectivism, uncertainty avoidance, power distance, masculinity–femininity, and long-term or short-term orientation.

❖ COMMUNICATION ACCOMMODATION THEORY

Have you ever caught yourself slipping into a southern drawl or using "y'all" while speaking to a native Texan? Maybe you have found yourself speaking in fast, clipped tones when talking with a New Yorker, or upon returning from a European vacation, friends point out that you suddenly sound more like Prince Charles than Charles Gibson. Do you speed up while talking with some colleagues, but slow your speech when speaking with others? Communication accommodation theory (CAT) can explain many of the changes in your speech and language use.

Originally conceived as speech accommodation theory (Giles, Mulac, Bradac, & Johnson, 1987) and later refined as communication accommodation theory (Giles & Coupland, 1991), CAT provides an informative platform from which to understand cultural differences and similarities with regard to speech and language. Essentially, Giles and colleagues argued that when interacting with others, individuals will accommodate their speech and language patterns, either by matching their partners' speech or by differentiating their speech and language use. In this section, we explain Giles and colleagues' notion of accommodation through both convergence and divergence. We also relate these concepts specifically to the communication of culture and to intercultural communication—that is, communication between members of different cultures.

Communicating Social Identity Through In-Groups and Out-Groups

Giles and Coupland (1991) assumed that individuals belong to a wide variety of social groups, such as groupings based on ethnicity, race, gender, and religion. Moreover, they maintained that these groups shape each person's collective identity. For example, "most ethnic minority groups in the United States have tended to form communities, however small, where they have other people of similar heritage to sustain their ethnic values, socialization practices, and culture" (Vivero & Jenkins, 1999, p. 9). Similarly, your marital status (married), your political alignment (Republican), your career (public relations director), and your ethnicity (Irish American) all represent various social groups that influence the way that you perceive yourself and that others perceive you.

Like it or not, human beings categorize information to simplify and create understanding. One way in which we commonly categorize others and ourselves is through these social identity groups; these clusters are divided into in-groups and out-groups, which were discussed in the section on Hofstede's dimensions. **In-groups** are social affiliations to which an individual feels that he or she belongs (Giles & Coupland, 1991). **Out-groups** are those social affiliations to which a person feels that he or she does not belong. In the workplace, for example, you may go to happy hour with members from your team or department but would feel out of place socializing with members of another department. Similarly, if you play on a company softball league, your teammates may become an in-group, even if you had not interacted previously.

In-groups and out-groups are important for understanding CAT. According to Giles and Coupland (1991), language, speech, and nonverbal messages all communicate one's in-group and out-group status. For example, if you have been around a group of teenagers recently, you may feel very much part of the out-group because your poor command of slang (language) and lack of body piercings (nonverbal artifacts) clearly differentiate you from them. When your teenage son says, "Hey! You don't need to be all up in the Kool-Aid" in response to your simple question of "Where are you taking your date tonight?" he has differentiated himself (a hip teen) from you (a stodgy middle-aged parent). Instead of simply saying "it's none of your business," his use of slang leaves you wondering what the heck he is talking about, thereby creating a gap between his generation and yours.

The use of slang to create in-group and out-group status applies to the workplace as well. Each profession has its own set of jargon or specialized language that not only gives precision to words and meanings but also helps to create and maintain a distinct in-group. Thus, jargon includes those individuals who have similar training and experience and excludes everyone else. A member of your company's information technology (IT) department may use computer jargon that intimidates the non–technology minded. For instance, when Karen calls her company's IT department with a question about a problem she is having with a Web site password, the help desk manager asks her, "What's your ISP?" Karen has no idea what an ISP is, much less which one she is using. In this instance, the help desk manager may use the jargon unintentionally when communicating with out-group members such as Karen and employees from other departments simply out of habit. Conversely, the manager may intentionally rely on jargon so as to intimidate the out-group members or to promote one's own credibility. Because she doesn't know what her ISP is, Karen may feel inferior, or she may perceive the help desk manager as possessing complex and invaluable information. Karen may even feel frustrated or annoyed because members of the help desk can't seem to explain things in plain English. Importantly, then, jargon is both inclusive and exclusive and should be used cautiously with out-group members.

Accommodation Through Convergence or Divergence

Individuals adjust their speech and conversational patterns either in an effort to assimilate with or to deviate from others (Giles & Coupland, 1991). When a person wants to be viewed as part of an in-group, CAT predicts that this person will accommodate by **convergence.** That is, you will alter your speech and behavior so that it matches that of your conversational partner. Speech includes word choice, pronunciation, pitch, rate, and even gestures such as smiling and gaze. For instance, elementary school teachers often converge their speech, using more expressive registers, slower speaking rates, and shorter words or phrases to accommodate their young pupils. When individuals match their speech, they convey acceptance and understanding. Interpersonal attraction also leads to convergence (Giles et al., 1987). That is, the more a person is likeable, charismatic, and socially skilled, the more likely you are to try to match his or her communication patterns.

Conversely, there are times when individuals don't want to be associated with a certain group or do find a person interpersonally unattractive; sometimes you want to differentiate yourself from a particular crowd. In this instance, you will alter your speech through **divergence**. Rather than match your partner's communication patterns, you will seek to make your speech different. Deliberately diverging from the speech of your partner signals disagreement or rejection. A kindergarten teacher may use a more stern tone when disciplining the class for misbehavior. Similarly, you may overhear your 16-year old neighbor conversing in strings of expletives with her friends simply as a way of countering adult authority. In addition to expressing disagreement or rejection of a speaker, divergence also illustrates one's cultural identity (e.g., a student's use of Ebonics when speaking with an English professor) or differences in one's status (e.g., a physician's use of elaborate medical terminology when talking with a patient).

Who Accommodates Whom?

It is worthy to note differences in accommodation across different cultural groups because these differences say a great deal about the importance of perceived status, authority, and cultural and social identity within our multicultural society. In her review of research, Larkey (1996) reported that when looking at race, ethnicity, and sex in the workplace, Euro-American male employees typically diverge; that is, they maintain their communicative style regardless of conversational partner because it is commonly defined as the "standard" in both the United States and much of Europe. Conversely, minority employees (including women and members of racial and ethnic minorities) typically must converge to this "standard" to achieve status within the organization. Persistent convergence may create cognitive dissonance (see Chapter 5) for minority members by placing them in a dilemma; maintaining their cultural and social identity is sacrificed when using the mainstream speech patterns that are expected and rewarded.

The Pitfalls of Accommodation

Importantly, accommodation is not always appropriate or effective (Giles & Coupland, 1991). When in doubt, individuals rely on social norms to inform their decision to accommodate or not. Norms are

Table 4.2 Consequences of Accommodation

	Positive Effects	*Negative Effects*
Convergence	Increased attraction Social approval Increased persuasion	Incorrect stereotypes of out-group Perceived condescension Loss of personal identity
Divergence	Protects cultural identity Asserts power differences Increased sympathy	Perceived disdain for out-group Perceived lack of effort Increased psychological distance

implicit expectations that guide social behavior; thus, we must rely on our perceptions of social appropriateness when determining whether to converge or diverge. Table 4.2 provides some consequences of accommodation. Note that there are both positive and negative consequences for both types of accommodation.

All told, CAT explains and predicts the experience of convergence and divergence in intercultural communication. The more we like a person or perceive ourselves as part of an in-group, the more likely we are to adapt and match our speech patterns. The more we want to communicate our difference, status, or unique cultural identity, the more likely we are to differentiate our speech from our partner's. Communicators must be aware, however, that accommodation is not always effective or well received.

❖ FACE-NEGOTIATION THEORY

In Chapter 3, we discussed the importance of "face" with regard to interpersonal communication and politeness theory. That is, individuals typically try to balance their own positive and negative face needs while also attending to their partner's face needs. Within the context of intercultural communication, the concept of face emerges again. This time, however, Ting-Toomey (1988, 1991a) used face to explain and predict the cultural differences associated with conflict management. Specifically, Ting-Toomey's research has illustrated differences found between individualistic and collectivistic cultures' face concerns and face needs. Predictably, differing face needs influence one's approach to conflict. When combined, face negotiation theory explains cultural differences in conflict as the result of combining differing face needs and conflict styles.

Combining Face With Cultural Orientation

Face-negotiation theory (FNT) begins with an understanding of face. As presented in Chapter 3, **face** is the desired self-image that an individual wants to present to others (Goffman, 1967; Brown & Levinson, 1978, 1987). Recall that face includes two dimensions: positive face and negative face. **Positive face** includes your need to be liked, appreciated, and admired; **negative face** emphasizes your desire to act freely, without constraints or imposition from others. Importantly, face is not a one-way concept; face also includes the recognition that those around us have their own face needs. Awareness of others' face needs (both positive and negative) is known as having **face concern.**

Noticeably, positive face and negative face are interdependent opposites; people typically desire both but usually can't achieve them simultaneously. Behaving so others bestow their approval on us (positive face) typically interferes with acting in an autonomous and unrestricted manner (negative face). Consequently, a tension or dialectic results in which you must choose between inclusion (wanting to be liked and associated with others) and autonomy (wanting to be free from responsibilities). Moreover, this tension creates a **face concern dilemma**—how do you address your own face needs when they may compromise your partner's face needs?

As presented earlier in this chapter, Hofstede's (1980) research categorized cultures along several dimensions. Central to FNT is the dimension of **individualism–collectivism**. To restate, individualist cultures privilege individual identity through the emphasis of individual goals, needs, and achievement, whereas collectivist cultures privilege a collective or group identity through the emphasis of group goals, needs, and achievement. As FNT posits, individualistic cultures are primarily concerned with negative face—that is, members of individualistic cultures prefer to present themselves as confident, self-directed, and independent (Ting-Toomey, 1988). Conversely, collectivistic cultures are primarily concerned with positive face; members of collectivist cultures are more likely to present themselves as likeable, cooperative, and interested in building relationships.

When considering these opposing orientations, it should be obvious that profound cultural differences can arise when trying to communicate; moreover, these differences can lead to misinterpretation and disagreement. Consider the example of an American executive who compliments a Japanese business partner's fluency in English while in front of other Japanese coworkers (Cupach & Imahori, 1993). The American believes his or her actions to be face enhancing—that is, giving someone a compliment is viewed as face enhancing. To the Japanese, however, such a compliment is actually face threatening because, by singling out one individual, the cooperative emphasis is damaged. Even the best intended messages, then, can lead to misunderstanding and intercultural conflict.

Toward a Global Understanding of Conflict Management

As you might imagine, conflict is of great interest to communication scholars and is a widely studied phenomenon. With regard to FNT, **conflict** is defined as either the perceived or actual incompatibility of values, expectations, processes, or outcomes between two or more individuals (Ting-Toomey, 1994). Among North American relationships, five conflict styles commonly emerge: avoiding, accommodating, competing, compromising, and collaborating (Kilmann & Thomas, 1977; Rahim, 1986; Thomas & Kilmann, 1974). These researchers likely did not think about the conflict styles in terms of being particular to "North Americans" (where they are most often tested) or cultural exclusion. As will become clear, however, these five approaches to conflict appear to exclude significant components of a collectivistic orientation.

According to Kilmann and Thomas (1977), these five conflict styles vary on two dimensions: assertiveness (concern for self) and cooperation (concern for other). Those who **avoid** conflict lack assertiveness and cooperation; they withdraw from or seek to evade conflict altogether. As such, there is little concern for self or for others. Individuals with an **accommodating** style cooperate with others but demonstrate little assertiveness, typically conceding to their partner's requests. Conversely, those who typically **compete** in a conflict situation are highly assertive but lack cooperation; they push their viewpoints on others, sometimes to the extent of sacrificing the relationship altogether.

A person with the **compromising** style has moderate concern for self and others; this individual is somewhat assertive and fairly cooperative.

Compromising typically involves a willingness to give up some demands to gain others. Finally, individuals with a **collaborating** style have a high regard for self and other, making the person very assertive and also very cooperative. Collaboration occurs when one actively seeks to create new solutions that meet both partners' interests without having to make the sacrifices involved with compromise. Importantly, conflict style is not a fixed trait; instead, it is a person's preferred response to conflict in a given situation. You can alter your conflict style depending on the partner involved and the circumstances at hand (Cupach & Canary, 1997).

Although Ting-Toomey (1988, 1991a) acknowledged the body of North American research showing support for the five previously mentioned conflict styles, she also maintained that these styles represent primarily a Western view of conflict. Ting-Toomey proposed that a global understanding of conflict management is remiss without examining issues of face. Consequently, her research extends the Western understanding of conflict management by viewing conflict styles on dual dimensions of **self-face concern** and **others-face concern.** Simply put, this means that individuals must consider their own positive and negative face needs (self-face concern) as well as their partner's positive and negative face needs (others-face concern). **Mutual-face concern,** then, is the recognition of both self- and others-face needs. In particular, FNT predicts a causal relationship between culture, face, and conflict style. Conflict is particularly salient for intercultural communication because, during conflict, both parties can easily lose both positive and negative face through face-threatening acts (see Chapter 3).

Indeed, research using FNT not only shows links between culture and face management, it also illustrates that when culture and face are combined, individuals can predict another's conflict management style (e.g., Ting-Toomey, 1988, 1991a; Oetzel & Ting-Toomey, 2003). After studying students' conflict responses in China, Japan, South Korea, Taiwan, and the United States, eight responses to conflict emerged (Ting-Toomey & Oetzel, 2002; see Figure 4.1). Although the terminology varies slightly, the first five conflict responses mirror those identified previously (e.g., Kilmann & Thomas, 1977): avoid, oblige (accommodate), compromise, dominate (compete), and integrate (collaborate). Interestingly, three additional styles emerged when considering Self-Face Concern and Others-Face Concern: emotional expression, passive aggression, and seek third-party help.

Figure 4.1 Eight Global Conflict Management Styles

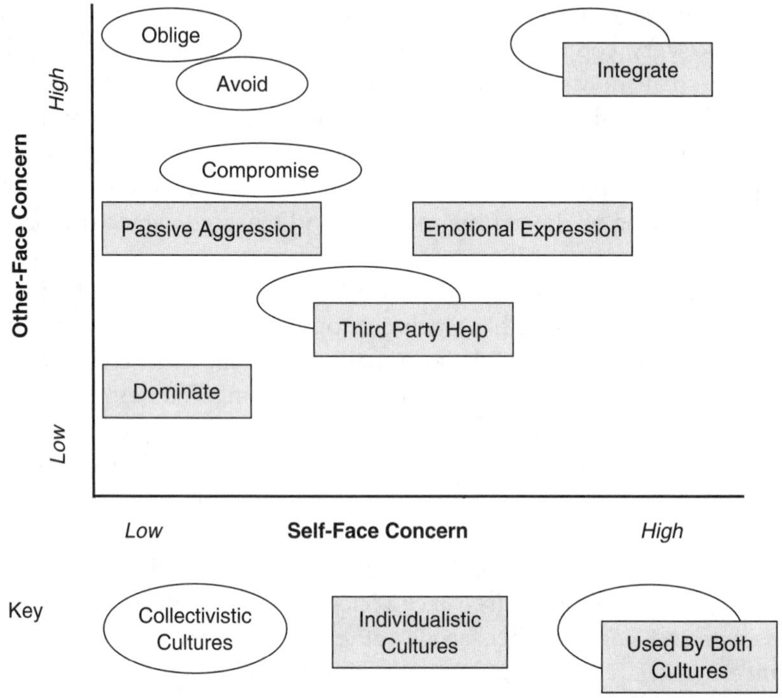

SOURCE: "Cross-Cultural Face Concerns and Conflict Styles: Current Status and Future Directions," by S. Ting-Toomey and J. Oetzel. In W. B. Gudykunst and B. Mody (Eds.), *Handbook of International and Intercultural Communication* (2nd ed., pp. 143–164), ©2002 by Sage Publications. Reprinted by permission of Sage Publications, Inc.

The **emotionally expressive** style refers to an affective response to conflict as opposed to a cognitive response. That is, emotional expression emphasizes a person's desire to react to his or her feelings or "gut reaction." A person who relies on a **passive–aggressive** style surreptitiously attempts to make his or her partner feel guilty. Passive aggression is more active than avoiding the situation altogether but less active than openly addressing the conflict; the passive–aggressive individual only drops blameful hints of the problem. Finally, the tendency to rely on **third-party help** means that the person is more comfortable asking a person outside of the relationship to help manage the conflict. Within the context of business communication, Asians often use such intermediaries to help preserve face (Ting-Toomey, 1992).

Americans typically use confrontational and dominating conflict strategies with a stronger win–lose orientation to preserve self-face (Ting-Toomey, 1992). Conversely, Asians prefer conflict avoidance in an effort to maintain mutual-face. More precisely, Taiwanese and Chinese rely more heavily on a compromising conflict style; when working with in-group (Japanese) members, the Japanese also rely on conflict avoidance. Notably, however, the Japanese mirror the American's more dominating conflict style when dealing with out-group (non-Japanese) associates. The Japanese's ability to switch between styles depending on in-group/out-group affiliations is particularly interesting and may help to explain Japanese appropriateness and effectiveness when communicating in global business relationships.

All told, Ting-Toomey's (1988, 1991a) face negotiation theory offers a more holistic view of conflict, particularly within the context of cross-cultural and intercultural communication. According to her causal model, one's cultural orientation (the degree to which one embraces individualism–collectivism) coupled with self- and others-face concerns predict one's likely repertoire of conflict responses. Importantly, intercultural conflict—that is, perceived disagreement between members of different cultures—may arise as a direct result of these cultural differences.

❖ GENDER AND COMMUNICATION: A TWO-CULTURE PERSPECTIVE

> Not biology, but gender prescriptions for women and men account for most differences in priorities, behaviors, attitudes, feelings, and self-concepts of the sexes. (Julia Wood in a dialogue with Kathryn Dindia, see Wood & Dindia, 1998, p. 30)

Examining sex and gender differences in communication is perhaps one of the most controversial and widely debated areas of communication research in recent decades (e.g., Canary & Hause, 1993; Wood & Dindia, 1998). Despite the number of popular self-help books proclaiming the idea that men inhabit one planet while women occupy another (e.g., Gray, 1992) or alleging that men and women "just can't understand" each other (e.g., Tannen, 1990), there is actually very little communication theory—or research—to support these stereotypical claims of widespread sex differences (Canary & Hause, 1993; Canary, Emmers-Sommer, & Faulker, 1997).

We have selected a modified two-culture approach (Maltz & Borker, 1982; Mulac, Bradac, & Gibbons, 2001) to discuss gender and communication for several reasons. First, as a "perspective," we take a broad approach to an area of communication that is widely studied but lacks theoretical understanding (Canary & Hause, 1993). Within our two-culture perspective, we have tried to encompass a number of current viewpoints. None of the theories are without controversy, however. Second, our two-culture view of gender differentiates one's biological sex from one's psychological and socially constructed (enacted) gender (Wood & Dindia, 1998). Finally, our two-culture perspective acknowledges more current understandings of men and women's interaction. That is, sex differences in communication are minimal at best; however, gender differences in communication do emerge when examined as a separate construct. Before explaining the two-culture perspective, we first define *sex* and *gender* as related to human communication.

Sex and Gender—What's the Difference?

How many times have you filled out a survey or questionnaire that asks, "What's your gender?" and then has a box to check for "male" or "female?" Really, what the survey is probably trying to determine is, "What's your sex?" You may scratch your head and wonder, "What's the difference?" The difference could be drastic or insignificant, depending on the context. When discussing messages and patterns between women and men in the context of communication, it is helpful to understand that there is a substantial difference between *sex* and *gender.*

According to Canary and Dindia (1998), **sex** is genetically determined; it is your biological makeup as either a male (with XY chromosomes) or a female (with XX chromosomes). With only very rare exception of genetic abnormalities, each of us is born as male or female, boy or girl. Thus, sex is a dichotomous variable; you are one or the other, not both or neither. Whereas sex is a biological categorization determined at conception, gender is far more fluid. **Gender** is "the psychological and social manifestations of what one believes to be male and/or female, which might—or might not—reflect one's biological sex" (Canary & Dindia, 1998, p. 4). In other words, gender is something that we "do"—it is a way of behaving that is categorized on a continuum that varies from masculine to feminine.

Importantly, it is society that assigns certain behaviors to each sex; in this way, gender is *related to,* but *not equated with,* sex. In Western culture, for instance, baby girls commonly leave the hospital wearing pink, whereas their baby brothers wear blue. Young girls receive baby dolls and tea sets and are told to be "sugar and spice and everything nice," while their brothers typically receive trucks and toy guns and are told not to "cry like a girl." As adults, women are still expected to be primary caregivers, while men are expected to be primary breadwinners. When boys and girls, men and women behave outside of these prescriptions, eyebrows raise, a person's sexuality may be questioned (e.g., assuming a male ballet dancer is gay), and boundaries are pushed.

Moreover, as societies evolve and change, so too does their conceptualization of gender. For example, in the United States during the 1960s, the likes of Marilyn Monroe and Jacqueline Kennedy epitomized femininity; "today Marilyn Monroe would be considered too fat to be a star, much less a sex idol" (Wood, in Wood & Dindia, 1998, p. 30) and Jackie Kennedy might be vilified as other, more recent First Ladies have been (e.g., Hillary Clinton, Nancy Reagan). In the 1950s, it was not considered masculine for a man to wear an earring or necklace; shoulder-length hair was considered effeminate or hippy-ish. Today, many men sport earrings, jewelry, and long hair as a sign *of* their masculinity (e.g., former Miami Dolphins running back Ricky Williams, WWF wrestling icon Triple-H).

Notably, not all communication researchers agree with or have made these distinctions between sex and gender in their research, often making for confusing findings. However, we support Canary and Dindia's (1998) view of sex as biologically determined and gender as socially constructed. Sex is essentially static, whereas gender is dynamic; as society changes, so does its view of how each sex "should" behave.

Sex Differences in Communication—Minimal at Best

Yes, men and women are different in many ways. However, communication research shows little support for the notion that men and women differ with regard to their *communication behavior* simply because of their biological sex. In fact, research suggests that we are more similar to the opposite sex than we are different. For example,

Canary and Hause (1993) used a statistical procedure known as meta-analysis to compare more than 1,200 studies looking at sex differences in communication. When combined, they found that one's biological sex accounts for less than 1% of differences in communication behavior! This means that 99% of differences in communication behavior are likely created by something other than simply having XX or XY chromosomes.

Gender Differences: Real or Imagined? A Two-Culture Perspective

Certainly, gender is related to biological sex, but it is not the same thing. As described under Hofstede's dimensions of culture, every known society has its own view of gender, its own prescription for how each sex should behave. As Wood described (in Wood & Dindia, 1998)

> Unlike sex differences, gender differences are cultivated, but not determined, by the distinct conditions of the lives of women and men as groups. Social ideologies prescribe that each group be allowed some and not other experiences (football and cheerleading; hunting and ballet), roles (damsel in distress, knight in shining armor; president, first lady; mother, father), personal appearance (grow a beard, shave legs; pectoral implants, breast augmentation), and professional options (human relations, executive; mommy track, no daddy track). (pp. 20–21)

Additional support for this idea of gender as a fluid behavior rather than as a sex-based trait comes from studies that put men and women in opposite gender roles. Wood (in Wood & Dindia, 1998) reviewed research that argues women become more aggressive, competitive, and confident when in professional roles that encourage these "masculine" behaviors, just as men become nurturing, supportive, and attentive when in caregiving roles that encourage such "feminine" behaviors.

Some research has examined gender (distinct from sex) and communication, yielding some interesting findings. Regardless of biological sex, having a relationship partner who exhibits a feminine (i.e., expressive) style of communication is positively related to (a) romantic relationship

Table 4.3 An Overview of Three Gender Theories

Theory	*Main Idea*
Standpoint theory	Men and women have different experiences, which shape the way they view the world. Because of these variations, men and women communicate differently.
Gender styles	Women use communication to establish connections with others, whereas men use communication to establish or maintain power over others.
Muted group	Because men have more power in society, language and meaning is biased toward a male perspective on life. Women must adapt and use male language or go unheard.

satisfaction (Lamke, Sollie, Durbin, & Fitzpatrick, 1994), (b) the use of positive and collaborative strategies for dealing with romantic relationship jealousy (Aylor & Dainton, 2001), and (c) decreased loneliness among long-distance friends (Dainton, Aylor, & Zelley, 2002). Masculinity has been associated with (a) more effective political campaign ads (Wadsworth et al., 1987), (b) more effective leadership in masculine-defined job roles (Eagly, Karau, & Makhijani, 1995), and (c) more strategic uses of communication (Aylor & Dainton, 2004).

Theoretical Examinations of Gender

The picture we have painted for understanding sex, gender, and communication is blurry at best, primarily because no single theory addressing the issue is without significant criticism. We have, however, summarized three influential theories of sex and gender differences in communication that have helped us to create this macro-perspective of understanding gender through a cultural viewpoint. Table 4.3 provides an overview.

Standpoint Theory. Developed first within philosophy to explain master–slave relationships (Hegel, 1807/1966) and later used in feminist scholarship (Hartsock, 1983), standpoint theory has more recently been applied to the field of human communication. A **standpoint** is a position from which you view and understand the world; the point in time, the location, and the experiences you bring to an observation influence your standpoint. Groups of individuals who share similar viewpoints and understandings also share standpoints. With regard to communication, standpoint theory argues that the differences in men and women's lives stem from imbalances in social, economic, and symbolic power (Wood, 1993). That is, many men and women come to an observation from different standpoints because the two groups have different social, economic, and symbolic experiences as a result of the gender expectations. Because boys and girls are socialized differently (Maccoby, 1990), boys and girls have different sets of rules, norms, goals, and meanings for their social experiences.

Importantly, these engendered standpoints do not provide comprehensive understanding—they are only partial snapshots. Similarly, standpoints are not fixed; "individuals may learn new rules, meanings, and forms of communication if they participate in communication cultures that foster skills and perspectives different than those learned previously" (Wood, in Wood & Dindia, 1998, p. 30). A significant problem with standpoint theory, however, is that it still assumes that most women assume a feminine gender and most men take on a masculine gender; there is little discussion of the world in between these two poles. Today, many girls are raised playing sports while their brothers are taught to cook; the number of stay-at-home dads is on the rise, while women continue to climb the corporate ladder. It appears that gender and sex are less intertwined than in previous decades.

Tannen's Gender Styles. You may be more familiar with the work of Deborah Tannen (1990); she has published several popular books, such as *You Just Don't Understand.* Tannen is a linguist who has applied a cultural perspective to conversations between men and women, arguing that

> male-female conversation is cross-cultural communication. . . . From the time they're born, they're treated differently, talked to differently, and talk differently as a result. Boys and girls grow up in different worlds, even if they grow up in the same house. And

> as adults they travel in different worlds, reinforcing patterns established in childhood. (p. 125)

Similar to standpoint theory, Tannen suggested that experiences shape our communication and understanding of the world, and women and men have different experiences. Rather than focusing on *why* men and women have different experiences, however, Tannen emphasized *how* the differences are manifested within conversation.

Tannen (1990) identified two primary differences in conversational patterns between men and women. She argued that men use conversation to maintain status or power, whereas women use conversation to build connection. This difference is particularly obvious in conflict, such that men are presumed to use language as a weapon, and women use language for expression. Additionally, she proposed that women focus more on how a message is said (expressive communication), whereas men stress the literal content of a message (instrumental communication). Importantly, Tannen views both ways of conversing as legitimate; she doesn't privilege one discourse over another or discuss issues of dominance and power—a point of criticism for feminist scholars (Troemel-Ploetz, 1991).

Although popular with the general public, Tannen's view of men and women in interaction is controversial among communication scholars. Her research methods have been widely criticized for using very small samples to make very large generalizations (Wood & Dindia, 1998). Additionally, she doesn't clearly differentiate sex and gender—is there something about a woman's biology that makes her more interested in building relationships? Or is it the way men are taught to behave that makes them more content focused?

Muted Group Theory. Adapted from anthropology, muted group theory is a critical theory that examines how power imbalances affect communication (see Chapter 1 for a definition of critical theory). Specifically, muted group theory argues that the English language is primarily a man-made means of communicating (Kramarae, 1981). As a result, many experiences of women (or of other minority groups for that matter) are left unarticulated, further serving to maintain an imbalance of power between men and women.

Muted group theory assumes that all language is bound by culture; that is, meanings are culturally derived (Kramarae, 1981). Similar to standpoint theory and gender style, muted group theory also assumes that men and women have grown up having different experiences. Kramarae has attributed these differences to power imbalances. Because men have had positions of power and dominance far longer than women, men have also had a greater influence in shaping language and meaning. For example, men who are sexually promiscuous are *womanizers, studs,* or *players.* Women who are sexually promiscuous are *tramps, sluts,* or *whores.* There is quite a different connotation between the terms. Kramarae stated that women have largely been excluded from creating meanings, leaving them muted or without adequate means to express their unique experiences. Women must either adapt and use male language or go unheard.

If best-selling book lists are any indication, the topic of gender and communication is certainly popular with the average American; communication researchers are also genuinely interested—and divided—on the subject. While stereotypical notions of what it means to be a male and a female flourish in the media, much controversy exists within the academic community as to whether these "differences" are manifested in actual interaction. What we do know is that biological sex alone seems to account for little in the way of communication differences. The construction, communication, and enactment of gender (and how gender relates to sex) are still up for debate and in need of a comprehensive theory.

❖ CHAPTER SUMMARY

We discussed four very different ways of examining culture and communication. **Hofstede's** five dimensions help create understanding of variations across cultures. **Communication accommodation theory** explains and predicts convergence and divergence in intercultural communication. By focusing on in-group versus out-group orientation, communicators can try to assimilate with or differ from their intercultural counterpart. **Face negotiation theory** offers a transcultural approach to conflict management. By incorporating cultural variations of facework, FNT demonstrates that conflict strategies are a by-product of one's culture and face concerns. Finally, we took a broad-based approach to gender and communication with the **two-culture perspective.** By distinguishing between sex and gender, a two-culture perspective illustrates that many differences in people's communication are socially constructed, not biologically determined.

Case Study 4 The Trouble With Tourists

Historic Philadelphia is booming as a travel destination. Among the many sites that tourists visit while in Philadelphia is the Granovetter Church,* a partially restored building nearly 300 years old that is noted for being a secret meeting place of the early founders of the United States. In 2002, nearly 1.5 million people visited the political and religious landmark, with an estimated one in seven hailing from a foreign country. The sheer number of tourists visiting the site, as well as the number who spoke languages other than English, combined to create significant challenges for the volunteers who provide guidance and interpretation to visitors. Unlike the nearby Independence National Park, which is run by the National Park Service, the Granovetter Church is still a congregation of the Presbyterian Church of the United States of America. All touring is done in coordination with a group of volunteers, who are managed by an oversight committee of the Philadelphia Presbytery.

During a general meeting of volunteers, it became apparent that the volunteers were having increasing trouble meeting the needs of international visitors, particularly with Japanese visitors to the park. Volunteers had difficulty explaining the general concerns and rules for behavior in what was in essence a place of worship. Further conversation among the volunteers brought to light that aggressive tour leaders were often the root of the problem. Such was the case with many tour leaders from an organization called Marzu Tours.

Marzu Tours frequently burst into the church with bullhorn in hand, talking in Japanese while an English-speaking interpretive presentation was in process. The group would push and shove to remain together throughout the presentation, interrupting and interfering with existing tour groups. Moreover, the Marzu Tour leaders would wander through the building on their own, often requiring a volunteer to run to prevent the tour from entering a sacrosanct area. Other tour operators and visitors frequently complained about these groups.

NOTE: *The location, history, and events of this story are entirely fictional. The Granovetter Church does not exist and is not based on any real building.

After years of avoiding the problem, Mark Hastings, the chair of the oversight committee determined that direct confrontation of the problem was inevitable. He began the process of trying to contact the director of Marzu Tours. His efforts led him to Yushiko Sato, a female employee of the company. Mark decided to be as straightforward and logical as he could be, even though he was actually frustrated and angry after wasting so much time with bureaucracy and red tape while trying to find the right person to talk with about the problem.

"Ms. Sato, we at Granovetter Church are having trouble with some of your tour guides. They do not wait their turn for admittance, they do not follow our rules for where they can go, and they seem to push their groups in front of other groups during the tours," Mark said.

"I am so sorry," Yushiko replied with a great deal of sincerity. "I will bring this to the attention of our director."

Mark hung up, satisfied that the problem would be resolved and impressed with the service he had received from Yushiko. Several months later, however, he was still receiving complaints about the company from the volunteers. He retraced his steps and contacted Yushiko Sato again. This time, he asked to speak to her director.

"That is a little difficult," Yushiko replied.

Mark was frustrated by the stonewalling. "This is a problem with a fairly simple solution!" he shouted.

"Mr. Hastings, you cannot change the Japanese. The Japanese are different," Yushiko calmly explained, with just a touch of condescension.

Mark refused to take the bait. "All of our visitors are important to us; the Japanese are not more important than others. I just want to level the playing field," Mark responded with what he thought was great patience. "Can we perhaps set up a meeting to discuss this in person?"

"I will see what we can do," Yushiko replied.

Two weeks later, Mark still had not heard back from Yushiko, so he called her yet again. He was as clear and firm as he could be. She agreed to have an in-person meeting the next week. Mark was a little bit late for the meeting because a rainstorm had flooded some of the roads leading out of the city to where the Marzu Tours office was located in the suburbs. He was shocked when he actually met Yushiko, who appeared to be very young and immature. The contrast between her innocent appearance and her clear distaste for his late arrival was intriguing. It was also very obvious that she was a low-level employee. He realized that the issue wasn't that she *would* not address the problem of her company's tour guides, but that she *could* not do so; she didn't have the authority.

Mark concluded the meeting by thanking Yushiko for her concern. He had given up on working with the company and decided that his volunteers would simply need better training to deal with Japanese tourists. To his bewilderment, Yushiko suggested that Mark meet the local director of the company. "Finally!" he thought. "Maybe now we'll get somewhere!"

Questions for Consideration

1. How might the troubles with the tourism company be explained by Hofestede's dimensions of culture? Make sure to look at both Japanese and American cultures.
2. Did either Yushiko or Mark ever accommodate? How? With what effect?
3. To what extent did Mark and Yushiko recognize each others' face needs during the conflict? What conflict strategies did they use? Were the strategies consistent with the predictions of face-negotiation theory?
4. To what extent might the problems that Mark and Yushiko experienced be related to gender?
5. Do any of the theories emerge as "better" than the others? Why do you believe this to be the case? What situations might surface that would make a different theory or theories better at explaining the situation?

5

Explaining Theories of Persuasion

Since the mid-1930s when Dale Carnegie first published his best-selling book *How to Win Friends and Influence People,* the notion of how to persuade others has been both a popular and profitable subject. Concurrently, with the rise of mass media and the pervasiveness of propaganda used in both World Wars, the study and understanding of mass-mediated persuasive messages became critical to understanding political and social change. Today, the importance of understanding the power of persuasive messages is greater than ever. According to Kilbourne (1999), "the average American is exposed to at least three thousand ads every day and will spend three years of his or her life watching television commercials" (p. 58). Clearly, we are inundated with messages of persuasion and influence in all aspects of our lives—relational, social, political, and economic. Accordingly, we believe that having an understanding of how persuasive messages work (or don't work!) is central for surviving in today's advertising and media-blitzed society.

❖ PERSUASION DEFINED

Persuasion is typically defined as "human communication that is designed to influence others by modifying their beliefs, values, or attitudes" (Simons, 1976, p. 21). O'Keefe (1990) argued that there are requirements for the sender, the means, and the recipient to consider something persuasive. First, persuasion involves a goal and the intent to achieve that goal on the part of the message sender. Second, communication is the means to achieve that goal. Third, the message recipient must have free will (i.e., threatening physical harm if the recipient doesn't comply is usually considered force, not persuasion). Accordingly, persuasion is not accidental, nor is it coercive. It is inherently communicational.

Many theories in this chapter are concerned with shifts in attitude, so it is important to make clear what we mean by that term. An **attitude** is a "relatively enduring predisposition to respond favorably or unfavorably" toward something (Simons, 1976, p. 80). We have attitudes toward people, places, events, products, policies, ideas, and so forth (O'Keefe, 1990). Because attitudes are enduring, they are neither fleeting nor based on whims. Yet at the same time, attitudes are *learned* evaluations; they are not something that people are born with. As such, attitudes are changeable. Finally, and perhaps most importantly, attitudes are presumed to influence behavior. To illustrate, your attitude toward a product will influence whether you buy the product.

In this chapter, we present four theories that explore aspects of persuasive communication. Although portrayed as theories of persuasion, each of these viewpoints can be applied to a wide variety of communication contexts. From well-crafted public relations campaigns designed to foster positive attitudes about a company to telling a story to convince a customer that a salesperson is honest, the theories presented highlight the varied ways to conceive persuasive messages. The four theories we discuss in this chapter include social judgment theory, the elaboration likelihood model (ELM), cognitive dissonance, and the narrative paradigm.

❖ SOCIAL JUDGMENT THEORY

Consider your personal and professional network. It is likely easy for you to come up with at least one example of a person with whom you cannot talk about a particular topic. Perhaps your father is a die-hard Democrat who will not listen to any conservative viewpoints. Or perhaps you know that your boss is incapable of having a discussion that involves spending any money. Social judgment theory suggests that knowing a person's attitudes on subjects can provide you with clues about how to approach a persuasive effort. Created by Sherif and associates, the theory focuses on peoples' assessment of persuasive messages (Sherif & Hovland, 1961; Sherif, Sherif, & Nebergall, 1965). Research using this theory has often focused on cognitive processes, but there are numerous implications for communicators seeking to persuade others.

Social judgment theory proposes that people make evaluations (judgments) about the content of messages based on their **anchors,** or stance, on a particular topic messages (Sherif & Hovland, 1961; Sherif et al., 1965). In addition to an individual's anchor, each person's attitudes can be placed into three categories. First, there is the **latitude of acceptance,** which includes all those ideas that a person finds acceptable. Second, there is the **latitude of rejection,** which includes all those ideas that a person finds unacceptable. Finally, there is the **latitude of noncommitment,** which includes ideas for which you have no opinion—you neither accept nor reject these ideas.

A person's reaction to a persuasive message depends on his or her position on the topic (Sherif & Hovland, 1961). Accordingly, the first step in the social judgment process is to map receivers' attitudes toward a topic. This task can be accomplished through an *ordered alternatives questionnaire.* The questionnaire presents a set of statements representing different points of view on a single topic (O'Keefe, 1990). The statements are listed so that they create a continuum; the first statement reflects one extreme view of an issue, and the last statement reflects the opposite extreme view. Respondents are asked to mark the statement with which they most agree (i.e., the anchor). They are then asked to indicate statements with which they generally agree or disagree (representing the latitudes of agreement and disagreement). Statements that are neither acceptable nor unacceptable are left blank (representing the latitude of noncommitment).

To illustrate, consider attitudes about the gap between the employment of Caucasian Americans and people of color. Recent statistics indicate that the jobless rate for Blacks is twice as high as that for Whites (Hammonds, 2003). Furthermore, although 29.7% of the workforce is classified as minority, just 14.9% of officials and managers are minorities. In contrast, White men represent 37.6% of the workforce, but 56.9% of officials and managers are White men (U.S. Equal Employment Opportunity Commission, n.d.). Simply presenting these statistics is likely to have sparked a response in you. For some, these figures might spark feelings of indignation about social inequities. For others, the statistics might spark irritation because we are discussing race. The fact of the matter is, your response is a perfect illustration of social judgment theory. Refer to Table 5.1, and consider the sample ordered alternatives questionnaire developed about the employment gap. By completing the instructions, you will have essentially mapped your own attitudes about the employment gap between White Americans and people of color. We will return to this questionnaire shortly.

Social judgment theory says that the map of an individual's attitudes about any given topic is a function of how **ego involved** that individual is about that topic. When an individual is highly ego involved with a topic, she or he believes that the issue is important, and the person typically holds an intense position (O'Keefe, 1990). Because the topic is one that has personal significance to the individual, it is considered to be central to their sense of self—hence, she or he is *ego-involved.*

Knowing whether a person is ego-involved allows the persuader to make certain predictions about the recipient of a persuasive message. First, *the more ego-involved a person is, the larger the latitude of rejection that person will have.* This prediction is based on logic; if you feel strongly about something, you are likely to reject anything that doesn't match your precise point of view. If you don't care as much about the topic, you are likely to be open to alternative possibilities. The second prediction is that *the more ego-involved a person is, the smaller the latitude of noncommitment.* Again, this hypothesis makes sense. If you believe a topic is important, you are likely to have thought about it, leaving little room for having no opinion or no knowledge. If you don't view the topic as important, you probably haven't spent much time crafting an opinion about it.

Our introduction of social judgment theory stated that people make judgments about messages based on their preexisting attitudes. How does this translate to the real world? Imagine that you work in the human resources department of a major corporation, and you would

Table 5.1 Ordered Alternatives Questionnaire

	Read each statement, and put a ✓ next to the statement with which you most agree. Then circle the letter of all statements with which you agree, and put an X through all statements with which you disagree.
____ A.	The gap between minority employment and White employment is due to a lack of ability among many minority members.
____ B.	The gap between minority employment and White employment is due to a lack of effort among many minority members.
____ C.	The gap between minority employment and White employment is due to a lack of education among many minority members.
____ D.	The gap between minority employment and White employment is due to a lack of role models for many minority members.
____ E.	The gap between minority employment and White employment is due to a lack of training and development for many minority members.
____ F.	The gap between minority employment and White employment is due to a lack of mentoring of minority employees.
____ G.	The gap between minority employment and White employment is due to an unwelcoming working environment for minorities in most organizations.
____ H.	The gap between minority employment and White employment is due to subtle and unintentional forms of racism.
____ I.	The gap between minority employment and White employment is due to active discrimination.

like to persuade the management team to do something about the employment gap between Blacks and Whites in your company. The first thing you need to do is to determine the management teams' attitudes about the topic. Where along our ordered questionnaire do they fall as a group? How ego involved are they? Once we do this form of audience analysis, we can predict how they might respond to particular messages. Quite simply, the theory asserts that messages that fall within the audience's latitude of acceptance will be viewed positively, and messages that fall within the audience's latitude of rejection will be viewed negatively.

Social judgment explains these responses through two processes, the contrast effect and the assimilation effect (O'Keefe, 1990). The

contrast effect occurs when a message is perceived as further away from that person's anchor than it really is—the receiver subconsciously exaggerates the difference between the message's position and his or her own position. This response happens when the message falls within an individual's latitude of rejection. The **assimilation effect** is just the opposite. When a message is received that falls within the individual's latitude of acceptance, the receiver subconsciously minimizes the difference between the message's position and his or her own position. Using the ordered alternatives in Table 5.1, imagine that Manager A's anchor is at the E statement, which explains the employment gap by a lack of training and development. Statements A and B are in her latitude of rejection, C–F are in her latitude of acceptance, and G–I are in her latitude of noncommitment. If you were to seek to persuade this manager to initiate a mentoring program for minority employees (linked to statement F), this manager will be easily persuaded. In fact, she will likely *assimilate* your message and believe your solution exactly matches what she thinks ought to be done, which isn't objectively the case.

Now, picture Manager B's attitudes. Manager B's anchor is at statement B, which explains the employment gap as due to a lack of effort among minority workers. Statements E–I are in her latitude of rejection, A–C are in her latitude of acceptance, and D is in her latitude of noncommitment. If you seek to persuade this manager of your plan to initiate a mentoring program, social judgment theory predicts that Manager B will not be persuaded. In fact, *contrast* is likely to occur, and this manager may accuse you of saying that the company is actively discriminating, a case you have not sought to make. The **boomerang effect** is when the message actually causes a person to change his or her mind in the direction opposite that desired. By the way, consider how the two managers' attitudes have mapped out. Which of the two is more ego-involved with the topic?

In sum, social judgment theory proposes that persuaders must carefully consider the pre-existing attitudes an audience might hold about a topic before crafting a message. If you send a message that falls in a receiver's latitude of rejection, you will not be successful in your persuasive effort. Moreover, if you send a message that is clearly in a person's latitude of acceptance, you are not persuading that receiver, you are only *reinforcing* what she or he already believes. True persuasion can only occur, according to this theory, if the message you send is in an individual's latitude of noncommitment or at the edges of his/her latitude of acceptance (Miller, 2002).

❖ ELABORATION LIKELIHOOD MODEL

Turning to our second theory of persuasion, the elaboration likelihood model (ELM) views persuasion primarily as a cognitive event, meaning that the targets of persuasive messages use mental processes of motivation and reasoning (or a lack thereof) to accept or reject persuasive messages. Developed by Petty and Cacioppo (1986), ELM posits two possible routes or methods of influence: centrally routed messages and peripherally routed messages. Each route targets a widely different audience. Accordingly, much like social judgment theory, ELM emphasizes the importance of understanding audience members before creating a persuasive message.

Slow and Steady: The Central Route to Persuasion

Petty and Cacioppo's (1986) model depicts persuasion as a process in which the success of influence depends largely on the way the receivers make sense of the message. As mentioned earlier, ELM presents two divergent pathways that one can use when trying to influence others. The more complex of the two paths is known as the **central route,** also referred to as an elaborated route. Centrally routed messages include a wealth of information, rational arguments, and evidence to support a particular conclusion. For example, during each election season, political hopefuls engage in speeches, debates, and roundtable discussions; each message is filled with elaborated and presumably rational information regarding the candidate's viewpoints, platform, and political history.

Centrally routed messages are much more likely to create long-term change for the recipient than are peripheral messages (discussed later); however, not all individuals are capable of receiving centrally routed messages. Importantly, ELM argues that centrally routed messages succeed in long-term change only when two factors are met: (a) the target must be highly **motivated** to process all of the information being given, and (b) the target must be **able** to process the message cognitively. For example, if you are not willing to sit through a 2-hour televised debate between presidential candidates, then ELM suggests that you do not have the motivation required to process an elaborated message in this instance. Alternatively, imagine that you are motivated to watch the candidates' debate, but the politicians' messages are so filled with jargon and complex issues of international policy that you do not understand them. In this case, ELM suggests that despite your motivation, the ability to understand the highly specific and intricate messages being offered is not present. The theory states that without *both* motivation and ability, an elaborated message is of little value.

Types of Elaborated Arguments. It should be apparent that understanding one's audience is critical when choosing the appropriate route; it is also imperative to understand the audience when constructing an elaborated argument (Petty & Cacioppo, 1986). In other words, it isn't enough to view your audience as motivated and able when considering the central route of persuasion. You must also consider how the audience members will likely react to the quality and arrangement of the arguments presented. Elaborated arguments can be measured as strong, neutral, or weak.

Strong arguments create a positive cognitive response in the minds of receivers while also positively aligning the receivers' beliefs with those views of the persuader (Petty & Cacioppo, 1986). Strong arguments inoculate the audience against counter-persuasion and are most likely to create long-term attitude change that leads to predictable behavior. Repetition is thought to enhance the persuasive effect of strong arguments; conversely, interruptions will diminish their effectiveness. **Neutral arguments** generate a noncommittal cognitive response from the receiver. In other words, no attitude change occurs, and the ambivalent receiver may instead turn to peripheral cues, or shortcuts to persuasion. Finally, **weak arguments** produce a negative cognitive response to the persuasive message. This negative response will not only prevent attitude change, it may, in fact, have a reverse or boomerang effect, thereby reinforcing the opposing point of view.

Taking a Shortcut: The Peripheral Route to Persuasion

Noted earlier, elaborated messages are ineffective when targeted participants are not capable and interested in the information (Petty &

Cacioppo, 1986). Although the persuader might prefer an involved audience so as to produce enduring change, it is unreasonable to expect every persuasive target to be motivated or skilled enough to understand the barrage of influential messages put forth each day. As a result, when motivation or ability is missing from the target audience, the persuader can use the **peripheral route** to persuasion. Peripheral messages rely on a receiver's emotional involvement and persuade through more superficial means. Returning to our political campaign example, it is common for presidential candidates to air 30-second commercials that focus on portraying feel-good images of their "family values," patriotism, character, and likeability. As well, some candidates use celebrity endorsements, such as having a famous person or group give public support. For example, a number of NBA players publicly supported Bill Bradley during his 2000 run for presidential nomination. Thus, ELM predicts that when the audience is unmotivated or unable to process an elaborated message, persuaders should focus on quick and easy ways to produce change. One significant drawback is that the peripheral route leads only to short-term change, if any change at all.

Types of Peripheral Cues. Cialdini (1993, 1994) identified seven common cues that signal the use of a peripheral message: authority, commitment, contrast, liking, reciprocity, scarcity, and social proof. Using **authority** as a peripheral cue, the persuader uses the perception of authority to convince the audience to accept the beliefs or behaviors presented. Parents often use this peripheral cue with their children: "Clean up your room because I said so!" This message may influence children to straighten the covers and hide the toys in the closet before grandma's visit, but it probably won't create long-term neatness.

Peripheral messages that rely on **commitment** emphasize a person's dedication to a product, social cause, group affiliation, political party, and so on (Cialdini, 1993, 1994). For example, some people publicly announce their commitment to a certain group or cause; they attend rallies, run for office, or wear pins, hats, and other logos that symbolize the affiliation (Canary, Cody, & Manusov, 2003). Similarly, wearing a polo shirt that displays your company's corporate logo demonstrates some amount of your dedication to the organization. Other people demonstrate their commitment more privately, for example, by sending anonymous donations to political campaigns or charitable organizations. Importantly, however, "people usually feel greater commitment to a cause if they are publicly committed to it" (p. 369).

One very common sequential procedure that underscores the commitment principle is the *foot-in-the-door* tactic (Cialdini, 1994). Here, a persuader convinces you to do something small first, like wear a campaign button. Then, the persuader asks to put a campaign sign in your yard; next the persuader may ask you to make a donation or to host a reception. The strategy is to convince you to agree to a small, seemingly innocuous request first. Once you agree and commit yourself to the campaign, it becomes harder to refuse larger requests because there is a threat of appearing inconsistent with your commitment.

Persuading through **contrast** or using **contrast effects** requires the communicator to set up uneven points of comparison (Cialdini, 1993, 1994). For example, asking a coworker if she could do you a "giant favor" and then contrasting the statement with a simple request ("Would you page me if FedEx drops off a package while I am in a client meeting?") sets up a disparity. By inflating the coworker's expectations for the "giant favor" requested and then contrasting it with a simple favor, it is more likely to result in compliance. Retail salespeople also use this contrast principle by "reducing" prices or by showing customers the most expensive item first (because anything else will seem cheaper in comparison).

Liking messages stress affinity toward a person, place, or object (Cialdini, 1993, 1994). That is, if we like you, we will like your ideas. Today's sneaker and soft drink companies often rely on such messages of liking. By using Britney Spears to sell Pepsi or Michael Jordan to sell Nike Air Jordan shoes, these companies expect that if you like Britney or Mike, you will also like their product (and will, they hope, buy it).

Messages of **reciprocation** try to influence by emphasizing a give-and-take relationship (Cialdini, 1993, 1994). For example, it is easier to persuade your sister-in-law to babysit your children if you have done something similar for her. Advertisers also use reciprocation; "Buy these steak knives in the next 10 minutes, and we will give you a free cutting board!" Here, the advertiser tries to influence the receiver by throwing in some extras. If you do this for us, we'll give you a freebie. Similarly, **scarcity** is a peripheral message that preys on people's worry of missing out on something. This "Quick! Get it before they're all gone" approach creates a sense of urgency for receivers. Home shopping networks and department stores use this strategy by imposing time limits on the sale of items; presumably, you won't be able to purchase the deluxe salad spinner after the sales event expires. Realtors also use this approach; alerting prospective buyers that an offer has been placed on a property creates a sense of urgency and may start a bidding war. A house that was "of interest" now seems that much more appealing when it may disappear from the market.

Finally, the peripheral cue of **social proof** relies on the age-old notion of peer pressure (Cialdini, 1993, 1994). Although you might mistakenly believe that only teenagers succumb to "everyone's doing it" mentality, adults are also swayed by messages of social proof. Within the workplace, for instance, many corporations participate in charity drives such as with the Red Cross or the United Way. Here, employees who participate in blood drives or fundraising are given pins to wear or balloons to display, thereby gaining influence by putting subtle pressure on other employees to "get on board."

If unaware of these techniques in the past, you should now be able to identify these seven peripheral cues—they are everywhere! Again, however, it is important to stress that these peripheral messages emphasize fleeting emotional responses and are not likely to create long lasting change.

Types of Peripheral Messages. As with centrally routed arguments, peripheral messages can be evaluated as positive, neutral, or negative (Petty & Cacioppo, 1986). **Positive peripheral messages** are those that are perceived favorably by the audience and create a positive affective state. Positive peripheral messages have a chance at yielding weak, positive changes in attitude. For example, if you are a fan of *The West Wing* and Martin Sheen publicly endorses Candidate X over Candidate Y, you may feel more positively about Candidate X. Notably, however, a change in attitude does not necessarily predict a change in behavior. For instance, you may believe that voting is an essential civic duty for American citizens; yet you may not vote in your local primary election because you don't think you are knowledgeable of the candidates. Here, we can see incongruence between a belief (voting is important) and behavior (failing to vote).

Neutral peripheral messages leave the receivers feeling emotionally ambivalent; they really don't know or care about the cue used to capture their interest (Petty & Cacioppo, 1986). If you don't know who Martin Sheen is or really care about his political views, then his endorsement of Candidate X will not create any attitude change, nor is it likely to influence your voting behavior. Finally, **negative peripheral messages** produce negative or disapproving emotional responses within the receiver. If you can't stand *The West Wing*, then Martin Sheen's ad endorsing Candidate X will likely irritate you. Thus, you are now left with a negative impression of Candidate X because of this person's "association" with an actor or TV show that you find objectionable.

To review, ELM makes very clear predictions, which are summarized in Figure 5.1. The theory predicts that if listeners are motivated and able to consider an elaborated message, persuaders should rely on strong, factually based arguments. Arguments can backfire if they are weak or poorly presented, however. Conversely, persuaders should focus on emotionally based peripheral messages if receivers cannot or will not consider an elaborated message. Importantly, persuaders must recognize that using a peripheral route guarantees no long-term change. Instead, effects, if any, will be minimal and fleeting.

❖ COGNITIVE DISSONANCE THEORY

It is often assumed that to persuade others to do something, an outside source simply has to provide enough ammunition to change another's attitudes or beliefs. For example, public health campaigns often presume that the best way to get a smoker to quit is to infuse the smoker with information about mortality rates, health problems, and the social stigma associated with smoking in order to change the person's attitude about cigarettes. If the smoker's attitude changes, surely he or she will stop smoking, right? After all, it doesn't make sense to engage in a habit that causes premature aging, various forms of cancer, and is banned in many public places.

According to cognitive dissonance theory, this line of thinking may seem logical but is potentially incorrect, possibly explaining why there are so many smokers who acknowledge the health and social risks yet continue to indulge in the behavior. Discussed in this section, cognitive dissonance theory (CDT) explains that persuasion is not simply the result of injecting new or refined beliefs into others. Instead, CDT

Figure 5.1 Elaboration Likelihood

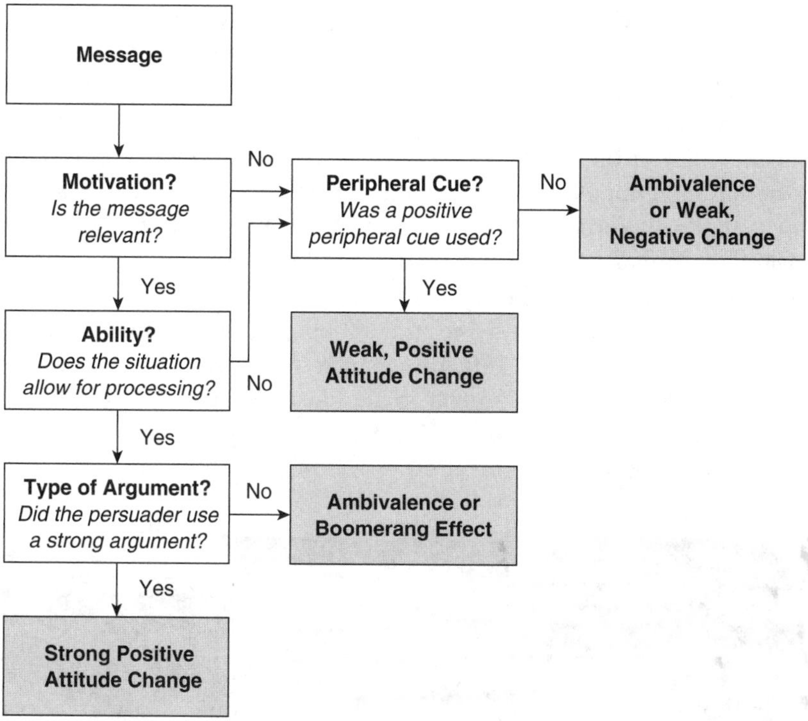

SOURCE: *Communication and Persuasion* (p. 4) by R. E. Petty and J. T. Cacioppo, 1986, New York: Springer-Verlag. Reprinted with permission of Springer-Verlag GMbH & Co. KG and the authors.

predicts that influence is often an intrapersonal event, occurring when incongruence between our attitudes and behavior creates a tension that is resolved by altering either our beliefs or our behaviors, thereby effecting a change.

Schemata: Creating Familiarity or Discomfort

According to Festinger (1957, 1962), when presented with a new or unfamiliar stimulus, individuals use **schemata**—that is, cognitive structures for organizing new information. Essentially, for new information to be understood or useful, we must find schemata with which to link the new stimulus to previously understood experiences. For example, when trying frogs' legs for the first time, many people claim that dish tastes "just like chicken"; in this case, the previous experience of being familiar with the taste of chicken serves as schemata for relating the taste of frogs' legs.

Importantly, however, when newly presented information is inconsistent with our previously established beliefs (i.e., schemata), we will experience an imbalance or dissonance (Festinger, 1957). It is this dissonance that becomes a highly persuasive tool because, according to Festinger, humans feel so uneasy with holding contradictory beliefs and actions that they will make every attempt to minimize the discomfort. In other words, when individuals behave in a manner that is incongruent with their beliefs, dissonance is created; dissonance creates discomfort. Because humans do not like to feel unnerved, individuals actively seek to change the situation to restore a balance between thought and action.

The Relationship Between Beliefs and Behaviors

Three possible relationships between beliefs and behaviors exist: irrelevance, consonance, and dissonance (Festinger, 1957). Briefly stated, **irrelevance** simply refers to beliefs and behaviors that have nothing to do with each other. For example, Cory's beliefs about preserving the environment and his position on gun control are completely unrelated. Thus, irrelevance is the absence of both consonance and dissonance. Second, **consonance** occurs when two stimuli or pieces of information are in balance or achieve congruence. For example, if Cory believes that recycling is an important way to maintain the environment, and he recycles everything from plastic bottles, to Styrofoam peanuts, to junk mail, it could be said that Cory has consonance between his beliefs (recycling benefits the environment) and his actions (he avidly recycles household waste). According to Festinger (1957), individuals prefer consonant relationships; that is, we strive to feel consistency between actions and beliefs.

Conversely, **dissonance** occurs when two stimuli or pieces of information contradict each other (Festinger, 1957). Continuing the previous example, if Cory believes that the environment is a precious commodity that deserves protection yet he drives an SUV for his 40-mile commute each day, he has created dissonance. Cory's beliefs (preserving the environment) and his actions (driving a gas guzzling SUV) are incongruent. CDT predicts that this dissonance will give Cory discomfort, at least until he can rationalize or augment the dissonance—either by shifting his belief (sure, the environment is important, but driving a car won't harm anyone) or by changing his behavior (trading in the SUV for an electric hybrid car).

Importantly, not all dissonance is created equally. That is, a *magnitude of dissonance* exists whereby some forms of incongruence produce greater discomfort than others (Zimbardo, Ebbesen, & Maslach, 1977). This magnitude of dissonance can be measured by three variables. First, the amount of dissonance one experiences is affected by the **perceived importance** of an issue. Recycling soda cans may not be as important of an issue when compared with driving while intoxicated. Similarly, spending $5,000 on a beach rental that turns out to be a dilapidated shack is far more devastating than spending $100 to watch your favorite football team lose. Second, the **dissonance ratio** affects the amount of discomfort one feels. The dissonance ratio is simply the proportion of incongruent beliefs held in relation to the number of consonant beliefs. If you hold a greater number of incongruent beliefs and behaviors compared with consistent thoughts and actions, you will experience more discomfort. Third, one's ability to **rationalize,** or justify, the dissonance also affects the amount of discomfort experienced when faced with conflicting beliefs and behaviors. The more you can justify these contrasting attitudes and actions, the less discomfort you endure.

A related issue is perception. Specifically, the perceptual processes of selective exposure, attention, interpretation, and retention can help minimize dissonance. CDT argues that an individual selectively perceives various stimuli so as to minimize dissonance. For example, with **selective exposure,** a person actively avoids information that is inconsistent with previously established beliefs or behaviors. Thus, a pro-choice supporter will likely avoid pro-life demonstrations and vice versa. Similarly, **selective attention** suggests that if you have to expose yourself to a situation that is incongruent with your beliefs, you will only attend to information that reaffirms your beliefs, disregarding any information that fails to support your views. Thus, if pro-choice supporters happen to come face-to-face with a pro-life demonstration, they will likely only attend to those details that support their previously held beliefs, for example, that pro-life supporters are religious "fanatics."

With regard to **selective interpretation,** CDT predicts that individuals will carefully decipher ambiguous information so that it is perceived to be consistent with our established beliefs. To illustrate, before Rosie O'Donnell publicly identified herself as gay, many of her fans interpreted her actions to be consistent with that of a heterosexual woman, such as her crush on Tom Cruise and her adoption of several foster children. When she revealed that she is, in fact, gay, her magazine readership dropped (O. Poole, 2002)—possibly because some subscribers could no longer hold the illusion that her ambiguous behaviors were those of a heterosexual woman. Finally, CDT maintains that individuals **selectively retain** information that upholds their viewpoints while more easily dismissing or forgetting information that creates dissonance. Accordingly, we conveniently forget how much was spent on that rundown beach house.

Persuasion Through Dissonance

By now, it should be understood that CDT assumes humans prefer congruency between beliefs and behaviors. When we engage in an action that opposes our attitudes, we experience distress known as dissonance. Depending on the importance of the issue and the degree of our discomfort, we are motivated to change our beliefs or behaviors (i.e., be persuaded). CDT is often considered a *postdecision theory,* meaning that individuals attempt to persuade themselves after a decision has been made or course of action has been enacted that the decision or behavior was okay (Gass & Seiter, 2003). The notion of buyer's remorse is an obvious example. After spending more than you feel comfortable with on a new home, car, vacation, or some other luxury item, you probably had to rationalize, or convince yourself, that the purchase was "worth" it. Thus, you try to reduce the dissonance created after making a decision to buy. Yet the question still begs: How can communicators use CDT as a tool to persuade others?

Recall that, according to CDT, motivation results from an individual's internal struggle to change beliefs or behaviors to restore consonance (Festinger, 1957). Consequently, if a persuader can create or exploit dissonance while also offering a solution to minimize the disparity, it is likely that the receiver will adopt these suggested new behaviors (or change beliefs).

In the case of buyer's remorse, sellers and real estate agents can capitalize on principles of CDT by reinforcing the wisdom of making certain choices. Realtors often encourage buyers to make a list of pros and cons before even looking for that new home with breathtaking views, a gourmet kitchen, or a sunken Jacuzzi tub (Light, 2002). This way, buyers can reduce dissonance that typically occurs after their bid is accepted by reinforcing their decision to purchase with the list of advantages. Home inspections and contingency clauses in the agreement of sale also help prospective buyers feel better about their decision to purchase.

Advertisers have also been using principles of CDT for decades, convincing consumers to buy their clients' products. For instance, the diet industry has made billions of dollars by preying on the average persons' insecurities about their appearance and body image. Most adults know that they should engage in exercise or physical activity on a daily basis; yet the majority of us don't. And although we may not be motivated enough to get off the couch and onto the treadmill, we are motivated to relieve the dissonance by purchasing so-called miracle products such as fat blockers, diet supplements, cellulite creams, and even low-carb beer. Thus, by presenting an easy alternative, these manufacturers help consumers to minimize their discomfort by realigning their beliefs and behaviors, if only on a temporary basis.

Within an organizational context, CDT predicts that by increasing employee commitments and loyalties, employee turnover could be reduced and satisfaction improved. That is, "once we've invested our time and energy or poured our hearts and souls into a cause, a person, an idea, a project, or a group we find it too difficult to let go" (Gass & Seiter, 2003, p. 69). If you have already invested years, overcome financial burdens, or forged meaningful relationships with coworkers, you are much less likely to leave an organization—regardless of pay or other adverse circumstances. Instead, you suppress second thoughts about other career opportunities, rationalize your corporate loyalty, and may even intensify your efforts to prove to yourself and others that the job is worth it.

We would like to offer a few words of caution, however. Take care when trying to capitalize on others' inconsistencies as a persuasive strategy for changing receivers' beliefs or behaviors. As Gass and Seiter (2003) noted, if you create too much dissonance, the receivers may simply create balance by changing their attitudes so as not to like you. Likewise, ethical issues abound when individuals plot to exploit consumers' or employees' dissonance for material gain. We believe that competent persuaders must think of each consumer or employee as an individual worthy of respect. If creating or magnifying another's dissonance strips that individual of self worth, then such techniques should be avoided.

In sum, CDT focuses primarily on an individual's psychological response to inconsistencies in beliefs and actions. Because dissonance produces distress, human beings seek to maintain consonance or the appearance of consonance whenever possible. This adverse effect may mean changing one's behaviors or realigning one's beliefs through some type of rationalization or selective perception. Although often a postreactive approach, communicators can use this knowledge of CDT to better target their persuasive messages. By offering a solution, product, or course of action that bridges the gap between receivers' incongruent beliefs and behaviors, communicators may influence receivers to use these methods to create cognitive harmony.

❖ NARRATIVE PARADIGM

Whereas ELM emphasizes the importance of strong, logical arguments for persuading a motivated and able audience, the narrative paradigm stresses the effectiveness of influence through narration—that is, persuasion through storytelling (Fisher, 1984, 1987). Using a more subjective theoretical orientation, Fisher argues that human beings are fundamentally storytelling creatures; therefore, the most persuasive or influential message is not that of rational fact, but instead a narrative that convinces us of "good reasons" for engaging in a particular action or belief.

Consider television advertising. Are the most memorable ads those that inundate the audience with facts about the products, or are they those that craft a memorable story? Since 1988 Budweiser has used the "Bud Bowl" saga to sell its beer during the Super Bowl. For more than 8 years, viewers watched the soap-opera story of a British woman and her attractive neighbor sipping Taster's Choice coffee.

Not all successful advertisements are long-term campaigns, however. One of the most memorable ads during the 2003 Super Bowl was Reebok's "Terry Tate Office Linebacker" ad, which demonstrated a unique way of maintaining office procedure: using a football player to handle discipline. The humorous vignette had little logically to do with athletic shoes, but it did tell a story. Current strategic marketing involves making products or brands "the central characters in their own story . . . brands within a marketplace could then usefully be conceived as romantic, tragic, heroic, or satirical" (Shanker, Elliott, & Goulding, 2001, p. 30).

As we explain subsequently, Fisher's (1984, 1987) view of communication contrasts much of Western thought that emphasizes rational decision making. Yet by juxtaposing a narrative worldview with a rational worldview, we hope that you will give some thought to this strikingly different way of considering communication and influence.

Fisher's Narrative Assumptions

Five assumptions drive Fisher's (1987) explanation of the narrative paradigm. First and foremost, Fisher proposed that what makes humans unique and distinct from other creatures is our ability and drive to tell stories. Importantly, narration, does not refer to "fictive composition whose propositions may be true or false" (p. 58); instead, **narration** includes the symbolic words and actions that people use to assign meaning. Fisher evoked the Greek term *mythos* to explain human communication primarily as a collection of stories expressing "ideas that cannot be verified or proved in any absolute way. Such ideas arise in metaphor, values, gestures, and so on" (p. 19). According to this view, not even the keenest expert knows everything about his or her area of specialization; there is an element of subjectivity in even the most "logical" of messages. Instead, your values, emotions, and aesthetic preferences shape your beliefs and actions. As such, individuals relay messages and experiences through stories as an attempt to capture these subjective experiences.

Second, the narrative paradigm suggests that because individuals' lives and understanding of reality are centered on these subjective narratives, people need a way to judge which stories are believable and which are not (Fisher, 1987). Here, Fisher argued that individuals use **narrative rationality**—a logical method of reasoning by which a person can determine how believable another's narrative is. Narrative rationality relies on **good reasons** as the basis for most decision making. As opposed to relying solely on argumentative logic, good reasons allow us to validate and accept (or reject) another's narrative based on the perceived truthfulness and consistency. Thus, coherence and fidelity are two ways to make this narrative judgment of "good reasons." When the narrative being used appears to flow smoothly, makes sense, and is believable, we say that there is **narrative coherence.** Similarly, when the narrative appears truthful and congruent with our own experiences, we say that there is **narrative fidelity.** To accept a narrative, an individual must perceive the narrative's fidelity first; without fidelity, coherence is irrelevant.

A related third assumption is that what a person accepts as a "good reason" is based on that individual's culture, character, history, values, experience, and the like (Fisher, 1984, 1987). In other words, what appears to have coherence and fidelity to one person may not appeal to another who comes to the narrative relationship with a different set of values and experiences.

Fourth, the narrative paradigm proposes that "rationality is determined by the nature of persons as narrative beings" (Fisher, 1987, p. 5). Rather than conceiving of reason as rooted only in fact and logical argument, Fisher argued that rationality—and therefore persuasion—stems from humans' ability to create a coherent story. Thus, piling on the facts about a political candidate's legislative record isn't what is persuasive for voters; what will influence constituents is a candidate's ability to share his or her experiences via narrative.

Finally, the narrative paradigm presumes that the world as humans know it is based primarily on sets of both cooperative and competing stories (Fisher, 1987). Importantly, individuals must use the logic of good reasons to choose among these narratives, thereby creating and recreating their social reality. Because "human communication . . . is imbued with mythos—ideas that cannot be verified or proved in any absolute way" (p. 19), Fisher believed that individuals must rely on narratives as the creation and recreation of a common understanding. The narratives we choose can fundamentally affect our life.

Table 5.2 Comparing the Narrative and Rational World Paradigms

Narrative Paradigm	*Rational World Paradigm*
1. Humans beings are storytellers.	1. Humans beings are rational.
2. Communication, persuasion, and decision making are based on the logic of good reasons.	2. Communication, persuasion, and decision making are based on sound arguments.
3. What one accepts as "good reasons" is determined individually by a person's culture, character, experiences, and values.	3. Strong arguments adhere to specific criteria for soundness and logic (e.g., Aristotle's use of the enthymeme).
4. Rationality is based on one's awareness of how consistent and truthful a story appears when compared with one's own (and others') lived experiences.	4. Rationality is based on the accuracy of information presented and on the reliability of the reasoning processes used.
5. People experience the world as a series of stories from which we choose. As we make these choices, we create and recreate reality.	5. The world and reality can be viewed as a series of logical relationships that are revealed through reasoned argument.

A Study in Contrasts: Comparing Narrative and Rational Paradigms

Mentioned earlier, the narrative paradigm contrasts with much of Western thought, including the Western emphasis on the rational paradigm. Table 5.2 presents the contrast between the narrative paradigm and the rational paradigm. Specifically, Fisher (1987) argued that *logos,* or purely rational arguments, have been unfairly privileged as the ultimate measure of rationality. For example, he cited Aristotle's preference for persuasion and intellectual arguments that are grounded first and foremost in *logos.* As previously discussed, the narrative paradigm assumes that little in our social worlds can be understood as purely fact; everything around us is shaded with the subjectivity of individual values and experiences. As such, "rationality is grounded in the narrative structure of life and the natural capacity people have to recognize coherence and fidelity in the stories they experience and tell to one another" (p. 137). Consequently, Fisher posited that *mythos* (narratives) and *pathos* (emotional appeals) are more meaningful to humans and, therefore, more persuasive.

Importantly, the narrative paradigm does not exclude logic (Fisher, 1987). Instead, Fisher argued that no rhetorical proof (ethos, pathos, or logos) should be regarded as more superior than the other forms of rhetorical proof. Fisher also maintained that humans should move away from dualistic approaches (i.e., that we are either rational or narrative) and embrace more integrated perspectives (i.e., that we are both rational and narrative).

According to the narrative paradigm, then, human communication and our understanding of "reality" relies heavily on narration. What's more, Fisher (1987) believed that the narrative is a more effective means of influence than deductive arguments such as the syllogism or enthymeme. Importantly, however, only when a narrative has the logic of good reasons and narrative coherence will it be convincing enough to permeate a receiver's consciousness and become translated into a change in action.

❖ CHAPTER SUMMARY

This chapter examined four theories of persuasion. Both social judgment theory and elaboration likelihood model argue that persuaders must carefully consider their audience before crafting a message. According to **social judgment theory,** the audience members' preexisting attitudes are important because sending a message that falls in a receiver's latitude of rejection will not result in successful persuasion. "True persuasion" occurs only when the persuasive message falls within a receiver's latitude of noncommitment or at the edges of his or her latitude of acceptance. **Elaboration likelihood model** also emphasizes the importance of knowing your audience. In this case, however, receivers must be motivated and able to process objective, elaborated messages. When the audience is unmotivated or unable to process such messages (or both), peripheral cues should be used. **Cognitive dissonance theory** explains persuasion as a postreactive response to inconsistencies in beliefs and actions. Individuals prefer to maintain consistency between beliefs and behaviors. Persuaders can take advantage of receivers' dissonance by proposing a solution, product, or action that attempts to close the disparity between incongruent beliefs and behaviors. Finally, the **narrative paradigm** views persuasion through a descriptive lens. That is, persuasion isn't so much a rational process as it is an emotional process based on storytelling. Importantly, narratives must have coherence and the logic of good reasons to be influential.

Case Study 5 CONNECTion Problems

CONNECT is an up-and-coming company that specializes in entertainment via telecommunications. A small business, CONNECT employs roughly 60 people and currently offers three products: a psychic network, a matchmaking service, and party-line access. Three separate product directors manage each of these three services. Ultimately, these directors are held accountable for their product as well as their staff.

Because of the company's small size, as well as the open attitude of upper management, CONNECT has created a unique environment where individual opinions are not only heard but encouraged. Employees value one another and the work they do because their own success relies on the company's success.

A collaborative work environment such as this has its downsides, however. For example, one drawback is the sheer abundance of new ideas (some good, some bad). Every idea and suggestion gets attention and needs to be researched—a time-consuming and often frustrating processes because many ideas lack the resources, practicality, and efficiency to be used.

As manager of the Media Department, Bryan Hopkins has worked for 2 years at CONNECT and currently supervises four employees. Bryan's chief responsibility is to oversee the selection and placement of print advertising. To an untrained eye, ad placement may seem simple; however, for advertising to be effective, CONNECT's procedure is fairly detailed. First, the Media Department purchases advertising space, usually in a newspaper or magazine. The Media Department then contacts the Graphics Department with an ad request, basically letting the graphics manger know what needs to be created (e.g., ad type, size, color, format) and when it needs to be completed. After completing the ad, Graphics sends the copy back to the Media Department for approval. Bryan checks each ad; only after he gives final approval is the ad then sent to the particular newspaper or magazine for publication. Although it seems tedious, Bryan designed this procedure himself and keeps it as streamlined as possible. The publication world runs on deadlines, so efficiency is critical.

Jim Martinsky, CONNECT's dating services project director, is extremely enthusiastic about CONNECT and his product. In Bryan's view, Jim is a perfectionist who tends to complicate and overanalyze things. Recently, Jim mentioned to Bryan that CONNECT might be changing its ad procedure. He wanted to schedule a meeting in the next few days to discuss the proposed changes. Jim also casually mentioned that he would like to be a part of the ad procedure process; for example, maybe the Media Department could show him each ad before giving final approval. As media manager, it was up to Bryan to determine the ad procedure, not Jim. What's more, Bryan didn't want to have someone peering over his shoulder and questioning his department's decisions.

"No way am I going to show this guy every ad that comes along!" Bryan thought to himself, "Jim will want to haggle over each comma and question mark, and it'll take months to get an ad published!"

Not wanting to appear difficult, however, Bryan decided not to say anything. He figured he would wait until the next meeting when he and the other directors could properly discuss Jim's ideas in more depth. He would bring research showing timetables, magazine commitment deadlines, and revenue charts to show how effective their ad placement has been since he took over a few years back.

Later that same afternoon, Bryan passed by the graphics department's studio and spotted Jim talking with Alison, the graphics manager. Jim caught Bryan's eye and waved Bryan into the room.

"Hey, Bryan! Come here—just for a minute. I've worked everything out." A bit perplexed, Bryan poked his head into the graphics studio. "Hey, Jim. I'm on my way to meet with the ad buyer for *HomeLife Magazine.* What's up?"

"I'm glad we ran into you! It's all set up. From now on, your department will show all ads to me before giving final approval," Jim declared, not defiantly, but rather, as if he had just solved a major world problem.

"Jim, I thought we were going to have a staff meeting to discuss this. In fact, I'm not even sure that there *is* a problem," Bryan replied.

"Well, Bryan, you know that we are always on deadline here. I wanted to get things in place before our next series of ads is due. You know what they say! 'Time is of the essence'!"

Bryan didn't know what to say. Keeping in mind Jim's overzealous approach and recognizing that his own stress level was high, Bryan answered with a quick "Uh . . . Okay, sounds good, I'll get back to you," and headed back out the door. Although Bryan firmly believed that Jim's wasn't a good idea, he also knew that discussing it while on his way to meet with an ad buyer wasn't the proper time or place to resolve it.

Later that afternoon, Bryan e-mailed Jim a meeting request to discuss the newly proposed ad procedure. It looked like there wasn't going to be a group discussion with the other project directors, so Bryan had to convince Jim on his own that the Media Department's current method was a good one and that it worked. At the very least, Bryan figured they could come up with a modified ad procedure that would not inconvenience anyone who was involved.

The next day, the two men met in an unoccupied office with the door closed. Bryan started the meeting, "Hi Jim, thanks for meeting with me today to discuss your new ad placement idea. Although I think your intentions are good, as the person responsible for ad placement procedure, I have some serious concerns about the plan you suggested." Bryan went on to say that Jim's idea simply was not practical for their deadline-driven industry. "Media places too many ads for too many of CONNECT's services; we can't run around and chase down all of the project directors for their approval when ad deadlines need to be met." Bryan expressed that Jim's new procedure created unnecessary steps, making it inefficient.

"I have an alternative solution," Bryan suggested, "one that combines your idea of having extra eyes look over the ads along with my belief that we shouldn't put up additional barriers in the approval process." Jim nodded, "Okay, I'm game–what's your idea?"

Bryan went on to explain his idea—graphics could show each ad to the respective project director for his or her approval prior to sending it back to Media for final approval. Bryan explained,

"This way, the Media Department's flow wouldn't be disrupted as much, and it would allow for the graphic artists and the project directors to work together on getting everything just right. This way, when Media does receive the ad, we could just do our normal checking routine before sending the ad out."

Jim indicated that he originally had suggested this idea to Alison in the Graphics Department, but that she had expressed the same concerns that Bryan just did. "Essentially," Jim said, "Alison told me it's simply inefficient; Graphics doesn't have time to chase down project directors for each ad's approval either."

As Jim began to feel as though a solution to the situation was hopeless, Bryan started asking some questions aimed at finding out exactly what the "problem" was. According to Jim, he had noticed some ads that were going out for his product that did not meet his approval. Bryan pressed Jim for more details; it turned out that "some ads" was really just two ads—one was a personal preference regarding layout, and the other was due to Jim's own forgetfulness about the ad he had previously approved.

When pressed even further, it turned out that the real issue was a communication problem between Jim and Sean, the graphic artist who typically worked on Jim's ads. According to Jim, they didn't get along well. Just recently, Jim noticed a published ad where an adjustment that he had requested Sean to make was not made; Jim lost trust in the ad procedure, fearing that these errors would continue to happen unless he was involved in some way.

Based on Jim's story, Bryan quickly recognized that Jim's problem was not with Media's ad procedure, but between Jim and Sean. Bryan also knew that changing the ad procedure was not going to fix a communication problem between the two men.

By listening to Jim's difficulties with working with Sean, Bryan realized that a slight change to the ad procedure, if done correctly, could benefit everyone. Together, Bryan, Jim, and Alison came up with a joint proposal. They would set up an in-box in each project director's office and in the Media Department. Once Graphics finished an ad, they would simply drop the ad in the project director's in-box. The project directors would check their in-boxes on a daily basis. If they agreed with the look of the ad and were happy with everything, they would sign off on the ad, and drop it in the Media in-box. Media would then check the ad as usual, give final approval, and then give Graphics the okay to send the ad. If, for some reason, a project director was not happy with an ad left in the in-box, he or she would go directly to Graphics to work out the problems. Once satisfied, the project director would sign off on the ad and then place it in the Media in-box for final approval.

This solution left the final approval in the hands of Media while also allowing all project directors to have a say in the ads, and it avoided any inefficiency in getting approvals because ads could now just be left in various in-boxes. Amazingly, all staff members involved agreed to this joint solution. A month later, all were satisfied with the new procedure.

Questions for Consideration

1. Consider the tenets of social judgment theory. How does the latitude of rejection operate within this case study? What about the latitude of acceptance? How could Jim and Bryan both have used SJT principles early on to avoid the confusion and conflict that ensued following Jim's initial proposal?

2. What peripheral strategies did Jim try to use to convince Bryan that there was a problem with the current ad approval method? Why didn't these strategies work? Would an elaborated message produce a different result? Explain.

3. In what way(s) does Bryan experience dissonance? How is this dissonance resolved?

4. It is only after Jim opens up and shares his personal experiences with the ad process that Bryan begins to understand and accept Jim's frustrations. Although not elaborated in the case study itself, imagine a narrative that Jim could have used to convey to Bryan his frustrations with the ad process and Sean, the graphic designer. Construct a narrative that demonstrates coherence and the logic of good reasons while convincing Bryan that there was a problem with the current ad approval method.

5. Which persuasion theory seems to explain the situation better than the others? Why do you believe this to be the case? Which situations might surface that would make a different theory or theories better at explaining the situation? What theories could you combine to make for an even better explanation of the encounter?

6

Explaining Theories of Leadership

Most U.S. corporations today are overmanaged and underled.
(Kotter, 1990, p. 103)

According to surveys, leadership skill is one of the top three qualities affecting hiring decisions (Egan, 1999). Yet despite centuries of studying leadership, scholars have yet to come up with a universal understanding of why some people function as leaders and others remain followers. Historically, leadership has been linked to particular traits (such as being knowledgeable or attractive); it has been categorized as having distinct styles; and it is recognized to be situationally dependent. This chapter focuses on four theories of leadership. The first two focus on styles of leadership. Likert's (1961) four systems proposes that one particular leadership style (or system) is superior to others. The transformational leadership approach focuses on a type of leadership in which leaders inspire others through communication. The final two theories focus on situational factors that influence leadership. Fiedler's (1967) contingency model recognizes that different organizational needs can be met by differing leadership styles. Finally, leader–member exchange theory addresses how the same leader can have dissimilar relationships with different followers. First, however, we define leadership as it is related to the study of communication.

❖ LEADERSHIP DEFINED

Leadership and management are frequently considered to be interchangeable concepts. Yet the quote presented at the opening of this chapter asserts that management and leadership are distinct concepts, requiring different skills and behaviors (Kotter, 1990). According to Kotter (1990), management is a formal position in an organizational hierarchy, whereas leadership is not based on a structural position. Anyone can serve as a leader, even if he or she was not necessarily hired to serve in that role. The major challenge of management is coping with complexity. With this challenge, managers need planning skill (e.g., setting targets or goals), budgetary skill (e.g., allocating resources to accomplish goals), and organizational skill (e.g., delegating, monitoring, and problem solving). The major challenge of leadership, on the other hand, is to cope with change (Kotter, 1990). Accordingly, leaders must demonstrate vision (e.g., negotiating the long-term direction of an organization), they must motivate people (e.g., persuading people to share in the vision), and they must empower people to accomplish what is necessary to achieve the vision. In short, to manage means to function within a structure; to lead means to create a structure in which to function. This chapter is focused on leadership theories related to communication. As you read the theories, consider to what extent each is describing good management versus good leadership.

❖ LIKERT'S FOUR SYSTEMS

As the founder and director of the Institute for Social Research at the University of Michigan, Rensis Likert's work has influenced a number of fields—including communication. He is probably best known for his work on leadership styles. Likert's (1961) theory suggests that there are four distinct leadership systems within an organization. Some of these systems are very traditional, reflecting classic views of organizations and organizational communication (e.g., hierarchy, specialization, bureaucracy). These systems are akin to management as we defined in the previous paragraph. Likert argued, however, that "new" leadership styles are increasingly necessary because, as the workforce becomes more educated, people are less likely to accept direct orders and close supervision. Table 6.1 provides an overview of the four leadership systems.

The first leadership style, **System 1,** is also known as the **exploitative authoritative system** (Likert, 1961). In this scheme, leaders motivate employees through threats and fear appeals. Communication is downward (moving from upper management down), with all decision making made at upper levels; leaders pass down orders issued by the highest levels of the organization. In fact, Richmond and McCroskey (1979) nicknamed this style the *tells* style, because the leader "tells" employees what to do. With these patterns of interaction, workers are often hostile toward organizational goals and may actively behave contrary to those goals. Not surprisingly, satisfaction and productivity typically are not high in these sorts of systems, and there is a high level of employee turnover.

The second leadership style, **System 2,** is the **benevolent authoritative system** (Likert, 1961). Like System 1, this scheme is also based on classical thinking about organizations; however, leaders tend to be less controlling when using this approach. Communication still tends to be downward in System 2, with decision making primarily at the top levels. Lower level employees may make decisions, but only using the mechanisms prescribed by upper levels. Lower level employees may attempt upward communication, but messages tend to be distorted to avoid the perception of giving management "bad news." Leaders tend to *sell* their point of view rather than telling employees what to do. In other words, workers are not only told what to do, but why it is the best way to do it, thereby softening the blow (Richmond & McCroseky, 1979). Finally, motivation in System 2 is achieved both through rewards and punishments. Outcomes such as satisfaction and turnover tend to be only slightly better than System 1, although productivity is fair to good.

System 3, also known as the **consultative system**, differs considerably from the first two systems (Likert, 1961). In this scheme, leaders typically use rewards to motivate workers, as well as occasional punishments; leadership is characterized by involving lower level employees in some decision making and goal setting. Specifically, workers are empowered to make lower level decisions that affect their specific

Table 6.1 Likert's Systems of Leadership

Issue	*System I "Tells"*	*System II "Sells"*	*System III "Consults"*	*System IV "Joins"*
Motivation	Fear, threats/ punishment, occasional rewards	Rewards and potential punishment	Rewards, some punishment, occasional involvement	Economic rewards, complete involvement
Level of responsibility (by level)	Upper = high Lower = less Workers = little	Managers = high Workers = little	Most feel responsible	Very responsible, goal oriented
Attitude toward others	Wide distrust	Subservient to supervisors, competition with peers	Cooperative, favorable, but some peer competition	Cooperative, trusting, confident
Satisfaction	Dissatisfaction with supervisors, organization, achievements	Dissatisfaction to moderate satisfaction	Some dissatisfaction to moderately high satisfaction	Relatively high satisfaction
Communication	Downward; subordinates suspicious; high distortion	Mostly downward, some upward distortion	Bidirectional, some initiative at lower levels	All directions at all levels, little distrust
Decision making	Made at top, unaware of lower level problems	Policy decisions at top, approved framework at lower levels	Policy and general at top, specific at lower levels	Made at all levels, management aware of lower level problems
Performance	Mediocre productivity, high turnover	Fair to good productivity, moderately high turnover	Good productivity, moderate turnover	Excellent productivity, low turnover

SOURCE: *New Patterns of Management*, by R. Likert, © 1961, by McGraw-Hill. Reprinted with permission of The McGraw-Hill Companies.

realm of work. More important, leaders set goals after having discussed problems and plans with their subordinates. This process of gathering employee feedback is what led Richmond and McCroskey (1979) to call this system *consults.* Because communication moves both upward and downward in System 3, competition between peers tends to be lessened, and condescension toward subordinates appears to be lower than in the first two systems. Not only is productivity good in this system, so are satisfaction and employee turnover rates.

Finally, **System 4** is known as a **participative system** (Likert, 1961). This scheme incorporates genuine participation among all levels in decision making and goal setting. Communication is extensive, regardless of rank; all employees are encouraged to interact with each other. Because employee participation determines organizational goals, all organizational members tend to accept these objectives. Moreover, motivation is achieved not only through compensation systems, but also by valuing all workers' skills and performance. Although a hierarchy may exist, all organizational members are respected and have a say in how the corporation operates. Because of the participation at all levels, Richmond and McCroskey (1979) termed this leadership style *joins.* Not surprisingly, Likert (1961) argued that System 4 management leads to the highest productivity and satisfaction and the least employee turnover. Likert's (1961) four systems move from what is believed to be the worst leadership style to the best, although Likert did acknowledge that each system might be effective given the appropriate situation. Moreover, Likert's approach suggests that although the systems are distinct, they actually reflect a continuum; each system blends together to form new patterns. Finally, although individual leaders might use any one of these four systems, Likert's perspective suggests that particular organizations foster particular leadership styles.

❖ TRANSFORMATIONAL LEADERSHIP

During the last 100 years, organizations have shifted from accommodating the industrial revolution to sustaining the information age. In the process, human beings have entered an era of global economy. Similar to Likert's (1961) pronouncement that leadership must change with the times, Bass (1997) argued that the global economy has shifted the type of leadership needed in current organizations. Thus, the second theory we consider contrasts two leadership styles—transactional and transformational—arguing that, although both can assist organizations in achieving goals, transformational leadership is superior for today's businesses.

The first style of leadership is *transactional leadership.* Bass (1985) argued that **transactional leaders** seek to achieve solid, consistent performance from subordinates. Here, leaders use bilateral exchange to achieve their goals. Specifically, leaders fulfill the needs of the employee in exchange for the employee meeting performance expectations. To illustrate, there are three primary characteristics of transactional leaders. First, transactional leaders work with subordinates to develop clear and specific objectives and promise rewards if these objectives are met (Bass, 1985). For example, a manager might meet with an employee to create performance standards jointly for an upcoming year. If the employee meets all of the standards, he or she will be rewarded with a raise.

Second, transactional leaders exchange rewards and promises of rewards for employee effort (Bass, 1985). Accordingly, a leader might reward an employee upon completion of a difficult task with an "Employee Excellence Award" or a financial bonus. In this case, the leader is not simply recognizing the completed goals, but is also rewarding people for the extra effort involved in attaining said goals.

Third, transactional leaders are responsive to the immediate self-interests of workers, particularly if the workers' needs can be met while also getting the job done (Bass, 1985). For example, consider a single parent who receives a phone call that her child is sick. A transactional leader would be supportive of the employee going home to care for the sick child if acceptable arrangements can be made to ensure that the work would still be accomplished, for instance, working late another day or negotiating with a co-worker to cover the required tasks.

In short, transactional leadership is responsive to employees and is clear and structured in terms of expectations. It is a natural result of bureaucratic systems. This leadership style focuses on meeting immediate needs as quickly and effectively as possible (Bass, 1985). Subordinates are respected and encouraged to participate in planning and decision making.

The second leadership style is **transformational leadership** (Bass, 1985). Transformational leadership is founded on particular attitudes and behaviors that support organizational change. Whereas transactional leadership seeks to achieve reliable and stable functioning, transformational leadership seeks to inspire exceptional performance (Bryant, 2003). At the center of transformational leadership is the ability to use subordinates' ideas and actions as a catalyst for *transformation*—moving ideas and actions toward the greater good of the organization.

Bass (1985) identified four facets of transformational leadership. First, **idealized influence** refers to efforts to establish positive attitudes among employees toward each other and toward the work itself. Associated with *charisma,* idealized influence involves taking risks, establishing trust, and promoting ethical standards. In so doing, the leader models ideal behavior for employees.

Second, **inspirational motivation** requires transformational leaders to present employees with a clear vision and a desirable future (Bass, 1985). Followers are motivated by the attainment of this vision and receive encouragement and support for doing so. As such, employees' self-interest is subsumed to the interest of the greater good.

Third, transformational leaders provide **intellectual stimulation** (Bass, 1985). The status quo is not taken for granted; transformational leaders challenge their own assumptions and encourage new approaches. Differences of opinion are addressed openly and without fear; leaders willingly acknowledge their own mistakes and recognize the superior ideas of others. Followers are encouraged to reject tradition as a means for operating and to challenge their own thinking.

Fourth, **individualized consideration** is considered the hallmark of transformational leadership (Bass, 1985). The transformational leader considers each individual's needs and abilities, while supporting development and mentoring efforts. In this way, the confidence of followers is enhanced, and subordinates can turn their attention from simple existence (i.e., keeping the job) to achievement and growth. Effectiveness is preferred to efficiency, and equity (considering outputs relative to inputs) is preferred to equal exchange (i.e., everyone receiving the same rewards).

Both transactional and transformational leadership are associated with achievement of organizational goals (Bass, 1985). Moreover, any given leader can be both transactional and transformative. Research has consistently shown, however, that transformational leadership is associated with greater individual and organizational outcomes (Bass, 1998). This outcome is likely because transactional leadership is rules based, competitive, and regulation driven; as such, it lacks flexibility. Employees are encouraged to look only at what affects them, because they are rewarded for their own performance. The transactional system provides little incentive to change unless the change benefits the individual directly.

Conversely, transformational leadership is more communication focused. The atmosphere is one of moral imperative, such that there are appeals to higher order motivation and needs. This leadership style engenders a team-based, cooperative, and participative atmosphere, which allows for greater adaptability and responsiveness (Bass, 1997). By focusing on common visions and mutual goal setting, transformational leadership facilitates both personal and organizational growth.

Only recently have scholars turned their attention to the next obvious question: if transformational leadership is so beneficial, what predicts the likelihood of an individual using this leadership style? Recent research has tentatively linked transformational leadership with a concept called *emotional intelligence* (Gardner & Stough, 2002; Palmer, Walls, Burgess, & Stough, 2001; Sivanathan & Fekken, 2002). **Emotional intelligence** (EQ) refers to a set of beliefs and skills that facilitate organizational performance (Goleman, 1998).

Simply stated, emotional intelligence is proposed as a counterpoint to traditional notions of intelligence, which privilege knowledge, training, and expertise in a particular field. In contemporary organizations, being "book smart" is not nearly as important as *emotional* intelligence, which references how well an individual works with people (Goleman, 1998). You are not born with emotional intelligence, nor do you develop it in early childhood: You learn and continue to develop emotional intelligence throughout the life span.

Five qualities are associated with emotional intelligence: self-awareness, self-regulation, motivation, empathy, and social skill (Goleman, 1998). Each is described in detail in Table 6.2.

Note that these qualities rest on understanding both oneself as well as others. Returning to the idea of transformational leadership, then, individuals high in emotional intelligence understand and manage the impact they are likely to have on others (based on self-awareness, self-regulation, and motivation) and are also likely to determine accurately how others feel (empathy) in order to influence others' behavior (social skill). To illustrate, imagine a situation in which an employee feels as if his or her work is underappreciated. A high EQ leader will recognize

Table 6.2 Components of Emotional Intelligence at Work

Component	*Definition*	*Qualities*
Self-awareness	The ability to recognize and understand your moods, emotions, and drives, as well as their effect on others	• Self-confidence • Self-deprecation
Self-regulation	The ability to control or redirect disruptive impulses and moods; the propensity to think before acting	• Comfort with ambiguity • Openness to change
Motivation	A passion for work for reasons beyond money or status; a propensity to pursue goals with energy and persistence	• Optimism • Commitment
Empathy	The ability to understand the emotional makeup of others; skill in treating people based on their emotional reactions	• Cultural sensitivity • People centeredness
Social skill	Proficiency in managing relationships and building networks; an ability to find common ground and build rapport	• Persuasiveness • Belief in cooperation

SOURCE: From "What makes a leader?" by D. Goleman, 2004, *Harvard Business Review, 82*, p. 88. Copyright © 2004 by the Harvard Business School Publishing Corporation; all rights reserved. Adapted and reprinted by permission of *Harvard Business Review*.

this employee's emotion and provide that person with appropriate feedback, thereby demonstrating transformational leadership through consideration of the employee as an individual (Palmer et al., 2001).

To summarize, transformational leadership is contrasted with transactional leadership. Both are effective leadership styles, but research indicates that transformational leadership is associated with higher personal and organizational outcomes. Transformational leadership involves charisma, motivation, stimulation, and consideration. These qualities can be developed through emotional intelligence. Individuals high in emotional intelligence will motivate others to achieve because these individuals understand themselves and others.

❖ CONTINGENCY MODEL

After many years of researching leadership styles, Fiedler (1967) hypothesized that leadership style alone cannot explain leadership effectiveness. Instead, Fiedler developed a model that included situational parameters when explaining leadership effectiveness. Specifically, Fiedler's contingency model suggests that leaders should adapt their behavior to situational constraints.

First, it is important to recognize that Fiedler (1967) recognized two distinct approaches, or styles, of leadership. A **task leader** focuses primarily on accomplishing particular organizational goals. This leadership style is associated with productivity. A **relationship leader**, on the other hand, emphasizes positive relations between all members of the group. These leaders are more concerned with satisfaction than achievement, focusing on maintaining group harmony. Note that the difference is a matter of degree; it is not that task leaders have no concern for relationships, but the focus is more on productivity than satisfaction. The converse is true for relationship leaders. They focus primarily on satisfaction, but productivity is also desired. Importantly, neither leadership style is inherently better than the other (Fiedler, 1967). Instead, the contingency approach makes predictions about which style will work in certain situations. Accordingly, the identification of situational constraints is the central focus of the contingency model.

Situational Constraints

Based on his research, Fiedler (1967) developed a scale of situational control that consists of three elements. Identified as the most important of the situational constraints, **leader–member relations** is the first element. Leader–member relations refers to the degree of trust and support followers provide to the leader. If leader–member relations are good, the leader can expect members to comply with directions. If leader-member relations are poor, the leader might be faced with followers who ignore directions or, worse, subvert policies.

The second situational factor, **task structure,** has four dimensions: (a) the *clarity* of the group's goals; (b) *path multiplicity,* or the number of potential courses of action available to the group; (c) *effect verifiability,* or the extent to which the effects of decisions are clear; and (d) the *specificity* of decisions to be made (Fiedler, 1967). A task is deemed structured if the goals are clear, there are relatively few different courses of action, the effects are verifiable, and the decisions are specific. Consider the following situation: a group of employees wants to hold a fundraiser to collect money for a charity. The goal of the task is clear, and the effects of the decision are easily verified (how much money was raised?). Although there are numerous ways funds can be raised, constraints of time and resources are likely to limit the options. Moreover, once a type of fundraiser has been determined (let's say a car wash), the decisions to be made are very specific: when, where, and how much to charge. In short, the task is relatively structured.

If the converse is true (i.e., the goals are unclear, there are numerous courses of action, effects are not easily verified, and the decisions are not specific) then the task is *unstructured.* Consider a small business that wishes to reorganize its administrative structure. In this case, many approaches might be undertaken, and the goal is not clear. Is there a desire for fewer administrators so that decisions are centralized? Or for more administrators so that power is distributed more broadly? How does one know whether the new administrative structure will be better or worse than the old structure? How many distinct decisions have to be made in the process of restructuring? Not only does the structure have to be considered, but also the compensation and the ultimate appointment of who fulfills which role in the new structure. In short, this sort of task is inherently unstructured.

The third situational constraint is the leader's **position power** (Fiedler, 1967). Recall that leadership is not based on a position in a hierarchy. If the leader has a strong position in the hierarchy, he or she is able to manage subordinates through rewards and costs. For instance, a manager might promise bonuses or threaten docked wages to motivate followers to comply. Leaders who do not have a strong position in the hierarchy must rely on other means of influence, however. In this case, the leader must ensure that he or she is not perceived as too bossy or controlling; instead, followers choose to conform to the leaders' requests based on respect or liking.

Fiedler (1967) combined the three situational constraints to make predictions about the most effective form of leadership. Note that Fiedler does not make specific predictions based on each of the three situational constraints but focuses on the interaction of the three to predict the most effective leadership style. The combination of the three constraints leads to a determination of **control over the situation.**

Fiedler predicts that in conditions of high control over the situation, the task leadership style will be most effective. Under moderate control, a task leader might be perceived as overly critical and anxious. In these cases, relationship-oriented strategies are warranted. Low-control situations, however, require the sort of direction provided by a task leader.

How do the situational conditions combine to indicate degree of control? Because of the complexity of looking at interaction, the predictions are best identified in visual form in Table 6.3. Note that there are eight combinations of the three variables. In four of the interactions Fiedler predicts that a task-oriented leadership style would be most effective. In the favorable situations identified in the first and second combinations, for example, followers enjoy a good relationship with the leader, and the task is highly structured. Accordingly, the leader is likely to have a high degree of control. Regardless of the leader's actual position of power, focusing on the task is unlikely to ruffle feathers, so the task-oriented style can be used effectively. Combination 3 is not as favorable because the task is unstructured. Still, the positional power of the leader combined with an established good relationship with followers allows a high level of control, and so a task orientation is perceived by followers as both appropriate and effective.

On the other hand, in Combination 8, things are going badly; leader–member relations are poor, the task is unstructured, and the leader has no position power. Combination 8 represents a low-control situation. This group is on the verge of disaster, according to Fiedler (1967). The contingency model predicts that task-oriented leadership is required to prevent the group from falling apart; someone needs to "take charge," or else paralysis and infighting will prevent either productivity or satisfaction from being achieved. At this point, a relationship style will be perceived as too little too late at best, and insincere at worst.

Fiedler (1967) argued that relationship-oriented leadership is appropriate in three conditions because of the moderate level of control over the situation. For example, in the moderately unfavorable conditions of Combinations 5 and 6, the model suggests using a relationship-oriented leadership style because the task is generally structured but the relationship is poor. By focusing on the relationship, the leader could prevent social loafing from diminishing what should be easy-to-achieve productivity. Combination 7 is more challenging; leader–member relations are poor, and the task is unstructured. Even with position

Table 6.3 Contingency Model of Leadership

Combinations	1	2	3	4	5	6	7	8
Leader–member relation	Good	Good	Good	Good	Poor	Poor	Poor	Poor
Task structure	Structured		Unstructured		Structured		Unstructured	
Formal leader–position power	Strong	Weak	Strong	Weak	Strong	Weak	Strong	Weak
Leadership	Task	Task	Task	Both	Relation	Relation	Relation	Task

SOURCE: *A Theory of Leadership Effectiveness*, by F. Fielder, 1967, New York: McGraw-Hill. Reprinted with permission of the author.

power, a task orientation is likely to be ineffectual, as followers are unlikely to tackle the difficulties of the job simply because a disliked superior has requested it. Instead, the leader would be wise to use a relationship-oriented strategy to try to inspire willingness and creativity among group members.

Combination 4 represents a unique challenge (Fiedler, 1967). Because the leader–member relationship is good but positional power is poor, the leader can use relationship-focused strategies to motivate followers. The task is unstructured, however, requiring a task leader to provide direction. In this case, Fiedler recommends using a balance of task and relationship leadership.

To summarize, Fiedler's (1967) contingency model suggests that different situations require different leadership styles. The foundation for which leadership style to use is grounded in the degree of control that the leader has over the situation. The three situational conditions are leader–member relations, task structure, and position power. In high- and low-control conditions a task-oriented style will be most effective. In moderate control situations, a more open, considerate, and participative style will be most effective because such a leader can address issues of low morale.

❖ LEADER–MEMBER EXCHANGE

The fourth and final theory we present takes yet a different perspective on leadership. Leader–member exchange (LMX) theory was developed in response to the majority of traditional leadership models that typically focused on leadership traits (i.e., enduring qualities that make a good leader) and leadership states (i.e., particular styles that can be developed by leaders to match particular situations). Instead, leader–member exchange theory argues that leaders actually treat each of their subordinates differently; there really are managerial "pets."

Developed by Graen and associates (Dansereau, Graen, & Haga, 1975; Graen & Uhl-Bien, 1995), LMX theory recognizes that leadership consists of an interpersonal relationship between a superior and a subordinate and that not all relationships are created equally. Because of limited amount of time and resources, supervisors cannot exert the same amount of energy with every employee. Accordingly, relationships between superiors and subordinates can be placed on a continuum.

At one end is **leader–member exchange relationships** (LMX relationships). LMX relationships, also called *in-group* relationships, are characterized by mutual trust, social support, and liking. There is much more interaction between organizational members in a LMX relationship than in other types.

At the other end of the continuum are **supervisory exchange relationships** (SX relationships). Interaction between the supervisor and the subordinate are defined entirely by the roles they perform and the contractual obligations provided by the organization. In short, SX relationships, also known as *out-group* relationships, are impersonal in nature, with little superior–subordinate interaction taking place.

At the midpoint of the continuum are **middle-group relationships**. Not surprisingly, these relationships involve elements of both LMX and SX. Interaction is often impersonal, but there are occasional provisions of social support. Moderate amounts of trust and liking occur between the supervisor and the subordinate. Individuals in the middle-group are often aware that they are not in the in-group, however. Figure 6.1 provides a visual representation of this continuum.

The practical implications of these varying types of relationships are profound in terms of organizational outcomes. LMX relationships are associated with higher employee job satisfaction, greater satisfaction with the manager, and higher organizational commitment (Nystrom, 1990; Vecchio, Griffeth, & Hom, 1986). Subordinates in these types of relationships also evidence more innovative behaviors and greater organizational citizenship (e.g., helping others with heavy workloads, providing assistance without being asked, listening to the problems of others, going out of their way to assist new employees, etc.). The converse is also true (Manzoni & Barsoux, 2002). Those who have an SX relationship with their supervisor report lower job satisfaction, less satisfaction with the manager, and decreased organizational commitment, and they engage in more nonconforming behaviors (e.g., taking undeserved breaks, being absent without notifying others, spending time on personal conversations, violating company rules, and complaining).

Obviously, LMX relationships are beneficial to an organization. What determines the type of relationship that will develop between any given manager and employee? Research points consistently to two factors. First, simple **liking** tends to have an impact. Dockery and Steiner (1990) found that liking was most associated with perceived similarity; the more perceived similarity between the manager and the employee,

Figure 6.1 The Leader–Member Exchange Continuum

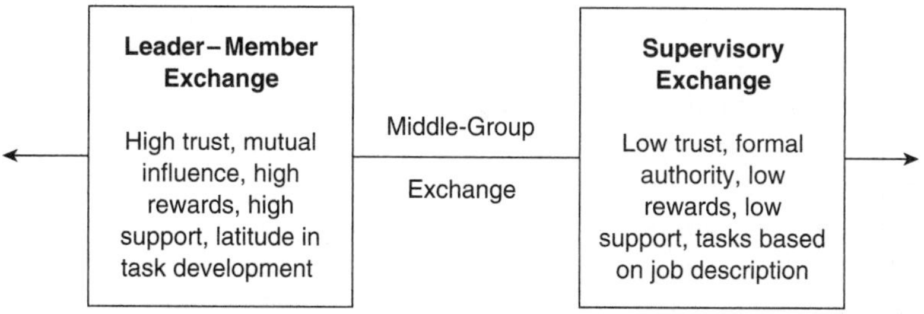

the more likely they are to have an LMX relationship. Accordingly, perceived similarity in terms of attitudes about family, money, career, strategies, goals, and education is beneficial to LMX relationships. Such attitudinal similarity is more important than demographic similarity (age, sex, race, etc.).

Second, **performance** has an impact. Interestingly, the causal route on performance isn't clear; does high employee performance lead to an LMX relationship, or does an LMX relationship lead to high employee performance? Both explanations make sense; it is likely that high-performing individuals will receive more trust and respect from their supervisor, but it is also true that people given trust and respect might perform at higher levels. Nevertheless, it seems that when a supervisor perceives an employee as highly skilled, she or he is more likely to develop a leader–member exchange relationship.

Unfortunately, the link between LMX relationships and performance is not as clean as researchers might like. One study found that poorly performing in-group employees were given high-performance ratings regardless of their actual performance, whereas the ratings of out-group employees were more consistent with actual performance (Duarte, Goodson, & Klich, 1993).

In sum, leader–member exchange recognizes that managers respond to employees in different ways. With some employees, managers develop strong interpersonal ties, called leader–member exchange relationships. Such relationships are associated with a number of positive outcomes. Other employees are out-group members; the supervisor's relationship with these employees is strictly based on the rules and roles designated by the organization.

❖ CHAPTER SUMMARY

This chapter focused on four theories of leadership. To start, we contrasted leadership with management. Management is a hierarchical position that entails planning, budgeting, and organizing. Leadership, by contrast, is not dependent on a particular position in a hierarchy. Leadership is achieved through vision, motivation, and empowerment. **Likert's four systems** identifies four styles of leadership, articulating that System 4, the participative system, is ideal. **Transformational leadership** suggests that exchange-based leadership, known as transactional leadership, is effective, but not as effective as transformational leadership. Transformational leadership is associated with emotional intelligence and consists of charisma, motivation, intellectual stimulation, and individual consideration. The **contingency model** of leadership suggests that multiple factors must be considered in predicting whether a task focus or a relational focus will be most effective. Finally, **leader–member exchange** theory suggests that leaders have different types of relationships with different subordinates, and the nature of the relationship is associated with differences in support and rewards.

Case Study 6 Saving Holmes Hospitality

Sally and Sam are coworkers at Holmes Hospitality, a medium-sized company that provides travel and event-planning services to corporations. During much of the 1990s, the company had experienced huge growth, as their client corporations expanded and required significant assistance with trade shows, corporate meetings, and travel incentives. Because of the terrorist attacks on the World Trade Center and the Pentagon, along with the flagging U.S. economy in the early years of the new millennium, Holmes was suffering. Many of their corporate clients went out of business, and the few that remained were no longer engaging in much corporate travel or sponsoring many major events. Any tensions that existed in the company before the downturn were magnified.

One significant source of frustration for Sally was the executive VP of Travel Services, Dick Sanderson. Both Sally and Sam reported to Dick, but the two had differing opinions about him. Sally believed that Dick treated the two employees differently. She pointed to the fact that Sam had received a bigger merit pay the year before than she had.

"But that's because I took on the big Steadway project," Sam exclaimed.

"Yes, but you were *assigned* the Steadway project. It's like he is careful to divvy out two projects to each of us, but your projects are the ones that will get you noticed, and mine are just run-of-the-mill sorts of things," Sally explained.

"Well, you should talk to him!"

"I've tried," said Sally, "but ever since I had to take a leave of absence when my mother was dying two years ago, it's like he doesn't trust that I'll be around. He always seems to forget that I finished every project, even though I took the time off. He just doesn't talk to me any more."

"Look, Dick is always asking our opinions on who should be doing what. The next time we have a meeting, make sure he hears some of your ideas. I'll try to shut up. Maybe he'll decide to pursue one of your ideas," Sam counseled.

"I don't want this to be a competition."

"It is and it isn't. Just don't screw up if he gives you something big!" joked Sam.

At the next department meeting Dick announced that because of the company's financial situation, Holmes Hospitality was going to have to generate new revenue, or it would close by the end of the year. Dick asked department members to work together to come up with some ideas to bring to the board about how to improve the financial picture of the company. The group members were a bit overwhelmed with this job. They spent a lot of time fighting over how they might be able to save money or whether it was even possible to find new clients during difficult economic times. Throughout the discussions, Dick focused on the task at hand, even when the group was experiencing a lot of tension.

After several months, the group had not come up with any solutions. Both Sally and Sam were worried that they were going to lose their job, but they were shocked when it was Dick who lost his job. Holmes Hospitality announced that Rob Caster, who had been the executive VP in charge of event planning, was going to collapse the Travel Division into his group. Apparently, Rob and his group worked together to create the idea that the company should expand their services to include videoconferencing and multisite meetings. The new services were extremely successful, and the company wanted Rob to tackle the challenges of the Travel Division as well.

Sally and Sam were both excited by the change. The people who worked for Rob were enthusiastic about working for him. They told Sally and Sam that Rob was the kind of person who made you believe that you could perform miracles. He gave credit where credit was due and was really good about building on people's strengths. Josh, one of Rob's employees, told Sally and Sam, "I have always been good at interfacing with clients, but I'm terrible when it comes to technology. I didn't want to look incompetent, so I never said anything, but Rob noticed I was uncomfortable with the technical tasks. He redistributed the workload so that I don't have to do them anymore, and I can deal with people."

At the first meeting of the newly blended divisions, Rob spoke to the employees, saying "Hospitality means more than friendly and generous service. If you look it up in the dictionary, it also means being open to new ideas. The new Holmes

Hospitality is going to continue providing the same great service to our clients that we always have. But I want you to challenge our assumptions about the right way to serve our clients. I want you to come up with new ways of meeting our clients' needs. Listen to each other, and listen to our clients. All of us can work together to create the kind of service that will keep us in business for the next millennium."

Both Sally and Sam left the meeting excited about the new beginning of the company that they worked for.

Questions for Consideration

1. Using Likert's four systems, which leadership style do you believe Dick Sanderson used, providing support for your beliefs from the case? Which leadership style do you believe that Rob Caster used? Provide support for your beliefs from the case.

2. Identify Dick's and Rob's transactional and transformational qualities, providing support for your beliefs from the case.

3. Dick's leadership style failed to help his group overcome the financial difficulties. Use contingency theory to explain where Dick might have gone wrong.

4. Use leader–member exchange theory to explain the differential relationships held by Sally and Dick versus that between Sam and Dick.

5. Do any of the theories emerge as "better" than the others? Why do you believe this to be the case? What situations might surface that would make a different theory or theories better at explaining the situation?

7

Explaining Theories of Group Communication

Whether you work for a production company, a publishing firm, or a Fortune 500 company, U.S. businesses are increasingly adopting a "team" structure. To succeed as a communication professional, an understanding of how groups work, as well as the principles and pitfalls of group decision making, is crucial to your career. In this chapter, we explain a broad range of group theories, from theories that explain all of group communication to more microscopic theories of group decision making and cohesion.

❖ GROUP COMMUNICATION DEFINED

Popular understanding implies that a *group* is simply a collection of people. Scholars studying group communication are more precise when using the term *group*, however. According to scholars, a **group** refers to *a system of three or more individuals who are focused on achieving a common purpose and who influence and are influenced by each other* (Rothwell, 1998). A group is different from an **aggregate,** which is simply a set number of individuals—say, the people standing at a bus stop or the people on an elevator. Moreover, a group is distinct from an organization. Organizations typically involve formal hierarchies (e.g., CEO, director, manager) and structured channels of communication (e.g., annual performance reviews, employee newsletters). In contrast, a group's structure and patterns of communication typically emerge through interaction (Rothwell, 1998).

Because of the increased use of team-based structures in organizations, it is also of interest to articulate the nature of **teams.** In an organizational setting, a team is an ongoing, coordinated group of people working together (Dyer, 1987). Teams are typically self-directed and self-regulating, meaning that typical chains of organizational command are suspended; teams are empowered to complete a task from start to finish. Not all groups are teams (if control is primarily external, for example), but all teams meet the qualification of being a group.

This chapter emphasizes understanding the communication that takes place within groups and teams. The four theories we present vary in focus. First, interaction process analysis provides a means to create a descriptive typography of the types of messages sent in groups and how they are perceived. Second, symbolic convergence theory explains the development of a group consciousness, including shared emotions, motives, and meanings. Next, functional group decision making centers on the tasks that communication achieves in the decision-making process. Groupthink, the final theory we discuss, describes how to recognize faulty decision making.

❖ INTERACTION PROCESS ANALYSIS/SYMLOG

Interaction process analysis (IPA) is a classic theory developed to explain patterns of group discussion, particularly in terms of leadership (Bales, 1953). The greatest accomplishment of the theory is the creation of a process for analyzing group communication. More recently, the theory has been expanded to provide a means for identifying and evaluating group networks and perceptions.

Bales's (1953) research shows that groups seek to achieve two goals: **task goals** (as evidenced by productivity) and **maintenance goals** (as evidenced by cohesion). Task performance requires communication geared toward achieving the groups' goals, such as asking for and receiving information or giving suggestions. Maintenance goals are achieved by socioemotional communication, such as expressing agreement, releasing tension, and demonstrating cohesion. The problem, according to Bales, is that these two goals are often in conflict with each other. Too much attention to the task can threaten group cohesion (which is considered to be a positive attribute of groups), and too much attention to maintenance can inhibit effective accomplishment of the task. Accordingly, groups must strive to reach an equilibrium, balancing task and maintenance needs.

Based on his research, Bales (1953) proposed a method for analyzing the functions of group communication, illustrated in Table 7.1. All group communication can be coded into one of the 12 categories. The first and fourth categories ("positive and mixed messages" and "negative and mixed messages") refer to socioemotional behavior. The second and third categories ("attempted answers" and "questions") refer to task behaviors. The lines connecting categories on the far right represent a means to identify particular strengths or weakness of the group, as evidenced by the problems these connections represent. By way of illustration, a group that spends little time dramatizing (Category 2) and shows too much tension (Category 11) has a problem of tension reduction. Research shows that healthy groups utilize approximately twice as much task talk as maintenance talk, and more positive socioemotional talk than negative socioemotional talk (Bales, 1953, 1970).

Moreover, IPA suggests that the same group might have two leaders, a task leader and a socioemotional leader (Bales, 1953). These situations occur because task leaders often cause tension and are therefore disliked; in response, social leaders emerge to diffuse this friction. Clearly, the task–relationship distinction is only appropriate in groups where the task is distinct from group cohesion; groups for which the primary task is social support are unlikely to develop separate task and relationship leaders (Wyatt, 1993). Indeed, Wyatt noted that the same communicative act can serve both task and maintenance roles.

Several decades after creating the interaction process analysis, Bales (Bales & Cohen, 1979) expanded on his earlier work by introducing a new means to evaluate groups. Called the System for the Multiple Level Observations of Groups, or *SYMLOG,* this technique focuses on the same variables identified as important in his interaction process analysis. SYMLOG is simultaneously a theory of group dynamics and

Table 7.1 Bales's Interaction Process Analysis Categories

Positive and mixed actions	1. Seems friendly (approx. 3%) 2. Dramatizes (approx. 6%) 3. Agrees (approx. 17%)
Attempted answers	4. Gives suggestions (approx. 8%) 5. Gives opinion (approx. 30%) 6. Gives information (approx. 8%)
Questions	7. Asks for information (approx. 4%) 8. Asks for opinions (approx. 2%) 9. Asks for suggestions (approx. 1%)
Negative and mixed answers	10. Disagrees (approx. 8%) 11. Shows tension (approx. 3%) 12. Seems unfriendly (approx. 1%)

a b c d e f

SOURCE: From *Personality and Interpersonal Behavior,* by R. F. Bales, 1970, Glencoe, IL: Free Press. Reprinted with permission of the author.

NOTE:

a = Problems of communication (6 & 7)

b = Problems of evaluation (5 & 8)

c = Problems of control (4 & 9)

d = Problems of decision (3 & 10)

e = Problems of tension reduction (2 & 11)

f = Problems of reintegration (1 & 12)

a practical method for measuring and changing group behavior (Bales, 1988). Specifically, group members evaluate themselves and all other members of the group on either their values or their behaviors to understand the group better, improve productivity, or increase satisfaction (Bales, 1999). This evaluation centers on three dimensions: forward–backward, positive–negative, and upward–downward.

First, group members rate each other and themselves on the extent to which they demonstrate **forward** (accepting authority) versus **backward** (rejecting authority) values or behaviors. An individual may emerge as high in forward values and behaviors (or high in F) or high in backward values and behaviors (or high in B). The forward–backward dimension might not emerge, however, either because the person manifests both forward and backward behavior and values or neither forward nor backward behavior and values. The same type of assessment is made for the other two dimensions, which are **positive** ("P"; friendly behavior) versus **negative** ("N"; unfriendly behavior), and **upward** ("U" or dominance) and **downward** ("D" or submissive).

Together, these three dimensions interact in such a way that a group member can be placed into one of 26 categories (reflecting one, two, or all three dimensions). To illustrate, an individual might emerge as strong in D (submissive) but does not emerge strongly on any of the other dimensions (Bales, 1999). SYMLOG suggests that D individuals are characterized as passive, saying little. Imagine, however, that the person is both strong in D and P (positivity). These two dimensions combine to create a description of a member who puts his or her trust in others and is appreciative toward other group members.

On the other hand, if a person is high in D but also high in N (negativity), the group member would be characterized as a person who passively rejects group activities; this person is likely to be resentful. If all three dimensions emerge as strong, the person might be classified as DNF. Such a person is identified as self-punishing, working too hard. Conversely, a DNB person would be predicted to withdraw effort because of perceived failure.

In short, each individual in the group is scored, and then all group members are plotted together in what is known as **field diagram.** This diagram presents a visual picture of the group. Based on this data, group coalitions and networks can be identified, as can perceptual barriers that impede group effectiveness. (For more details about SYMLOG, go to www.symlog.org)

In sum, Bales (1953; Bales & Cohen, 1979) presented a theory grounded in his own research about the nature of communication in groups. The norms he referenced can be used to study the roles that individuals enact in groups (task vs. maintenance), leadership emergence in the group (who speaks most often, using what types of statements), and communication problems within the group. As such, the theory has strong practical applications.

❖ SYMBOLIC CONVERGENCE THEORY

The next group theory we discuss is symbolic convergence theory (SCT). Although considered a general theory of communication, SCT was developed within the traditions of small group communication and has been applied most frequently to this context (Bormann, 1982). Specifically, Bormann and colleagues took special note of the positive and mixed actions identified by Bales's (1953) interaction process analysis (described in the previous section). Focusing on the categories of "seems friendly," "dramatizes," and "agrees," SCT was founded on the idea that group members cooperatively create and sustain a shared consciousness, including shared meaning, through interaction. Specifically, SCT focuses on two aspects of group communication: the creation of a group identity and the ways that group identity influence norms for behavior.

Central Concepts

As with many theories, a number of concepts are critical for understanding the explanation of group communication provided by SCT. The most important concept is a **fantasy theme.** The term *fantasy* can be misleading. According to SCT, fantasy does not refer to something that is desired or something that is fictional; rather, it refers to a creative understanding of events that fulfills a psychological or rhetorical need (Bormann, 1982).

A fantasy theme starts with a **dramatizing message**—a joke, pun, figure of speech, anecdote, double entendre, or metaphor, among other things (Bormann, 1996). These messages do not refer to present happenings; instead they reference events that have happened in the past or that are anticipated for the future. Moreover, dramatizing messages always include some level of emotional revelation, typically including both a surface level and a deeper level (Bales, 1970). For example, imagine that Missy has recently solved a problem for her work team. When walking into her next team meeting, Jim starts singing the theme from *Mighty Mouse* ("Here she comes to save the day!"). This message serves the surface function of tension release but also serves the deeper function of recognizing the value of the work that Missy did. Sometimes these messages are sent and immediately dropped, but if the rest of the group responds to the dramatizing message, a fantasy theme has emerged.

Continued embellishment of the fantasy theme can result in a **fantasy chain,** which is when the fantasy theme is developed through group interaction and enters group consciousness (Bormann, 1982). If, for example, the "superhero" theme develops and is built on by other group members, a fantasy chain has emerged. At a later meeting, group members might name a difficult supervisor after a comic book villain or they might joke about the superpowers that would be needed to accomplish a project on time.

According to symbolic convergence theory, building fantasy chains results in group cohesion, a process termed **symbolic convergence** (Bormann, 1982). In other words, the emergence of a fantasy chain transforms the group from a collection of individuals to an identifiable group with a group consciousness. Consider the superhero fantasy chain. Imagine a subsequent meeting that includes the original work team as well as other organizational members not part of that team. Again, Jim whistles the *Mighty Mouse* theme, and all of the original team members laugh—they understand the reference. The individuals who were not a part of the original team may feel left out, however, because they don't understand the joke. Bormann, Cragan, and Shields (1994) argued that

> when people have a shared fantasy theme, they have come to share a consciousness that can be set off by a commonly agreed upon symbolic cue. Only those that have shared the fantasy theme to which the inside-joke refers will respond in an appropriate fashion. (p. 281)

In this way, group identity can be established symbolically.

Any given group might have numerous fantasy chains. That is, the same group that chains the superhero fantasy theme might also use sports metaphors when referring to business situations (*"You really hit that one out of the park, Jane"* or *"It's third and long and we have to go for it if we're gonna win"*). In addition, the group might have a stock story about a team member who failed to follow procedure and lost his job. New members might be told the story as a cautionary tale, and current members might be sanctioned by being told, *"Don't be a Don!"* The ways that various fantasy chains combine within a group leads to a **rhetorical vision.** A rhetorical vision is a unified way of viewing the world. Consider the three fantasy chains just described: superheroes, sports, and sanctions against violating rules. All three fantasy chains share a common way of viewing the world. All three suggest that the world is clearly divided: right and wrong, good and evil, winners and losers. If you are on the side of good you play hard and win; if you are on the side of evil you will lose. This rhetorical vision provides a set of implicit norms for group behavior.

In addition, the process of symbolic convergence affects decision making (Bormann, 1996). For instance, building a sense of common identity and shared meanings fosters group members' creativity in decision making. Moreover, group consciousness and shared motivation also influence assumptions and preferred processes by which decisions are made. In fact, Bormann contended that group members might create fantasy themes about the decision-making process itself.

Figure 7.1 seeks to provide a visual representation of the process of symbolic convergence. Starting at the upper left-hand side of the diagram, a group member sends a dramatizing message. If others in the group interact as a result of that message, a fantasy theme has emerged. If and when group members embellish that fantasy theme, a fantasy chain results. When studying a group, observers can examine the fantasy chains to uncover the underlying rhetorical vision that provides the group with a sense of cohesion and implicit norms for behavior.

The discussion of SCT thus far implies that the theory is concerned only with events internal to a group. One of the strengths of the theory, however, is that it links groups to other social systems, such as a larger organization or a social movement (M. Poole, 1999). For example, a rhetorical vision might start in a group and spread to other parts of an organization. Conversely, the rhetorical vision of a larger organization might restrict the types of fantasy themes generated within a group.

❖ FUNCTIONAL GROUP DECISION MAKING

The third theory moves beyond a general focus of communication in groups to a more specific focus on decision making. Gouran and Hirokawa (1983, 1986, 1996) are the key researchers associated with the functional approach to group communication. A **function** refers to what communication does. An apology serves the function of relationship repair, or a joke can serve the function of tension release. As such, their approach to decision making focuses less on what is

Figure 7.1 The Symbolic Convergence Process

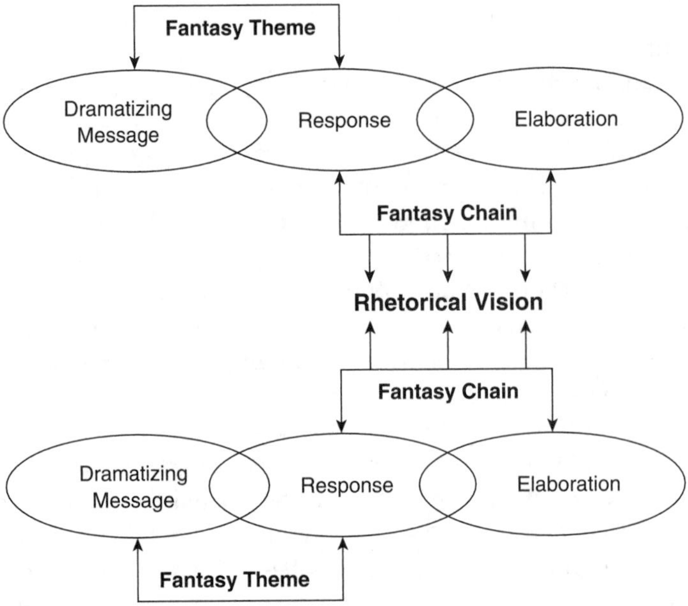

actually said, and more on what the communication in groups *does;* how does it function?

Gouran and Hirokawa began theory development by asking the basic question, "Why do some groups make good decisions while others make bad ones?" (Hirokawa, see Miller, 2002, p. 219). Their model argues that the answer to this question has to do with whether the group has successfully accomplished four functions, which they call **requisite functions** (Gouran & Hirokawa, 1983). These functions are highlighted in Table 7.2.

The first function is **problem analysis.** This means the group must take a realistic look at the nature, extent, and likely causes of the problem. A thorough analysis often involves information gathering. As an example, let's consider a group that has convened to address the larger organization's continued budget shortfall. The functional group decision-making theory suggests that the group should spend a significant amount of time analyzing the actual gap between essential and realized revenues, the implications of the budget shortfall, as well as

Table 7.2 The Four Functions of Decision Making

Function	*Means of Achievement*
Problem analysis	Focus on the nature, extent, and likely causes of the problem. Be careful to differentiate between problems and symptoms of problems.
Goal setting	Identify what an ideal solution would "look like." What are the necessary elements, and what would be ideal but not necessary?
Identify alternatives	Generate a large number of possible solutions: Quantity matters more than quality at this point.
Evaluate and select	Evaluate each alternative using the established goals.

the possible causes for the shortfall. Was it too many expenditures? Slow growth in sales? Or is it just a normal downturn in the economy, which might bounce back? The answers to these questions are important because recognizing the root cause and implications for the problem will determine what form the solution should take.

Second, the **goal setting** function necessitates that all members are clear about what they are trying to accomplish (Gouran & Hirokawa, 1983). Returning to our example, the group members studying the budget shortfall need to be clear about their goals (e.g., are they an advisory group that can only make recommendations, or are they an actual decision-making group?). Typically, this goal setting function also requires group members to develop criteria; these criteria, or standards, will be used to evaluate possible solutions. Thus, our example group should also determine the requirements for a solution. Some sample criteria might include the following: budget cuts shouldn't exceed more than 5%; the implementation of the solution must be possible to achieve within 6 months; and the solution must support the organization's mission.

The third function is the **identification of alternative solutions.** Here, group members brainstorm to generate many possible solutions, maximizing the likelihood that a good solution is ultimately chosen (Gouran & Hirokawa, 1983). *Brainstorming* requires that the group members come up with as many solutions as possible while following these rules: (a) don't evaluate ideas; (b) don't clarify ideas; (c) encourage zany ideas; (d) expand on others' ideas; (e) record all ideas with no reference about who contributed; and (f) encourage participation from everyone (Rothwell, 1998).

Fourth, the group must **evaluate and select the solution** (Gouran & Hirokawa, 1983). To accomplish this task, group members must evaluate the possible solutions generated in the previous function; specifically, the members must compare the possible solutions with the criteria they developed in the second function. Both positive and negative characteristics of the proposed solutions should be considered before selecting the solution that best meets the groups' goals (Gouran & Hirokawa, 1983). Returning to our example decision-making group, the chosen solution will likely be different if the group determined that the problem was slow sales growth rather than overexpenditure.

Functional group decision-making theory states that all four functions need to be accomplished to maximize the likelihood of an effective decision and that no one function is more important than another. Hirokawa (1994) acknowledged, however, that a specific problem might make a particular function less challenging to accomplish. For example, because some problems are particularly obvious, problem analysis will be relatively easy to accomplish. Other problems might naturally have few possible solutions; again, generating alternatives might not be a time-consuming task. On the other hand, there are some problems that impede the effective accomplishment of the four functions. They include ignorance of the issue, relying on faulty facts, operating under misguided assumptions, failure to evaluate the alternatives adequately, making illogical inferences, disregarding group procedures, or suffering from undue influence by one of the group members (Griffin, 2003).

Despite appearance of a logical order to the requisite functions, research suggests that it doesn't matter whether they are completed in a particular order; it only matters that the functions are all completed (Hirokawa, 1994). The performance of the functions is more important than the sequence. Nevertheless, Hirokawa found that groups tackling complex problems tend to follow a similar path. Specifically, the pattern suggests that an analysis of the problem tends to happen first, but that the group then cycles back and forth between goal setting and identifying alternatives. Once criteria are established and the group is satisfied with the proposed alternatives, they move on to evaluation and selection.

Finally, functional group decision-making theory makes particular claims about communication in groups. The theory argues that "communication is a social tool used to accomplish effective decision-making" (Hirokawa & Salazar, 1999, p. 169). As such, it proposes that human beings actively construct group experience based on their communication. Gouran and Hirokawa (1986) specifically posited that three types of communication exist in small groups. **Promotive** discussion is communication geared toward one of the requisite functions. **Disruptive** communication diverts, retards, or frustrates the ability of the group to achieve the requisite functions. Disruptive communication might include social communication. Finally, **counteractive** communication, or messages that return a disrupted group back to the requisite functions, is likely to be most important for group decision making.

Relatively narrow in scope, the functional perspective focuses solely on the task communication associated with small group decision making. It is the promise of improved group success that makes this theory one with significant practical application for communication, business, and other professions. The next theory we discuss, groupthink, also has such practicality.

❖ GROUPTHINK

Whether or not you know the details of the theory, it's likely that you've heard the term *groupthink*. Developed by Janis (1972), the notion of groupthink has bridged the gap from the realm of academics into popular culture. We performed a *Lexis Nexis* search of the term and found literally hundreds of hits during the past year, with the term being referenced in major newspapers, magazines, and even newsletters. Clearly the concept is being used—but is it being used the way that Janis intended?

Defined, **groupthink** is a dysfunctional "way of deliberating that group members use when their desire for unanimity overrides their motivation to assess all available plans of action" (Janis, see Miller, 2002, p. 193). As such, groupthink was designed to explain and predict how bad decisions are made by groups. At its core, the notion of groupthink represents a failure of the group to demonstrate critical thinking. When groups "go along to get along" the end result of the decision-making process is likely to be less effective than if group members question the information at hand, being careful to look at the problem from a variety of perspectives.

Janis (1982) articulated three **antecedent conditions** to groupthink. According to Janis, these preexisting conditions make it more likely that groupthink will occur. Note that the existence of the antecedent conditions does not guarantee that groupthink will occur. Instead, these are what Janis calls "necessary but not sufficient" conditions. The antecedent conditions are high cohesion, structural flaws, and situational characteristics.

First, **cohesion** refers to the degree of connection between group members, or a sense of solidarity (Janis, 1982). Because groupthink emphasizes the preservation of group harmony, a high degree of cohesion is necessary for groupthink to occur. Yet Janis's notion that cohesion might engender bad decision making is novel. Think about your own workplace; in how many "team-building" activities have you taken part? If you are a full-time student, how many of your classes have started with "icebreakers" so that the class might feel more connected to each other? Typically, workplace cohesion is viewed positively, but Janis warns that cohesion might make people reluctant to "rock the boat"; yet rocking the boat might be necessary to make the best possible decision.

The second antecedent condition, **structural flaws,** refers to problems with the way the group is organized (Janis, 1982). Janis identified four specific structural flaws, any one of which might lead to groupthink. First, **group insulation** means that the group is somehow isolated from the larger world. Perhaps they meet so frequently with each other and so infrequently with others outside the group that they are disconnected from the larger system. Perhaps the group hasn't had direct experience with the problem at hand. This insulation might lead to an inability to process adequately all of the information necessary to make an effective decision. The second structural flaw is **biased leadership.** If the leader already has his or her mind made up or has a personal stake in the decision, group members might defer to the leader simply because of the power differential, regardless of whether the leader's solution is good. Third, a **lack of procedural norms** can lead to groupthink. Not having a process in place for how to make a decision can happen either because the group has not taken the time to create the process or because the group fails to follow the process.

In either case, following a standard process can prevent the group from inadvertently missing a key component of the decision-making process. Last, too much **homogeneity** is problematic. Homogeneity refers to similarity; group members who are very similar—in background, values, or beliefs—are less likely to challenge each other's ideas.

The third and final antecedent condition is **situational characteristics** (Janis, 1982). In short, groupthink is more likely to occur in times of **high stress.** This high stress might come from pressures from outside the group. Groups that work in the pharmaceutical industry experience stress from Federal Drug Administration requirements. Television network executives experience pressures from advertisers. Sometimes external forces place undue pressure on the group through operating constraints, threats, or legal requirements. High stress might also come in the form of **time pressures;** the more rapidly a decision has to be made, the less likely that all possible solutions have been adequately studied.

Stressors don't always come from outside the group, however (Janis, 1982). Groups that have experienced **recent failures** may lose confidence in their decision-making ability, and the loss of confidence might create a self-fulfilling prophecy. The final category of situational characteristics is **moral dilemmas;** if a group feels that the viable alternatives represent ethical challenges, they are more likely to fall prey to groupthink. Consider a situation where a group can come up with only three solutions to a problem, but two of the three are deemed ethically inappropriate—the group is likely to pursue the third option, regardless of how good it might be.

Again, these three antecedent conditions are necessary, but not sufficient, for groupthink. In other words, all three conditions must be present to some degree for groupthink to occur; however, simply because these circumstances exist doesn't guarantee the occurrence of groupthink. Instead, Janis (1982) argued that you have to examine how the group operates to observe **symptoms of the groupthink process.** He identified eight symptoms that are grouped into three categories: overestimation, closed-mindedness, and pressure toward uniformity.

The first classification of symptoms falls into the category known as **overestimation of the group** (Janis, 1982). Overestimation occurs when group members have an inflated view of the group's abilities. Two specific symptoms to look for are **illusion of invulnerability** (a belief that the group won't or can't fail) and a belief in the **inherent**

morality of the group (a belief that because the group is good, the decisions the group makes have to be good). Note that both of these symptoms are representative of a level of unwavering confidence in the group and its abilities. As such, group members might not feel it is necessary to analyze critically the decisions being made.

Janis (1982) labeled the second category of groupthink symptoms **closed-mindedness**. These symptoms demonstrate polarized thinking, which means viewing the world in extremes. Things are perceived either as good or bad, right or wrong. If they are good, they are wholly good; if they are bad, they are wholly bad. If a decision is right, it must be completely right. Two specific instances of this category are stereotyping out-groups, and collective rationalization. First, **stereotyping** out-groups refers to the process of demonizing other groups and their leaders. Frequently, images of good and evil are invoked, such as former President Ronald Reagan's designation of the Soviet Union as the "Empire of Evil." When other groups are portrayed as uncompromisingly bad, it is easier to justify decisions that might put those groups in jeopardy. **Collective rationalization** means that the group members tend to justify their decisions by talking themselves into it. As an example, consider a group that spends only 5 minutes coming up with a solution, and 25 minutes discussing why they are right in making the decision. Rather than critically analyze the decision, group members come up with a litany of reasons to defend why it's a good decision.

The third and final symptom of groupthink is organized around the notion of **pressures toward uniformity** (Janis, 1982). When groupthink occurs, it is not only because the group has an inflated view of themselves or because they demonstrate polarized thinking; it is also because individual group members actively suppress critical thinking. **Self-censorship** means that group members tend to keep their mouths shut when experiencing doubts. Often they feel as though everyone else is "on board" with the decision, so they are afraid to go out on a limb with their concerns. This tendency also highlights the **illusion of unanimity**, which means that group members perceive that consensus has been reached, even if it really hasn't. As such, silence tends to be interpreted as consent. In fact, **self-appointed mindguards** are careful not to present any contrary information, even if they know it exists; in other words, a self-appointed mindguard engages in self-censorship. If someone actually does question the decision, a group experiencing groupthink will often place **pressure on dissenters**; challenges to the group are squashed.

Table 7.3 Groupthink Processes

Antecedents		*Symptoms*
Cohesion		**Overestimation of group** • Illusion of invulnerability • Belief in morality
Structural flaws • Insulation • Biased leadership • No procedural norms • Homogeneity	**Groupthink**	**Closed-mindedness** • Stereotypes • Collective rationalizations
Situational characteristics • High stress • Time pressure • Recent failures • Moral dilemmas		**Uniformity pressures** • Self-censorship • Illusion of unanimity • Self-appointed mindguards • Direct pressure on dissenters

To prevent groupthink, Janis (1982) recommends that group members take the following steps: (a) encourage critical evaluation; (b) avoid having the leader state a preference; (c) set up several independent subgroups to study the problem and propose solutions; (d) discuss what is happening in the group with people outside of the group; (e) invite outsiders into the group; (f) assign someone to be a devil's advocate; (g) monitor the group for the symptoms; and (h) take time between the initial decision and the confirmation of the decision to give people time to analyze the decision critically.

Table 7.3 presents an overview of the antecedents and symptoms of groupthink. As you can see, Janis (1982) identified a large number of factors that exist before the group begins deliberating, as well as factors that are recognizable while the group is deliberating. Groupthink itself—the tendency to avoid critical thinking so that cohesion can be maintained—occurs somewhere in between antecedent conditions and the symptoms.

❖ CHAPTER SUMMARY

In this chapter, we discussed four distinct theories of group communication. **Interaction process analysis** predicts that the enactment of specific behavioral types can indicate group roles, leadership, and problems. **Symbolic convergence** suggests that particular types of messages called fantasy themes contribute to a sense of group identity or consciousness. An examination of these fantasy themes and how they might combine provides a rhetorical vision that provides the principles by which the group operates. **Functional group decision making** delineates specific tasks group members need to complete to make an effective decision. Finally, **groupthink** provides a means to understand why group members make poor decisions through a particular focus on cohesion, structural faults, and situational constraints.

Case Study 7 The Gifted Group

A new leader brought renewed enthusiasm at the Brunswick County Conference & Visitors Bureau, Inc. (BCCVB), the official tourism promotion agency for Brunswick County, Pennsylvania. Under her leadership, the bureau underwent both programmatic and physical expansion. Shortly after the BCCVB relocated its offices and visitor center to a newly constructed building, the executive director decided to create a gift center committee. The purpose of the committee was to devise a plan for a visitor center gift shop—something the BCCVB had never had—in which a variety of merchandise bearing the Brunswick County logo could be sold to visitors.

The committee consisted of the following five BCCVB staff members: John Maher, communication assistant; Laura Doherty, office manager; Nannette Kearny, membership director; Lisa Berman, assistant director; and Donald Johnson, corporate sales manager. The newly formed group was highly cohesive; they had worked together for more than 5 years, and they were all committed to the vision of the visitor's bureau developed by the executive director. The committee was given 3 weeks, meeting as often as they deemed necessary to devise a plan detailing how the BCCVB would establish a visitor center gift shop. The timeframe was difficult to achieve given that the group members still had to perform the duties of their regular jobs, but all of the members were committed to doing so.

The first meeting turned out to be a "meeting of the minds" to establish a consensus as to how the group would move forward. Because of their cohesion, committee members were sociable, gregarious, and comfortable working with one another. As a result, members spent a good 15 minutes at the onset of the meeting catching up with one another. Donald, the group clown, decided that an important first step was to come up with a name for the committee, and he decided that the group members should be known as the "gifted group." This name lead to much laughter and joking that it would be the first time Donald had ever been called "gifted" in his life.

Lisa Berman also participated in this social interaction but took naturally to a leader-type role when it came time to discuss business matters. She made an effort to focus the committee's attention to the matter at hand—the gift shop—and enabled the group to transition from social-related to more task-related communication. At that point, the committee began discussing the overall idea of a gift shop and how to devise a plan that details how to initiate such a venture. The group quickly came to a rather dramatic realization following this discussion: nobody on the committee had any retail or gift shop experience. Committee members, undoubtedly discouraged by this realization, became reluctant to move forward. The meeting closed, however, with John recommending that each member research visitor center gift shops before the next gathering. Donald and Nanette initially disagreed with the proposal, saying they didn't have time to do so. Nannette asked Laura if she would be willing to do the research, and Laura quickly complied. However, Lisa pointed out that if each person did a little research, no one person would be overburdened. She persuaded the group members to take on the task as a whole.

At the second meeting, each committee member arrived with an impressive arsenal of visitor center gift shop research. Again, the first 10 or 15 minutes were devoted to socializing. And again, Lisa had to work to get people back on task. At first, Donald fought with Lisa for control of the meeting. He continued joking around, calling one of the organizational members not on the committee "special Ned." When Lisa tried to get the group back on task again, Nanette responded, "Hey, not everyone can be considered gifted," and the group continued laughing. Lisa tried to remain lighthearted because she wasn't the official leader, but she was frustrated that others were wasting time. She remarked, "We won't continue to be considered gifted if we don't get this done." Donald responded, "Uh oh, teacher is mad. Are you gonna keep us after school if we don't hit the books?" At this, everyone laughed, including Lisa.

Finally turning to the job at hand, the meeting entailed a thorough investigation of each member's materials and a lengthy discussion about how the group would use the research to proceed.

The committee decided to compile the research that related most directly to the BCCVB and to set a calendar indicating how, armed with such information, they would move forward with subsequent meetings. Collectively, the committee established a heavy meeting schedule, with a meeting scheduled every day for the remainder of the 2-week timeframe.

Each meeting flowed in a manner very similar to that of the first and second meetings. The first 10 or 15 minutes of every meeting, even as the deadline drew near, were set aside for social interaction. Donald would joke around and the others would follow his lead. Then, the committee would either progress naturally toward the task at hand, or Lisa Berman would comment about moving forward or getting down to business and eventually the group would do so.

Toward the end of the second week, group energy was sagging. Everyone had been devoting a significant amount of time not only to the meetings, but to "homework" each tackled in between the meetings. At this point, John's role shifted from group member to group cheerleader. He encouraged others when they became frustrated or tired. He reminded everyone that although the short timeframe meant that they weren't running a marathon, the work they were doing wasn't a sprint either. Donald responded, "What, we're doing the 800 meter?" Nanette retorted, "Well, hell, that's my problem, I'm out of shape!" John joined in, saying, "Actually, the hurdles were always my specialty! But yes, it is an 800-meter race; we need to keep a rapid pace, but we can't all-out sprint the whole time."

After the 3 weeks were over, the group presented their final proposal to the executive director. Following the meeting, Laura presented all of the members a track jersey with the words "The Gifted Group" written across the chest.

Questions for Consideration

1. Describe each of the group members in terms of the interaction categories described by Bales. Then consider Bales's SYMLOG; how do you think the group members perceive Lisa?

2. Discuss the elements of symbolic convergence as related to the group. How do you think symbolic convergence might have affected the decision-making process?
3. Using the functional model, was the decision likely to be effective? Why or why not? Describe how and when each function emerged.
4. What is the likelihood that groupthink occurred? What antecedents are present? Do you see any symptoms of groupthink?
5. Do any of the theories emerge as "better" than the others? Why do you believe this to be the case? What situations might surface that would make a different theory or theories better at explaining the situation?

8

Explaining Theories of Organizational Communication

> *Businesses give a great deal of lip service to the importance of communication. Managers often give speeches about it to their employees and customers. Employees and customers listen and nod their heads. Sometimes they shake their heads. That's the problem. Employees and customers listen, but often that's the extent of their participation. Corporate information usually flows from the top down. (Parkinson, 2003, para. 1–2)*

Recognize this scenario? One of the most intriguing paradoxes of corporate life is how often organizational members stress the importance of communication, yet how little many of these members know about organizational communication. In Chapter 1, we argued that popular culture tends to oversimplify the communication process. Nowhere is this more evident than in the organizational setting.

❖ ORGANIZATIONAL COMMUNICATION DEFINED

Before introducing theories of organizational communication, first let's define what we mean by an organization. An **organization** is characterized by a group of people who coordinate activities to achieve individual and collective goals (Miller, 2003). Note that this definition is not referring only to incorporated entities, nor only to profit-making enterprises. The definition we are using includes obvious examples of organizations, such as IBM or Johnson & Johnson, as well as less obvious examples, such as the Boy Scouts of America, your local pizza parlor, or an intramural volleyball league. In short, think broadly as you read these theories of organizational communication. These theories are likely to apply not only to businesses where you work or frequent; they also hold true for any structured leisure activities you might pursue.

Communication within organizations typically serves three functions or purposes (Shockley-Zalabak, 2002). First, communication serves a *relationship* function. The relationship function refers to the centrality of communication in socializing organizational members and integrating them into their work environment. Second, communication serves an *organizing* function, which means that communication guides, directs, and controls organizational activity. Third, communication serves a *change* function. It is through communication that organizational members analyze, problem-solve, adapt, and innovate.

This chapter focuses on four theories of organizational communication: organizational identification and control, Schein's organizational culture model, structuration theory, and Weick's organizing theory. The first, organizational identification and control, emphasizes the relationship and organizing functions mentioned above. The remaining three theories—organizational culture, structuration, and organizing—emphasize all three functions of organizations.

❖ ORGANIZATIONAL IDENTIFICATION AND CONTROL

As indicated in Chapter 7, organizations are increasing their use of team-based structures to improve quality, engender creativity, and increase employee involvement (Deetz, Tracy, & Simpson, 2000). Although these are the *stated* goals of work teams, research suggests that team-based structures also serve another purpose: *control over employees* (Barker, 1999). Consequently, organizational identification and control (OIC) theory centers on the way that an individual's connection to the organization influences behavior and decision making in team-based structures (Barker, 1999). Three main concepts tie the theory together: **control, identification,** and **discipline.**

Control

First, and quite simply, "an organization needs control to get things done" (Miller, 2003, p. 210). There are, however, several forms of control that an organization might utilize. Based on Edwards's (1981) delineation, an organization may exert control through three methods. **Simple control** involves direct, authoritarian control. This method is analogous to Likert's (1961) system one and system two forms of management (see Chapter 6). It is the classic way of controlling employees.

The second method of control is more subtle. **Technological control** involves the use of technology to manage what can and can't be done in the workplace (Edwards, 1981). A factory assembly line is a perfect example; employees must go exactly as fast as the assembly line is moving, no faster and no slower (as the classic episode of *I Love Lucy* in the candy factory illustrated). Employees on an assembly line can only take prescribed breaks, as well, because the whole line must be shut down if one person takes a break. A more contemporary example of this type of control is the limitation of computer technology. How often have you been told by someone, "the program won't let us do that?" What sorts of technology you do or don't have access to and the ways that technology does or does not work serves as a means of organizational control.

The third kind of control is **bureaucratic control** (Edwards, 1981). Undoubtedly, you are familiar with the term *bureaucracy,* and it is usually associated with negative perceptions. Edwards, however, was referring to the vision of bureaucracy first articulated by Max Weber, a German sociologist. Writing at the turn of the 20th century, Weber argued that modern organizations are served best by a hierarchical system of rules, with rewards and punishments drawn from those rules. That hierarchy is evident in contemporary organizations through company policies and formal procedures. Employee handbooks and other such formalized rule systems are the clearest example of bureaucratic control.

These three forms of control are the ways that power has typically been exerted in organizations. Tompkins and Cheney (1985) suggested that changes in organizations during the latter part of the 20th century have shifted the way that control is wielded. With the growing use of team-based organizations, and organizations grounded in participation and empowerment, Tompkins and Cheney identified two additional types of control: unobtrusive and concertive. First, **unobtrusive control** is based on shared values within the organization. Put simply, in the "new" organization, management's job is to create a vision and mission for the organization. When organizational members make decisions based on the vision or credo of the organization, they are not making those decisions because they are forced to, but because they believe in the mission of the organization—they identify with the organization. Thus, the commitment to organizational values controls employees.

Similarly, **concertive control** is based on interpersonal relationships and teamwork (Tompkins & Cheney, 1985). More obvious than unobtrusive control, concertive control happens when coworkers develop mechanisms to reward and control behavior that influences the team. For example, Barker (1999) suggested that group members can discipline nonconforming coworkers through direct criticism, monitoring, the use of silence, and social pressure, among other things. As with simple control, concertive control is obvious and direct. It is not, however, a managerial function in this system, but happens among hierarchical equals. Table 8.1 provides an overview of the types of control.

Identification

OIC's second major concept, **identification,** refers to the sense of oneness with or belongingness to an organization; when individuals experience identification, they define themselves in terms of the organization (Mael & Ashforth, 1992). Evidence of identification happens when you listen to organizational members speak. Often they will say things such as, "we don't operate that way here" or "we launched a new product today." In these cases, the organizational member is adopting the persona of the organization—she or he may have had little to do

Table 8.1 Organizational Identification and Control

Type of Control	*Example*
Simple	• Commands • Threats
Technological	• Assembly lines • Removing computer games from workplace machines
Bureaucratic	• Employee handbooks • Employment contracts
Unobtrusive	• Identification with organizational values • Decision making based on organizational mission
Concertive	• Monitoring of other team members' performance • Coworker pressure on nonconforming members

with the new product, but there is a sense of pride in and ownership of the product because of identification.

Discipline

Pulling together the concepts of control and identification, Barker (1999) and colleagues (see also Tompkins & Cheney, 1985) suggested that discipline is achieved through a sense of responsibility to the work group because members identify with their organization and because they share common values and a vision for the organization. When individuals are faced with a decision, they will rely on organizational values to make that decision—there is no need for top-down management directives. If an individual is not behaving in concert with organizational values, work group members tend to censure that individual.

Notably, according to OIC theory, superiors need not do the disciplining themselves; the norms for behavior generated by the organizational mission and values coupled with the identification of organizational members work in concert to maintain organizational control. Thus, the creation of organizational missions and visions might have the explicit function of driving the organization's business, and work teams might provide a mechanism for employee empowerment, but these initiatives also serve the implicit function of constraining employees.

❖ ORGANIZATIONAL CULTURE

The notion of organizational visions and values provides a nice segue to our next theory of organizational communication. Organizational visions are often considered part of organizational culture. Many theories and concepts are associated with organizational culture, and not all of them paint a consistent picture (for an overview, see Modaff & DeWine, 2002). Not recognized as a formal theory per se but as a model for understanding communication in organizations, Schein (1985, 1992) focused on the elements that comprise an organizational culture and how organizational cultures assist individuals in making sense of their experiences. His model will be the approach to organizational culture we highlight. According to Schein (1992), **culture** refers to a pattern of shared assumptions that have been invented, discovered, or developed by a given group and are taught to new members as the correct way to perceive, think, and behave. Although this definition seems to imply that organizational members are consciously aware of organizational cultures, Schein argued that this is not always the case; frequently organizational members are not aware of the cultural assumptions they hold. Moreover, culture is something that emerges from interaction and continuously develops, although it is resistant to change.

Schein's (1992) model includes three levels of culture: artifacts, values, and assumptions. Although all three make up a culture, he believed that the third level, assumptions, is at the crux of organizational culture, and that the first two levels, artifacts and values, may simply reflect the more abstract and subconscious assumptions shared by organizational members.

Level 1: Artifacts

Artifacts refer to the observable evidence of culture (Schein, 1992). They may take the forms of physical entities, such as architecture, dress, and documents, but they also consist of patterns of behavior. These patterns of behavior can take the form of rituals, acronyms, forms of address, approaches to decision making, and management style. Table 8.2 lists some examples of artifacts.

Although artifacts are by definition observable, interpreting what the artifacts mean may not always be obvious (Schein, 1992). For

Table 8.2 Cultural Artifacts and Behaviors

Artifact/Behavior	*Examples*
Architecture	Open floor plan, cubicles; offices with windows; size of offices; rented suites versus owned campus
Technology	Type of phone system used; up-to-date versus archaic computers/computer systems; availability/type of Internet connection, e-mail, portable digital assistants (PDAs)
Dress	Business attire versus casual attire; casual Fridays; dress codes
Forms of address	Titles used, versus first names; differences in address by hierarchical level
Decision-making style	Autocratic versus participatory; rapid versus slow; conservative versus risk taking
Communication patterns	Formal versus informal; friendly versus distant; use of acronyms, unique terms, myths, stories; rituals

SOURCE: From *Organizational Communication: Approaches and Processes (with InfoTrac)* (3rd ed.), by K. Miller, ©2003. Reprinted with permission of Wadsworth, a division of Thomson Learning: www.thomsonrights.com. Fax: 800-730-2215.

example, imagine an organization that develops a pattern of using formal titles among organizational members. According to Miller (2003), such a behavioral artifact might mean that the organization is a very formal one. On the other hand, it might simply mean that organizational members hold each other in high esteem, and wish to show each other respect. Or, it might be an indication that the organizational members dislike each other and seek to maintain distance. Thus, while this level of culture is readily apparent, it does not provide much substance to an understanding of organizational culture. Attention must be turned to higher levels for such understanding.

Level 2: Values

The second level of culture is organizational members' **values,** defined as preferences about how situations should be handled (Schein, 1992). These preferences represent shared beliefs about how things ought to happen. By nature, values are intangible, but organizational members are typically able to articulate them. Organizational leaders are frequently the source of values; for instance, research shows that the values held by the founder of a company strongly influenced the values described by other employees (Morley & Shockley-Zalabak, 1991). Certainly, literature suggests that leadership is, by definition, the ability to shape members' perceptions of the task and the mission of the organization (Barge, 1994). Accordingly, it's not surprising that organizational members are persuaded to adopt the values of organizational leaders.

Still, simply because a leader articulates a value system does not make it so. Importantly, championed values are not always authentic values, as is evident when the ideals expressed do not match behavior (Schein, 1992). Consider, for instance, two organizations that claim to value *innovation.* When scrutinizing the artifacts of the first organization, observers notice that the company encourages risks and gives employees time to experiment. Failures are not punished; in fact, the company encourages employees to talk about failures, because one person's failure might be the solution to another person's problem. A significant portion of the annual budget is earmarked for research and development. In this case, the artifacts seem to support the value of innovation. At the second company, however, failure is not an option; people who fail are punished. The organization is resistant to change and has very rigid systems to implement even the smallest change. Little of the budget is slated for research and development, and employees are kept so busy maintaining the current product line that they have virtually no time to develop any new ideas. In fact, employees have facetiously created the company slogan, "We don't innovate, we duplicate." Clearly, these artifacts do not seem to suggest that the value of innovation is actually practiced. The point is that espoused values are not always identical to the actual values of the organization; just because it appears in the mission statement does not mean it reaches the level of everyday practice.

Level 3: Basic Assumptions

The final level of culture is the most difficult to identify because it is often taken for granted by organizational members. **Basic assumptions** refer to the viewpoints organizational members hold about the world, including perceptions, thoughts, feelings, and beliefs. These assumptions are subconscious because they have been reinforced over and over again as the organization faces challenges. Basic assumptions lie at the heart of organizational culture because such presumptions are made uniformly throughout the organization (Schein, 1992).

Specifically, organizations develop assumptions about the nature of reality, time, space, human nature, and human relationships, among other things (Schein, 1992). These concepts are relatively profound philosophical commitments to things, such as the "right" way for people to interact with each other, whether human beings are by nature good or evil, and whether truth is singular (i.e., there is one absolute Truth) or conditional (e.g., some things are true at some times in some places for some people).

Although this notion sounds complex, such assumptions have a substantial impact on organizational life. Morton (1999) illustrated this effect through an analysis of assumptions in child welfare agencies. Specifically, a fundamental assumption of one child welfare agency might be that people are capable of changing. Such an assumption will affect the everyday decisions that are made because organizational members will spend energy seeking to develop and reward individuals rather than punish them for past infractions. Yet a different organization might hold the assumption that the best predictor of future behavior is past behavior. In this case, organizational members are likely to view individuals who have made previous mistakes as risky prospects likely to repeat those mistakes.

According to Schein's (1992) model of organizational culture, an analysis of assumptions could assist organizational members in generating a coherent blueprint for how the organization should operate. This prediction is not always the case. Some organizations might simultaneously hold seemingly conflicting assumptions. For example, employees of a Catholic institution of higher learning may be challenged by incompatible assumptions; for instance, assumptions that the Catholic Church makes about "truth" may contrast the assumptions that some of the university's academic disciplines hold about "truth." Such contradictory assumptions might cause problems for members who are seeking to behave in concert with organizational assumptions. How the organization reconciles these inconsistent assumptions determines the overarching organizational culture.

To summarize, Schein (1985, 1992) proposed three levels of culture: artifacts, values, and assumptions. Although there may be surface inconsistencies within and across these levels, a careful analysis of the patterns that emerge will give observers an understanding of the organizational culture. These cultures are created by employees, with particular emphasis placed on the impact of those at the highest levels in the organization, but much like structuration theory described in the next section, organizational cultures also constrain how organizational members communicate.

❖ STRUCTURATION THEORY

Originally proposed as a general theory of social interaction (Giddens, 1979), structuration theory served as a springboard for M. Poole and McPhee (McPhee, 1985; M. Poole, 1985, 1988; M. Poole & McPhee, 1983) to explain organizational communication processes. At the core of structuration theory is the notion of structure. Poole (1988) argued that structures are featured characteristics of organizations: "Division of labor, organization of workflow, arrangement of people into hierarchical positions, the use of budgets all are the hallmarks of the organization, and all involve the imposition of structure" (p. 1).

According to Poole (1988), structures serve five primary functions in the organization: they provide a means for *coordination and control*, they assist members in defining their *identities* in the organization, they provide a means to *monitor member performance*, they help the organization to *relate to its environment*, and they serve a *symbolic function*, indicating to both organizational members and outsiders the nature of the organization. Despite the importance of structures in organizations, Poole's theory contends that structures are not as permanent as you might think; they require constant maintenance and repair. Specifically, communication is the means by which structures are developed, maintained, and changed. This process is known as **structuration.**

Assumptions

There are two major assumptions of structuration theory. First, the theory assumes that humans are actors who make choices in their behavior (Giddens, 1979). This assumption, also called **agency,** means that people have free will in terms of their communicative behavior. The second assumption is that organizations are produced and reproduced through structures in interaction (Giddens, 1979). This assumption requires people to understand what Giddens means by the terms *structure, production,* and *reproduction.*

In this context, *structure* does not match popular understandings of the term. **Structure** is not a physical entity, but a set of *rules and resources used by an organization in order to meet its goals.* A **rule** is *how* an organization should accomplish its goals. Think of rules as either formal or informal prescriptions for how to do things. A formal rule might be a company policy that says everyone must show up by 8:00 a.m., and an informal rule might be that organizational members believe decisions are made by consensus. **Resources** refer to the properties that organizational members rely on to get things done. Two types of resources are available to members. **Allocative resources** refer to material forms of assistance, such as time and money. **Authoritative resources** refer to the interpersonal characteristics of organizational members, such as cohesion, experience, and status.

With the understanding that structures (rules and resources) are central to organizational life, we turn to the second premise of the theory; *organizations are produced and reproduced through structures in interaction.* Through their behavioral choices, organizational members create (**produce**) structures. To illustrate, organizational members who act as though time is more important than money will create a structure (i.e., a rule) that making rapid decisions is more important than making cost-effective decisions. The impact of this structure lives on, however. Future organizational members can refer back to this rule and then prioritize their decision making so that time efficiency is more important than fiscal conservation. As such, they have reinforced (or **reproduced**) the rule that was initially created. Through interaction, the structure is produced and reproduced; individuals have created it, but they are also constrained by it.

This notion that organizational members' action (agency) both creates and constrains interaction is known as the **duality of structure.** Note that the idea of agency stands on its own; human beings have complete free will with regard to their behavior. The notion of structure is intertwined with human action, providing a subtle force. Ellis (1999) characterized agency and structure as "braided social entities" (p. 127). Throughout the process of structuration, human beings have the choice to change the rules or adjust the resources available to them in their interaction, but they feel pressured by the constraints of previous actions.

Moreover, these activities often occur at low levels of consciousness. Organizational members are not always aware of structures, nor of their ability to change structures.

Influences on Structure

Two additional ideas are important before discussing the applications of structuration theory within organizations. First, structures are often borrowed from larger groups (M. Poole, Seibold, & McPhee, 1985, 1986). For example, a work group may **appropriate,** or borrow from, the structures of the larger corporation, such as the organizational culture. As such, the group is not starting from scratch, but relying on the structures already available to them prior to interaction. Similarly, organizations can appropriate larger societal structures, such as individualism, patriotism, or capitalism. This behavior would be considered appropriation from society.

Second, structuration theory assumes that all social interactions include elements of communication, morality, and power (Poole et al., 1985; 1986). The **communication** element dictates that organizational members operate within a given set of meanings or understandings. As such, their language choices are important. A worker might use particular words such as *competitive* or *innovative* as a symbolic reflection of the rules of the organization. These words are the *buzzwords* or the *in terms* of the organization. The idea of **morality** means that organizational norms about what is and what is not acceptable behavior affect the agency, or actions, of organizational members. Finally, **power** means that the implicit power structures (e.g., equality, or hierarchy, or authority) affect the interactional choices made by organizational members.

Applications of Structuration

Structuration theory is complex, with a large number of abstract concepts. Yet the theory does provide some concrete advice for organizational members (M. Poole, 1988). This advice is captured in Table 8.3. Note that the advice mirrors some of the buzzwords of corporate America today. For example, the first proposition focuses on the importance and power of restructuring. Although occasionally used as a euphemism for *layoffs,* true restructuring means having a flexible organization.

Table 8.3 Practical Implications of Structuration

Advice	*Explanation*
Plan for restructuring	Assume that restructuring is a normal part of organizational life; have explicit conversations with organizational members about what the structures are and how they are used.
Communicate why	Don't just present the details of the structure to organizational members, explain the philosophy behind it. This will allow members to reproduce the structure creatively.
Experiment	"Test drive" structures to determine whether they work in the intended ways, and assess unintended consequences. Listen to organizational members' responses to ideas and problems with structures.
The dangers of writing	Putting structures into writing (policy manuals, user's manuals, etc.) gives everyone the same information, but written structures are easily misunderstood and manipulated.
Capitalize on ambiguity	Ambiguity is useful; it allows interpretation and does not alienate members who disagree with the details. Members can show initiative within general guidelines that they can't within specific guidelines.
Temporary structures	Using temporary structures, such as task forces, allows members to recognize that all structures are transitory; it calls to the forefront the process of structuration, reinvigorating members' agency.
Beware of expertise	Expertise often means a narrow perspective; nonexperts can bring new ways of looking at creating structures.

Note, too, the advice that suggests that expertise should be viewed with some caution; calling in consultants might not be the best way to resolve a problem, according to structuration theory.

An additional area of focus concerns **organizational climate.** Much like the climate of a city, organizational climate refers to what it *feels like* to be in a particular organization (Miller, 2002). Thus, an organization can be described as *laid back* or *stressful*, *friendly* or *formal*. From a structuration approach, climate is a structure of an organization; it is produced and reproduced by organizational members' interaction. Because climate is considered a structure, it is a collective attitude, meaning that it is widely experienced and has far-reaching effects within the organization (M. Poole & McPhee, 1983). For example climate affects the communication of organizational members, as well as their productivity and satisfaction. A description of climate that is shared throughout an organizational system is called a **kernel climate.**

Climate can also be differentially interpreted and experienced within the same organization (M. Poole, 1985). This aspect of climate is **surface climate.** Surface climates can vary dramatically between and among hierarchical levels, and from one subgroup of the organization to another. To illustrate, if one department of the organization is characterized by cooperation and support, members of that department might experience the climate of the organization positively. Individuals from a different department, however, might interact with suspicion and distrust, creating quite a different climate for those organizational members.

Notably, according to a structuration approach, the same kernel climate might result in different surface climates (M. Poole, 1985). Consider, for example, a kernel climate of *flexibility*. Examples of this kernel climate in action might include rules and resources that allow employees to work the hours they wish, to select the tasks they are most interested in, and to work at their own pace. One group of employees might experience this structure as fostering a creative and supportive atmosphere, which would be the surface climate for them. These employees would interact with each other in such a way that flexibility would facilitate personal and organizational success. A different group of employees might experience this structure as unorganized and demotivational; why work hard if the organization doesn't care what you do or when you do it? How do you know what to do if no one tells you? The surface climate for these employees might produce and reproduce a structure of apathy and frustration.

In sum, structuration theory states that organizational members have the power to form their own organization through the rules they create and modify in their interaction. This theory also recognizes, however, that previous rules become structures that impinge on the organization's communication in the future, such that members feel pressure to abide by earlier decisions.

❖ ORGANIZING THEORY

The previous theories in this chapter have linked communication processes to organizational processes. The fourth and final perspective, Weick's (1969) organizing theory, takes this link one step further by stating that communication *is* the organization. Instead of viewing organizations as containers in which communication occurs, Weick argued that communication is what constitutes an organization. Instead of examining an *organization* (a noun), Weick examined the process of *organizing* (a verb).

With roots in Darwin's theory of evolution, information theory, and systems theory (see Chapter 3), organizing theory assumes that organizations exist in an **information environment** (Weick, 1969). Rather than focusing on the physical environment, Weick's theory is concerned with the massive amounts of information that organizations have available to them. Information comes from internal and external sources. Importantly, organizations depend on information to accomplish their goals. The challenge of processing all of the available information is a Herculean task.

In addition to issues of quantity, managing the information environment is difficult because much of the information that organizations deal with is unpredictable. The term **equivocality** references the ambiguity of information available to organizations (Weick, 1969). Messages are equivocal to the extent that there may be multiple understandings of the information. Equivocality is different from the concept of uncertainty. When individuals are uncertain about a message, they can gather more information to reduce uncertainty. However, when individuals find a message to be equivocal, they do not need additional information; instead, they must decide which of multiple interpretations is the best fit. Consider the example of an individual who has to decide how to invest her money. The state of the economy is equivocal; some financial planners argue that the stock market will pick up, and so she should invest in the stock market, whereas others suggest that because the market is poor and looks like it will continue to perform poorly, she should invest in real estate. Gathering more information is likely only to add to the equivocality. In the end, she has to interpret the state of the economy for herself, but her interpretation is only one of many interpretations that can be made.

According to Weick (1969), one way to reduce equivocality is to rely on **rules** (also called **recipes).** The term *rule* most often refers to guidelines for behavior, and Weick's use of the term is consistent with this conceptualization. Typically, organizations have rules, or guidelines, for analyzing both the equivocality of a message as well as how to respond to messages. These rules are developed to make a process more efficient, and they are generally based on past successes. There are many obvious examples of rules, such as rules for who to contact to accomplish certain tasks, rules about specific forms to be used, and rules about processes to be followed. Rules can also be less formalized. For example, an organization might have had past success with increasing profits by reducing packaging costs for its products. Accordingly, the next time corporate earnings are in question, the stock response is to seek to reduce packaging costs: Cost reduction has become a rule.

Rules don't always work, and there isn't always a rule for every situation. Organizing theory suggests that a second way to reduce equivocality is for organizational members to engage in communication cycles known as **double interacts** (Weick, 1969). Double interacts are suited for instances of high equivocality because they require organizational members to develop interdependent relationships in the process of communicating. Recall that in Chapter 3, we discussed the concept of *nonsummativity:* The whole is greater than the sum of its parts. Weick's theory is grounded in systems principles, and so he argued that greater involvement among organizational members can produce greater results in reducing equivocality.

A double interact consists of an act, a response and an adjustment (Weick, 1969). An **act** is a communication behavior initiated by one person or group of people. The receivers of the message communicate in return, which is considered a **response.** This two-way exchange of messages is the one most typically used to understand the communication process. Weick proposed that genuine communication requires a third step, an **adjustment** to the information that was originally received. This adjustment can take several forms. It might be a confirmation that the information has been understood. If the information is still equivocal, the adjustment might be additional information gathering.

To illustrate, the marketing department of a major manufacturing company has created a new product configuration to be sold only at

Walmart. They approach production with the new idea, but members of the production team respond by telling marketing that the configuration they have sold cannot be produced on the current assembly lines. Marketing amends the proposal so that the customer receives the specialty product and the production department can utilize existing equipment and materials: act, response, adjustment.

At the beginning of this section, we stated that Weick (1969) was more concerned with the process of organizing than with the entity of an organization. Double interacts are the process of organizing; according to Weick, they are literally the links that hold an organization together. Weick also believed, however, that organizing is an evolutionary process. Much like Darwin's theory of evolution, which suggests that organisms become extinct if they can't adapt to their environment, organizing theory maintains that organizations that don't adapt to their environment will collapse. Accordingly, Weick proposed a three-stage process of **sociocultural evolution** for organizations.

The first stage of sociocultural evolution is **enactment** (Weick, 1969). Enactment occurs when members of an organization take note of equivocal information in their information environment. Recall that equivocal information can be interpreted in multiple ways. Recognizing that there are multiple interpretations and acting to put into process a mechanism for making sense of the information are at the heart of enactment.

The second stage is **selection** (Weick, 1969). In seeking to reduce equivocality, organizational members must choose how to respond. As described earlier, organizational members can choose between *rules,* or standard guidelines for how to respond, and a *double interact,* which is a communication process that allows members to adapt solutions to the problem.

The third stage is **retention** (Weick, 1969). Retention is a form of organizational memory. What was done and how it was done is stored, formally or informally, so that organizational members can refer to it again. Notice what is happening here; even if organizational members go through a double interact to reduce equivocality, in this stage the double interact is retained as a new rule or guideline for behavior for future use. Accordingly, retention should be used sparingly. Figure 8.1 provides a visual illustration of sociocultural evolution.

Figure 8.1 Weick's Model of Organizing

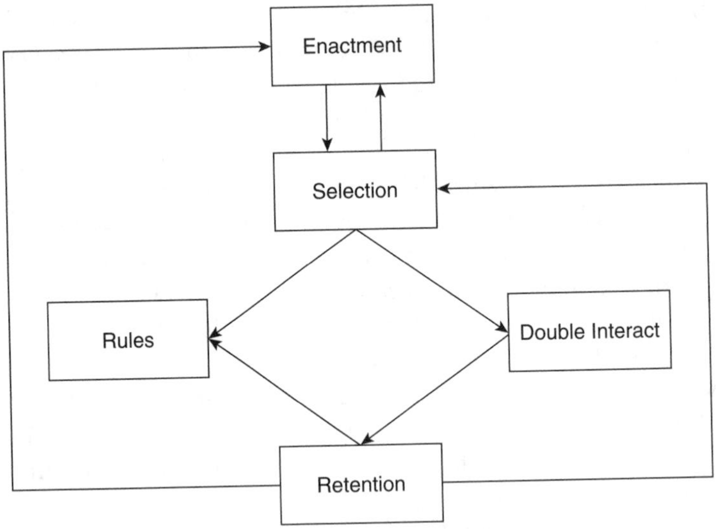

To complete the analogy with Darwin's theory of evolution, Weick's (1969) theory of organizing posits that organizations exist in a complex information environment. This environment is complex because organizations have to deal with equivocal information. Organizations that don't adapt to equivocality, whose members don't utilize double interacts to resolve new forms of ambiguity, will not survive and flourish. In short, change is the key to organizational success, and change occurs through the process of communicating.

❖ CHAPTER SUMMARY

This chapter introduced four theories of organizational communication. In brief, **organizational identification and control** proposes that when organizational members identify with the values of an organization, they can be controlled through self-discipline and peer pressure. Schein's model of **organizational culture** suggests that there are three levels of culture: artifacts and observable behaviors, values, and basic assumptions. His model proposes that basic assumptions are at the heart of organizational culture. Next, we discussed structuration. **Structuration theory** states that organizational members produce and reproduce structures through their communication; communication simultaneously creates and constrains organizational life. Finally, Weick's **theory of organizing** argues that organizations must process equivocal information in order to succeed.

Case Study 8 A Time of Transition

Financial Consulting Associates (FCA) has approximately 200 trained financial advisors who service clients via telephone. In addition to these financial advisors (or sales force), the division has about 50 marketing and strategy employees. The call center is located in two separate regions, one in the Northeast, and one in the Southeast. Approximately 6 months ago, a new senior management team took over the division, creating a skeptical and demoralized staff.

Before the new team's arrival, management encouraged the sales force through monetary rewards (i.e., production credits) from which they made significant commissions on sales. The new management team changed the emphasis from sales to client satisfaction. The variable compensation component was removed from the sales employees' salary structure. This new compensation plan gave no rewards to salespersons, meaning that a financial advisor could sell nothing or a great deal and still bring home the same amount of pay. Sales employees were informed of this change and had one-on-one meetings with their managers to discuss the impact of the change. Essentially, the members of the sales force who once brought in high commissions were seeing a 10% to 20% drop in their pay. Current management placed the emphasis on client satisfaction and client service, which became new catch phrases in the presentations given to the sales floor. As imagined, the rate of attrition skyrocketed and left remaining sales and non-sales employees questioning the direction and goals of the business. These views were explicitly expressed in a number of employee surveys conducted for the management team.

The new leader, Steve Eagle, was committed to communicating with all employees. This commitment generated a series of Town Hall meetings during which he made presentations to employees to clarify priorities and answer employee questions. At the first Town Hall meeting after the compensation change was announced, Eagle received the following question from the audience: "What is our mission and vision at the FCA if we are not expected to sell? Could you give us any direction on what this organization is becoming?" The question was an honest one, trying to uncover what sort of creed employees should be following. At the same time, the question was getting at what many employees were thinking: "Is the direction or idea behind this organization something I want to stick around and be a part of?" Eagle told the workers that he had not yet constructed a mission or vision, but he had some ideas. In closing, Eagle promised that he would get back to the employees with an answer.

Senior management had an independent researcher make recommendations based on *Best in Class: Client Satisfaction Organizations.* In addition, management solicited advice on how to shift the emphasis from sales promotion to client service. The specific recommendation from the researcher was the following: Construct an FCA vision (philosophy, purpose, or commitment) that reflects the desire to achieve superior client satisfaction. Place a strong emphasis on integrating this vision into the culture through the hiring process, training of managers and financial advisors, coaching and feedback, measurement and reward systems, and ongoing development.

With this recommendation and pressure from employees, Steve Eagle drafted the mission and vision of the business. He then took the mission and vision to his off-site meeting with a select grouping of his managers and used the statements as an exercise to solicit feedback. The outcome of the off-site meeting did not change or alter the statements based on employees' comments or concerns. Upon returning from the offsite, Eagle took his mission and vision statement and decided to present it at an upcoming Town Hall meeting with employees. The Financial Consulting Associates Mission and Vision were presented as follows:

Mission: To assist our clients in realizing their financial goals.

Vision: We will be a customer-focused organization that listens to our clients and adapts to meet their needs. By placing the customer first, we will be a leading provider of financial advice, service, and solutions.

FCA's new mission and vision were unveiled at an FCA Town Hall meeting, held jointly at both the Northeast and Southeast locations. Normally at these meetings, employees received a business update from management; instead, the usual format was dismissed and the presentation of the mission and vision took top billing. Steve Eagle had handpicked a team of various managers and nonmanagers on both the sales and nonsales side of the business to present the mission and vision statements. He quickly introduced the team as having worked on these statements and turned the presentation over to them. They took turns reading the statements. The presentation was less formal in tone but, unlike previous meetings, did not spark any discussion or questions. Following the Town Hall meeting, banners displaying the mission and vision were placed around FCA and on the cafeteria's electronic message boards. Following the Town Hall meetings, human resources conducted a short anonymous survey consisting of six questions (four multiple choice and two open-ended) to gauge the success of the meeting. The majority of respondents reported that they both understood the mission and vision as presented and understood how the mission and vision affected their role in the organization. A number of respondents raised concerns about other issues within the organization and how the mission or vision could be upheld with so much change.

Questions for Consideration

1. Do you believe that FCA is using unobtrusive control effectively during the transition? Why or why not? Do you believe that concertive control will exist during the transition? What needs to happen to allow these forms of control to emerge?

2. At what level do you believe the new mission and vision are operating: artifacts, values, or assumptions? Do you believe the new leader will be able to change the organizational culture at FCA? According to Schein's model of culture, what will need to be done to accomplish this?

3. Using structuration theory, what was the old "structure" in place at FCA? How are the rules and resources changing? What is the current climate, and how might it vary for different people in the organization?

4. Using Weick's theory of organizing, do you believe that the company has used double interacts? Based on that determination, what sort of predictions might you make about the future success of FCA?

5. Do any of the theories emerge as "better" than the others? Why do you believe this to be the case? What situations might surface that would make a different theory or theories better at explaining the situation?

9

Explaining Theories of Mediated Communication

Events such as the tragic shootings at Columbine High School, teenagers' dangerous attempts to mimic the outrageous and often dangerous stunts from MTV's television show *Jackass*, and the public's panic surrounding recent news events such as SARS (severe acute respiratory syndrome), mad cow disease, kidnappings, and Anthrax only seem to heighten popular belief that mass communications must some how be to blame (Sparks, 2002). Interestingly, and despite this commonly held view, scholarly research often conflicts with popular beliefs and even contradicts other scholars' work. Intellectual and political debate remains over *who* are most affected, *to what extent* these individuals are influenced, and *why* some people are more affected than others. In this chapter, we present four of the most influential and often controversial theories that attempt to explain and predict media use and media effects. These theories include agenda-setting theory, cultivation theory, social learning theory, and uses and gratifications theory.

❖ MASS COMMUNICATION DEFINED

The study of mass communication is fundamentally concerned with **the media,** or complex organizations that distribute messages to the public. *The media* is not the same as mediated communication, however. **Mediated communication** refers to any communication in which something exists between the source and the receiver. This "something" can refer to technology, which is the case when talking about the media, but can also refer to other things. A person who is deaf might have a sign-language interpreter when communicating with hearing individuals; this example also is mediated communication, because the interpreter is *between* the source and the receiver. Finally, there is mass communication. **Mass communication** refers to mediated communication between a source and a large audience that is often unknown by the source. The notion of an "unknown" audience is important; with mass communication, message senders don't necessarily know their audiences' motivations, biases, and so on. Additionally, the opportunity for audience members to provide feedback to the source is limited and slow; consequently, the source can't adapt easily. Film producers hope that many people will go to see their film, for example, but they don't know who exactly might see the film; if reviews (feedback) are bad, the film producers can't do much to change the film. All mass communication is mediated, but not all mediated communication is mass. Think about e-mail and the telephone; these forms of communication are mediated, but they are not typically used to communicate with a large, unknown audience.

❖ AGENDA-SETTING THEORY

McCombs and Shaw (1972) were among the first communication scholars to test and support their ideas of media influence within the realm of political news. Before their study of the 1968 presidential campaign, it was widely held that the news media simply reflected the public's interests, covering issues about which audience members already knew, believed, or wanted to understand in more detail. In this way, many assumed that the news media simply act as mirrors of public interest. According to this viewpoint, presidential hopeful Howard

Dean's postcaucus "scream" during the campaign of 2004 was aired repeatedly because the public wanted to know more about this candidate.

McCombs and Shaw (1972), however, had a hunch that something wasn't quite right with the "news media as a reflection of society" theory. Instead, they argued that public opinion is shaped, in part, by media coverage, particularly with regard to political news and political campaigns. Rather than the news media simply providing a reflection of the public's interests, McCombs and Shaw posited the reverse equation—that is, the public reflects what is presented by the news media. In other words, McCombs and Shaw conceived that the news media present audiences with an "agenda" for what events the public "should" consider as important. Relying on several assumptions, McCombs and Shaw were able to test this "agenda-setting function" of the news media.

Two key assumptions guide agenda-setting theory. First, McCombs and Shaw (1972) argued that the news media have an agenda. That is, the news media tell audiences what "news" to consider as important. Importantly, however, the media's agenda is viewed as somewhat limited. Using Cohen's (1963) well-known quote discussing the limited effects of media, the agenda-setting function suggests that the news media provide "not what to think . . . but what to think about" (p. 13).

Second, McCombs and Shaw (1972) believed that most people would like help when trying to understand and evaluate politics and political reality. Because people need assistance with determining their political viewpoints, audience members come to rely on news media to point out topics of importance.

Drawing on these assumptions and using media coverage of the 1968 presidential election as an opportunity to study agenda-setting theory, McCombs and Shaw (1972) predicted a causal relationship between the news media's coverage of the candidates (Richard Nixon and Hubert Humphrey) and subsequent voters' perceptions. In other words, McCombs and Shaw hypothesized that voter perceptions of Nixon and Humphrey and their campaign election issues would form *after* and *based on* the content of campaign coverage presented within various media outlets.

To test their prediction, McCombs and Shaw (1972) derived two primary criteria for measuring the media's agenda: **length** and **position** of a news story. Newsprint and broadcast news media (such as TV or radio) contain limited space or time for reporting a given story.

Furthermore, on television and radio, time is money. Similarly, for newspapers and news magazines, space is money; like TV and radio, advertisers and subscribers support the publications to the extent that not every news story can possibly be reported in any one publication.

What McCombs and Shaw (1972) found, and what other researchers have continued to support through numerous studies of the subject, is that a clear association exists between what the news media present to audiences and what the audiences perceive of the issues reported. Their study could only find a correlation, not ascertain causality, however (see chap. 1 for a review of research). Ten years after McCombs and Shaw's initial hypothesis, Iyengar, Peters, and Kinder (1982) supported the causal relationship through experimental research studies. In other words, these researchers found that what the news media present as important is then perceived by the public as important. This causal notion of agenda setting is further developed through the concept of framing.

"Framing" the News

It is hypothesized that the news media's success in telling viewers and readers "what to think about" stems from the media's ability to **frame** issues (McCombs & Shaw, 1972). Much like an art gallery director's choice of which frame to place around a given painting, the media are believed to frame news events. Whereas the gallery director chooses a frame that highlights or de-emphasizes certain features of the painting, perhaps nuances in color or angular shaping of objects, news media **gatekeepers**—the handful of news editors who set the agenda—also select, emphasize, elaborate, and even exclude news stories or parts of news stories to create a certain effect for the audience. As Griffin (2003) reported, "75% of stories that come across a news desk are never printed or broadcast" (p. 394). This is probably a good thing because it is estimated that the average person can only follow three to five ongoing news stories at a time; however, when considering the large number of news stories, or parts of news stories, left on the editing room floor, it may give you pause to wonder what *has* been left out? Although it is difficult to know which stories or aspects of stories have been excluded, a savvy reader or viewer can take a critical examination of the news event presented. Table 9.1 provides an overview and example of framing.

Table 9.1 Framing the News

Process	*Example in Action*
Selection	During the spring of 2003, a newly classified disease known only as severe acute respiratory syndrome (SARS), erupted in parts of eastern Asia and southeastern Canada and made U.S. national news headlines. Thus, news editors selected the strange disease as an important event.
Emphasis	Nearly all of the SARS stories emphasized the increasing number of those diagnosed with the illness, the number of lives lost because of SARS, and cities thought to be most affected by the illness; thus, these news depictions stressed the disease's danger.
Elaboration	During the spring of 2003, U.S. troops were in Iraq after a brief invasion that overthrew Saddam Hussein. Although war coverage had been the elaborated story for many weeks, by May 2003, SARS coverage had eclipsed much of the military and international news.
Exclusion	Very few news stories discussed what precautions could be taken to prevent the disease or how to treat the disease if infected. Virtually no stories discussed how unlikely it was for U.S. citizens to catch SARS, particularly while living domestically and not in targeted cities.

We should note that although agenda setting focuses on the gatekeeping ability of the media, other people besides journalists, editors, and broadcasters can influence the media agenda. Public relations professionals, lobbyists, and even the president of the United States can influence what the media cover as news (Huckins, 1999; Peake, 2001). Accordingly, media professionals might, either consciously or unconsciously, frame news coverage, but it can also be deliberately manipulated by other parties.

Issues and Individuals Most Affected

Obviously, the news media do not affect every issue nor every audience member, and those who are affected will not necessarily be affected in the same way. As McCombs and Bell (1974) argued, even despite the media's ability to influence, individuals' thoughts, opinions, and actions are not predetermined by the news media's agenda. Certain issues are more likely to influence audience thought, and certain individuals are more likely to be influenced by these issues. First, the media are particularly effective in creating public interest in political issues, such as stories about the candidates and their campaign strategies, and in chronic social issues, such as human rights violations, chronic disease, and teen violence. Topics unlikely to be affected by the media include consumer issues that deal with personal spending, taxes, and personal finance because individuals already have their own opinions of such private matters.

Similarly, individuals have differing needs for external advice or direction, also known as the **need for orientation.** This need for orientation depends both on a topic's *relevance* as well as on a person's *uncertainty* about the issue at hand. For example, child-care issues are typically more relevant to viewers who are parents, and especially to those who have not yet made up their mind about how to handle child care. Viewers who are not parents or who have their minds made up about the topic are not likely to experience the agenda-setting effect.

In sum, agenda-setting theory states that gatekeepers selectively determine an agenda for what's news. By selecting, excluding, emphasizing, and elaborating certain aspects of the news, public opinions are inevitably shaped and influenced. Thus, the news media influence their audiences to think about selected issues in a certain light.

❖ CULTIVATION THEORY

Like agenda setting, cultivation theory also emphasizes media effects. Unlike agenda-setting theory, which has been used to study the framing of "news" within a variety of media, the origins of cultivation theory focus almost exclusively on one medium: television (Gerbner, 1998; Gerbner, Gross, Morgan, & Signorelli, 1980; Signorelli, Gerbner, & Morgan, 1995). Specifically, George Gerbner and colleagues have spent nearly 4 decades specifically examining the portrayal of **violence** on TV. These researchers argue that the inescapable violent content of current television programming influences audiences' view of social reality. Specifically, cultivation theory predicts that viewers who watch lots of TV will overestimate the occurrence of real-life violence, thereby perceiving the world as a "mean and scary" place. Before explaining cultivation theory's causal thesis in more detail, we explain several assumptions.

First, cultivation theory assumes that television has become central to American life and culture (Gerbner, 1998). Nearly 99% of Americans have at least one television in their home and watch, on average, 7 hours of TV programming each day. Because of its ubiquity, Gerbner believes that TV has become the principal source of stories and storytelling in the United States. Whereas neighbors and family members used to gather around the dinner table, sit on the front porch, or stand on the street corner sharing stories about what happened during the day or recounting the local gossip, individuals and families now watch NBC's "Thursday night lineup" and are hooked on legal dramas such as *C.S.I.;* water-cooler gossip is centered around which member of the *Sopranos* is going to get whacked next. Thus, Gerbner maintains that television has usurped personal conversation, books, religion, and any other medium as the primary source for storytelling and that the stories being told are not "from anyone with anything relevant to tell. They come from a small group of distant conglomerates with something to sell" (Gerbner, 1998, p. 176).

Second, cultivation theory assumes that TV influences audience perceptions of social reality, thereby shaping American culture in terms of how individuals reason and relate with others (Gerbner, 1998). In other words, through TV's selective and mass-produced depiction of current events, stories, dramas, comedies, and the like, only certain aspects of social life are presented. Importantly, Gerbner does not suggest that television programming seeks to persuade audiences to think or act in a particularly way; instead, he argues that the repetitive representation of commercialized social life is what audiences come to expect and believe as more or less normative.

A final assumption is that television's effects are limited (Gerbner, 1998), meaning that TV is not the only factor, nor necessarily the greatest factor, that affects an individual's view of social reality. Although this statement of "limited effects" sounds like backpedaling, Gerbner et al. (1980) argued that the *consistency* of television's effect is more telling than the *magnitude* of the effect. In other words, the effects of TV may not be huge, but they are consistently present and do make a significant difference in the way people think, feel, and interact.

Violence? What Violence?

Before testing the prediction that watching television violence leads to a negative outlook of the world, *violence* must be defined and objectively quantified. Specifically, Gerbner and colleagues (Gernber et al., 1980; Signorelli et al., 1995) have consistently and objectively defined violence as the "overt expression of physical force (with or without weapon, against self or others) compelling action against one's will on pain of being hurt and/or killed or threatened to be so victimized as part of the plot" (p. 280). This definition includes cartoon violence, comedic or humorous violence, and so-called accidental violence; the definition excludes more ambiguous messages such as verbal assaults, threats, and inconsequential gestures, such as sticking out one's tongue or giving someone the finger.

Using this definition of violence, Gerbner and his associates (Gernber et al., 1980; Signorelli et al., 1995) created the **violence index,** an objective research instrument that uses content analysis to measure the prevalence, frequency, and role of characters that are involved in TV violence (for an overview, see chap. 1). Researchers have assessed violence annually and have studied more than 30 years of television programming (Gerbner, 1998). Year after year, they have repeatedly found that the prevalence, frequency, and role of TV violence during daytime (8:00 a.m. to 2:00 p.m.) and primetime programming (8:00 p.m. to 11:00 p.m.) differ little. In fact, more than half of primetime programs contain violent content, with about five violent acts per episode; children's programs are worse, averaging 20 violent acts per hour. Heroes and villains alike engage in equal amounts of violence.

Not only does research indicate that TV shows are markedly violent, cultivation research also illustrates an imbalance with regard to who is victimized (Gerbner, 1998). Specifically, the victims of TV violence are disproportionately of minority backgrounds; African American, Latino, underprivileged, elderly, disabled, or female TV characters are more likely to be victims of violence than are White, middle-class, male characters. Moreover, Gerbner's 30-plus years of research shows that these same minority groups are vastly underrepresented during primetime. For example, U.S. Census data indicates that 12% of the population is Latino; however, the Children Now research institute (2001) reported that Latinos represented only 2% of primetime TV characters. In other words, a **symbolic double jeopardy** exists in which minority persons are significantly less visible on TV than in real life, but these TV characters are much more likely to be portrayed as victims of violence. Not surprisingly then, minority audience members worry the most about being victimized as result of TV viewing.

What Effects? For Whom?

Importantly, violent TV doesn't affect everyone; cultivation theory predicts that individuals' social attitudes grow more pessimistic as their TV viewing increases. In other words, the more TV you watch, the more likely you are to view the world with suspicion and believe that danger lurks around every corner. Gerbner et al. (1980) separated heavy viewers, or "television types," from light viewers. Television types average 4 or more hours of TV viewing each day, whereas light viewers report watching 2 hours of TV or less each day. As predicted, television types erroneously believed that their chances of being involved with violence were 1,000 times greater than crime statistics suggest; these viewers overestimated criminal and police activity and were more likely to agree with statements such as "most people will take advantage of you if they could" (Gerbner et al., 1980).

According to Gerbner (1998), these pessimistic television types suffer from a **mean world syndrome.** Figure 9.1 provides a visual depiction of the differences between heavy and light television viewers. Televised reality doesn't match actual reality, and heavy viewers are partially influenced by television reality, whereas light viewers are not. Interestingly, research indicates that light viewers selected certain programs to watch and then turned off the TV, whereas heavy viewers tend to graze, watching whatever shows caught their attention (Gerbner, 1998).

How Does Cultivation Take Place and With What Effect?

Cultivation theory research suggests that viewers' attitudes are cultivated in two ways: mainstreaming and resonance (Gerbner, 1998). **Mainstreaming** implies that viewers, heavy viewers in particular, develop a common view of social reality based on their frequent exposure to the repetitive and dominating images, stories, and messages depicted on television. Thus, these television types are likely to perceive

Figure 9.1 Heavy Versus Light Television Viewers' Attitudes

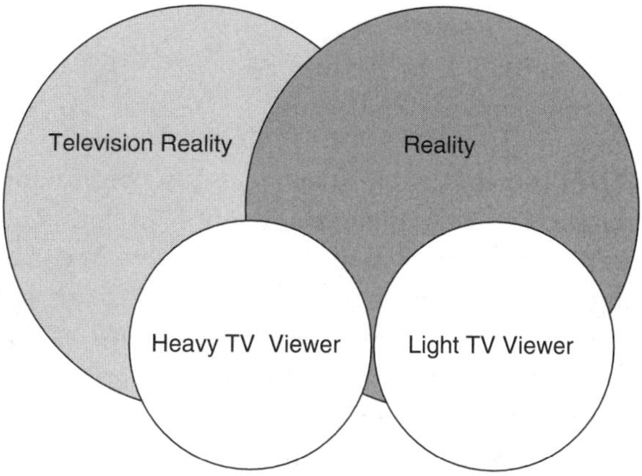

the world in ways that parallel TV's theatrical portrayal of life—as more corrupt, more crime ridden, and more violent.

Resonance is the second way that cultivation is thought to occur (Gerbner, 1998). Resonance involves congruency between viewers' own violent experiences and that which they see on TV. In other words, when individuals who have actually faced acts of violence in their own lives then watch violent television programming, they are forced to replay their own life situations again and again. The TV violence reinforces, or resonates, with their personal experiences and only serves to amplify their suspicion of a mean and scary world while rejecting the vision of a life without such aggression.

More recently, researchers have used cultivation theory to study the mainstreaming and resonance processes of other cultural beliefs besides violence—for example, cultivation of TV viewers' perception of gender roles, personal relationships, parenting, work life, and political views (Gerbner, 1998).

To review, cultivation theory assumes that the power of television is ubiquitous, with its primary message being violence. Moreover, this violent content of TV programming negatively affects heavy viewers by creating a pessimistic attitude about people and the world. Thus, individuals who watch 4 or more hours of television each day are exposed to a greater number of violent incidents and transfer that media exposure to their beliefs about the real world in which they live.

❖ SOCIAL LEARNING THEORY

Bandura's (1977) social learning theory has also been widely used to study the effects of media violence. In contrast to cultivation theory's prediction that TV violence influences attitudes rather than behavior, social learning theory posits that people learn and use aggression as a result of viewing violent media. Discussed earlier, television is one medium in which violent action is common and rewarded. For Bandura, then, watching violent behavior on TV means viewers learn that aggression is a successful means of solving problems; in turn, these viewers may become more prone to act aggressively. We discuss several assumptions of social learning theory next.

Generally speaking, Bandura's (1977) central claim is that "most human behavior is learned observationally through **modeling**: from observing others one forms an idea of how new behaviors are performed, and on later occasions this coded information serves as a guide for action" (p. 22). In other words, you can learn plenty about relationships, social norms, and acceptable behavior simply by taking note of what others do (and of the consequences) in particular situations. Bandura also noted that learning through observational modeling saves individuals time and embarrassment from using a behavioral trial-and-error approach; "learning would be exceedingly laborious, not to mention hazardous, if people had to rely solely on the effects of their own actions to inform them what to do" (p. 22).

Importantly, this notion of learning through observation contrasts with classical learning theory. According to classical learning, humans learn primarily through the trial and error of doing, by improving on their own actions, not through observational modeling. Intuitively, however, Bandura's (1977) idea of learning through observation makes sense. For example, even if you are not a parent right now, you probably have learned quite a bit about raising children from observation—from reflecting on your own parents' child-rearing methods, as well as by watching friends, siblings, and TV parents interact with their children. Thus, social learning theorists believe that you can learn quite a bit by watching what others do (and don't do), as well as by noting others' reactions to your behaviors. You can then decide which behaviors to emulate and which to overlook.

Beyond the general premise of social learning, Bandura (1986) has also demonstrated specific concern with what individuals (children especially) watch and subsequently learn from repeatedly viewing mass media images. Like Gerbner, Bandura is particularly troubled by the amount of violence portrayed on TV; however, repeated exposure to other forms of media violence such as in music and movies certainly could come into play. Bandura proposed that individuals who repeatedly watch TV violence then *learn how* to behave in violent ways themselves. Thus, social learning theory doesn't simply claim that watching TV violence makes viewers violent. Instead, the theory predicts a more subtle link: watching violence teaches viewers *how* to be violent; if viewers know how to do something, they are more likely to do it, particularly when the perceived rewards are great and consequences are few.

Four Stages of the Social Learning Process

Certainly, not every child who watches *The Three Stooges* or *Yu-Gi-Oh!* lashes out and hits other kids over the head, just as not every adult who watches *The Sopranos* or *Walker, Texas Ranger* uses guns or fisticuffs to solve work disputes. Thus, other factors come into play. Specifically, a causal relationship between viewing TV violence and behaving aggressively is predicted based on four successive stages of behavioral learning: attention, retention, reproduction, and motivation (Bandura, 1977). Figure 9.2 provides an overview.

Attention Processes. Using social learning theory, you can't learn much if you don't pay attention to a particular behavior. Thus, selective **attention** to a given situation is critical. Bandura (1977) noted that attention processes are determined by both the observers' characteristics and the arrangement of intended behaviors. In other words, the observer needs to be attentive and the actions in question need to be worthy of notice. Obviously, TV stations and other mass media outlets want to make money. To do so, they need audiences. Programmers, scriptwriters, advertisers, and even actors need viewers' attention. Bright colors, rapid edits, the use of popular songs, dazzling special effects, and nudity are just a few of the ways the media seek to gain our attention.

Figure 9.2 The Social Learning Process

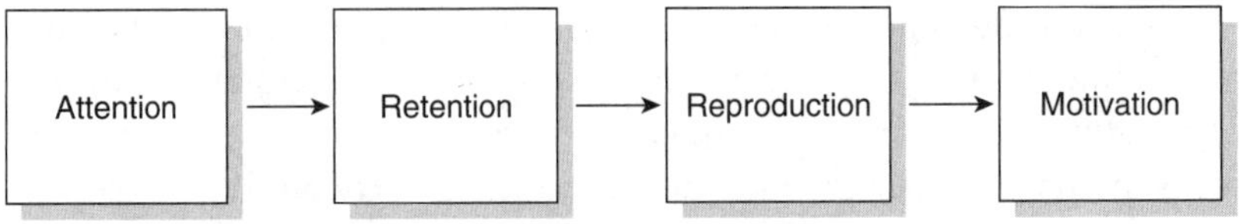

Retention Processes. Learning through observational modeling is not inherently a negative process. In fact, learning by observing has many positive aspects. For example, you can learn how to cook by watching *30-Minute Meals* on the Food Network. Importantly, social learning theory posits that humans can learn without actually engaging in a particular behavior if they can visually and verbally store the images to which they have attended (Bandura, 1977). In other words, you have to **retain** the observed behaviors to learn from them.

The learning process is more complicated than simply watching and mirroring another's behavior. Instead, social learning is a cognitive process wherein individuals observe, organize, remember, and mentally rehearse behavior (Bandura, 1977). "Observers who code modeled activities into either words, concise labels, or vivid imagery learn and retain behavior better than those who simply observe or are mentally preoccupied with other matters while watching" (p. 26).

Motor Reproduction Processes. It only makes sense that to engage in a modeled behavior, one must have the motor skills necessary to **reproduce** the activity in question. You might attend to and remember how to tie a chicken before roasting, but if you do not have the strength, coordination, or motor skills necessary, you will not be able to replicate the behavior with much success. As Bandura (1977) noted, individuals can typically execute a fairly accurate demonstration of a new behavior through modeling; they then refine the action through self-corrective adjustments based on feedback and focused demonstrations of behavioral segments that have only been learned in part.

Motivational Processes. The last piece of social learning theory is **motivation** (Bandura, 1977). To go from observation to action requires the ability to replicate the behavior as well as the desire, or motivation, to use the learned action. Motivation is, in part, inspired by perceived rewards or punishments. In other words, if you perceive that you will be rewarded as a consequence of engaging in an observed behavior, it is likely that you will enact the behavior. If, however, you perceive that you will be punished as a result, your motivation to use the behavior diminishes.

Importantly, Bandura (1977) recognized that many factors influence one's ability to observe and then engage in a given behavior. He noted that not every person will correctly reproduce every behavior. This failure to match the model's actions may stem from a variety of factors, such as neglecting to observe the relevant activities, incorrectly remembering the events, forgetting aspects of the learned behavior, lacking the physical ability to perform an action, and failing to be inspired by incentives.

Social Learning and Media Violence

As a theoretical construct, social learning represents an impartial process; it is not inherently negative or positive. As Bandura (1977) argued, social learning is simply a primary means by which humans learn. When applied within the realm of mass communication, however, research shows that such modeled learning can be hazardous, particularly for viewers of media violence (e.g., Bandura, 1986).

Stated earlier, Bandura (1986) emphasized the violent content found on television's entertainment programs and in TV newscasts. In both cases, Bandura argued that violent acts grab viewers' attention. Aggressive behaviors such as kicking, punching, and biting are also easy to remember and reproduce. Then, when fictitious characters and real-life individuals are rewarded for their aggression, a positive incentive is introduced.

Importantly, the distinction between observation and motivation is a critical determinant in the social learning process. It is not simply the observation of violence that leads one to engage in violent behavior; it is the positive reward associated with aggressive action that entices one to mimic observed behaviors (Bandura, 1977; Bandura, 1986; Bandura, Ross, & Ross, 1963; Huesmann, Moise-Titus, Podolski, & Eron, 2003). If violent behavior is denounced, viewers are less likely to copy the aggression. Note that it is not enough that "bad guys" are punished on television; many of the "good guys" are rewarded for using violence to triumph over the bad guy. Indeed, as Bandura (1986) argued, "given that aggressive life styles are portrayed as prevalent, socially acceptable, and highly functional, it is not surprising that viewing violence is conducive to aggressive conduct" (p. 292).

In sum, social learning theory predicts that humans learn through a four-step process: attention, retention, motor coordination, and motivation. For communication scholars, media producers, parents, and viewers, social learning theory adds a new level of complexity to TV and media. That is, if individuals are exposed to media aggression that is easily replicable and socially rewarding, viewers, particularly young audience members, are more likely to turn to such violence themselves.

❖ USES AND GRATIFICATIONS THEORY

Uses and gratifications theory (UGT) represents a somewhat different means by which to analyze and explain mass media. Rather than look at how the media might "affect" an individual—for example, by causing a person to behave more aggressively or to think more pessimistically—UGT focuses on *why* a person uses the media. Specifically, UGT maintains that because humans have options and free will, individuals will make specific decisions about which media to use and when to use them (Katz, Blumler, & Gurevitch, 1973). The choices and decisions that you make are based on personal needs and values that you wish to fulfill. Thus, you can select among various media to gratify your individual needs. Discussed in more detail, several theoretical assumptions guide UGT.

Three primary assumptions drive our discussion of uses and gratifications theory. First, and unlike many other theoretical approaches to studying mass communication effects, Katz et al. (1973) believed that audience members actively use various media to fulfill certain needs or goals. Thus, media usage isn't passive, involuntary, or coerced; instead, today's mass media represent numerous options available to fulfill a person's social or psychological needs and values. In this way, UGT suggests that media use is **active** and **goal driven** based on individuals needs.

Second, mass communication isn't something that *happens to you;* nor do mass media do *anything to you.* There is no magic spell cast by media owners to coax your viewership. Instead, UGT maintains that a person must identify his or her need and make a media **choice** (Katz et al., 1973). Individuals choose to surf the Internet, watch TV, or listen to the radio. In this regard, the term *media effects* is misleading. Katz et al. did not believe in the simple "straight-line effect" whereby a given medium causes people to think or behave differently. According to Katz et al., audience members choose a medium and allow themselves to be swayed, changed, and influenced—or not. You choose to turn on the TV and watch; the television doesn't turn on itself and watch you.

Third, media outlets **compete** with other available means of satisfying personal needs (Katz et al., 1973). Stated differently, there are many ways to fulfill individual needs. If you feel frazzled after a hectic day at work, you may fulfill your need to relax and unwind by watching a sitcom (mass media) or escaping to the movies. Alternatively, you may meet your needs by taking a run in the park, practicing yoga, or soaking in a warm bath with a glass of wine. Thus, the mass media represent only a handful of alternatives available to you. Next, we present reasons that individuals use the media and how media exposure can gratify various social and psychological needs.

Why Do We Watch What We Watch?

McQuail's (1987) typology lists four common reasons that humans use the mass media: entertainment, information, personal identity, and integration and social interaction (see Table 9.2). First, media are used to **entertain.** Individuals can relax, escape from daily problems, feel some form of excitement or emotional catharsis, pass time, experience sexual arousal, and simply enjoy an artistic pleasure. You may relax by listening to a soothing CD while on your commute home from a long day at the office. You may have watched *The Matrix Reloaded* to experience the extraordinary thrill of science fiction or *Titantic* to experience an emotional connection. Your children may watch Barney on DVD while riding in the back seat of your car to prevent boredom. Similarly, you may turn on a TV sitcom as a diversion from the daily grind.

Second, various media outlets and content are used to **inform** (McQuail, 1987). This information function of the media presents individuals with opportunities to learn about current and historical events,

Table 9.2 Uses and Gratifications

Gratification	*Examples*
Entertainment	• Listening to a Barry White CD to set a romantic mood • Watching *The Texas Chainsaw Massacre* to experience a thrill • Surfing the Web because you have nothing else to do
Information	• Seeking advice about practical matters, like how to cook a turkey (Food TV) • Finding out the weather so you know what to wear to work
Personal identity	• Reading *Vogue* or *Esquire* so you know how to dress and be considered stylish • Watching *7th Heaven* because you like the show's values
Personal relationships and social interaction	• Listening to the Sports Radio Network on your drive to work so you can talk about it with your coworkers • Watching *Survivor* every week to bond with your family

to obtain advice, and to feel secure or satisfy curiosity by acquiring general knowledge. Thus, you may turn on news radio for the weather, traffic updates, and local sports scores. You probably have watched or read about local, national, and world news to find out what is going on in your neighborhood as well as in the world. You may read an advice column for investment strategies or etiquette protocols. You may use the Internet to scour real estate Web pages and research the dimensions of your dream home.

Third, people use the media to reflect, reinforce, or contrast their **personal identity** (McQuail, 1987). In other words, individuals can choose among various media and media content to gain insight into or assist in the development of their own attitudes, beliefs, and sense of self. For example, many Americans tune into the *Oprah Winfrey Show* to listen to guests' incredible "life changing moments" or to hear advice about becoming more compassionate. Likewise, a person often acquires a deeper sense of self by comparing, and perhaps contrasting, one's self with characters portrayed in various media. For instance, you are probably familiar with the hit show *Seinfeld*. Although you may find the characters of Jerry, George, Kramer, and Elaine to be hilarious with their warped sense of life, you also are apt to compare your own experiences and attitudes with theirs. Are you that self-centered? That neurotic? That kooky? That insecure? We hope not! But that is exactly the point of the show—to present extreme personalities that audience members can at once relate to and simultaneously ridicule for their triviality.

A fourth and final reason is that people turn to various media for **personal relationships and social interaction** (McQuail, 1987). Media exposure can help individuals to learn about or connect with others through comparisons of interpersonal relationships and social situations. Certain media can even serve as a substitute for real-life relationships by offering companionship. Monday morning water-cooler gossip about the latest twist on *The Sopranos* creates a sense of community. Following the relationship blunders of the women of *Sex and the City* allows viewers to compare and commiserate about their own relationship foibles. Reading a magazine article about the growing trend of stay-at-home dads or a newspaper interview with successful single moms may provide readers with an opportunity to consider another type of family arrangement.

In brief, uses and gratifications theory maintains that people have many options from which they deliberately select to meet personal needs. Thus, the media don't do anything to you; you are not a drone hypnotized by a mass spell of TV and radio waves. Rather than taking the approach that the media directly (and negatively) affects audiences, UGT takes the perspective that individuals actively make specific media choices based on four common needs.

❖ CHAPTER SUMMARY

In this chapter, we presented an overview of five theories of mediated communication. **Agenda-setting theory** states that the media do not tell us what to think, but they do tell us what to think about. **Cultivation theory** suggests that the social perceptions of individuals who watch large quantities of television are skewed toward the reality presented on television; television types believe in a mean and scary world. **Social learning theory** argues that the world might indeed become more violent, as television viewers model their behavior on what they see on television *if* the program has gained their attention, they have retained the actions, they are able to reproduce the actions, and they are provided with motivation to emulate the actions. On the other hand, **uses and gratifications theory** argues that audience members are active; they use the media forms that will provide them with the individual gratifications that they seek.

Case Study 9 The Gay Agenda

According to gay-rights activists, "the people sitting in the back room of the gay rights movement weren't plotting to bring you *My Big Fat Gay Summer*" (Smith, quoted in von Sternberg, 2003, p. 1A). Nevertheless, during the summer and fall of 2003, gays and lesbians were all over broadcast media. The hit show of the summer was *Queer Eye for the Straight Guy,* a makeover show featuring five gay "lifestyle experts" who assist clueless heterosexual men on how to dress stylishly, cook, and live with panache. On a weekly basis, the NBC sitcom *Will & Grace* reigns as one of the most highly rated television shows. In the political sphere, the U.S. Supreme Court ruled that sodomy laws are unconstitutional. The Episcopal Church of America made a landmark decision to approve an openly gay bishop. On news shows, opinion columns, and talk radio, the possibility of gay marriage is being hotly debated, with the states of New Jersey, Vermont, and Massachusetts in various stages of debating gay unions. The media have also covered other officials performing gay marriages despite the gray zone of legality. If you believe the media hype, gay is good. Or, at the very least, gay is important.

Interestingly, both sides of the political spectrum are criticizing the increasing presence of gay individuals and gay issues in the media. Those who actively seek gay rights are frustrated that the gay characters presented in the mainstream media appear as extreme stereotypes. Vinay Menon (2003) of the *Toronto Star* argues that gay stereotypes are "masterfully disguised" but extremely common. Richard Roeper (2003), of the *Chicago Sun Times* and television's *Ebert & Roeper,* writes that *Queer Eye for the Straight Guy* is "dripping in stereotypes—the gay Team is populated with flamboyant quipsters, while the makeover targets are inevitably amiable dunces" (p. 11).

Still, Anne Stockwell (cf. Holston, 2003), arts and entertainment editor for *The Advocate,* a gay and lesbian news magazine, believes that proposed television programming for the 2003–2004 season that features committed gay couples is a positive development, no matter how stereotypical the portrayal. "We used to see similar fears aroused by black people who were visible on television," she stated (p. D10).

And fears there are. Letters to the editor and talk-radio callers have frequently referenced the media's capitulation to the Gay Agenda. Both the media and gay rights activists express puzzlement over the exact nature of the so-called Gay Agenda, but the term appears frequently in the rhetoric of the religious right. According to Christian groups, the Gay Agenda is promoting homosexuality as an acceptable lifestyle while also providing gays and lesbians with special status by making them a protected class under state hate-crime laws. A Web site run by the nonprofit organization Stop Promoting Homosexuality International (SPHI; 1999) provides an extensive description of the strategies of the Gay Agenda. Referencing an article called "The Overhauling of Straight America," SPHI describes the means used by gay activists:

> At least in the beginning, we are seeking public desensitization and nothing more. We do not need and cannot expect a full "appreciation" or "understanding" of homosexuality from the average American. You can forget about trying to persuade the masses that homosexuality is a good thing. But if only you can get them to think that it is just another thing, with a shrug of their shoulders, then your battle for legal and social rights is virtually won. And to get to shoulder-shrug stage, gays as a class must cease to appear mysterious, alien, loathsome and contrary. A large-scale media campaign will be required in order to change the image of gays in America. (Kirk & Pill, 1987/2003, para. 10)

Is the religious right correct? Does the increased presence of gay issues in the media have the effect of making gays more acceptable in mainstream America? Are they teaching impressionable children how to live the gay lifestyle? Randy Barbato (see Zurawick, 2003), producer of *The AMC Project: Gay Hollywood,* believes that masculine identity in the United States is undergoing a shift because of increasing visibility of gays in the media. Barbato concluded, "the primary reason that things have changed in terms of male identity on television is the success of gay programs or programs with gay characters" (p. D5).

Lawrence E. Mintz (see Zurawick, 2003), a professor of pop culture at the University of Maryland in College Park, isn't sure the effects are quite that strong. He asserts, "One of the ways we work through such social issues is with popular culture. We look at images of gay men in a television series like *Will & Grace* and decide Will is OK, but maybe Jack (Sean Hayes) is not. It's a safe, symbolic way to figure out how we feel about the issues and struggles that have real consequences in the larger society" (p. D5).

On the other hand, television networks are not likely to be making programming decisions based on the social ramifications that might occur. "The success of *Will & Grace* had a huge impact on the industry. In television, the bottom line is always money, and ratings equal money. What we're seeing now is a response to the ratings success of shows like *Will & Grace*," stated Barbato (in Zurawick, 2003, p. D5).

Questions for Consideration

1. How can agenda-setting theory be used help to explain audience members' and critics' reactions (both positive and negative) to media coverage of gays and lesbians? How has the media "framed" this issue (i.e., through selection, emphasis, elaboration, and exclusion)?
2. Although Gerbner's testing of cultivation theory has typically focused on TV violence, cultivation theory can be used to explain the ways in which television "cultivates" other beliefs and behaviors. For example, a recent study showed that participants who regularly watch soap operas and romantic comedies had more idealistic expectations of marriage (Segrin & Nabi, 2002). With that in mind, how can cultivation theory be used to explain the belief that the increased presence of gay issues in the media will have the effect of making gays more acceptable in mainstream America—a viewpoint held by both sides of the issue (e.g.,

Stockwell and SPHI)? What might cultivation theory's concepts of mainstreaming and resonance explain or predict about audience members' beliefs of gays and lesbians based on television portrayals?

3. Critics of the media's gay-friendly programming, such as SPHI, argue that the media teaches children how to live a gay lifestyle. Similarly, although coming to the issue from the opposite perspective, Barbato and others maintain that masculinity in the United States has been redefined based on "the success of gay programs." Both views seem to suggest that social learning theory is at work—how so? Use the concepts of attention, retention, reproduction, and motivation to explain your answer.

4. Uses and gratifications theory (UGT) proposes that individuals actively make choices about how they use various media to fulfill different needs. What would UGT predict about the so-called effects (positive or negative) of gay programming? How would UGT explain the success of "gay programming" such as *Queer Eye for the Straight Guy* and *Will & Grace?*

5. Which theory do you think best explains the issues and effects (or lack thereof) of homosexual programming? How could you combine several theories to make a stronger explanation or prediction of audience responses to the media's presentation of this issue?

10

So What Should a Communicator Do?

In Chapter 1, we asserted that the most competent communicators are those who understand the underlying principles of communication. We proposed that scholarly theory provides a means to obtain that understanding. We proceeded to inundate you with 32 theories, each of which introduced several new concepts and each of which illuminated a somewhat different aspect of the communication process! The purpose of Chapter 10 is to help you make sense of it all. In the following pages, we identify influences and effects consistently identified in research using the theories. In the end, we genuinely believe that application of the individual theories, as well as a synthesis of commonalities across the theories, can assist professionals in enhancing their communication skill.

❖ COMMUNICATION COMPETENCE

Because we believe that one of the goals of studying communication theory is to make you a better communicator, we should articulate more clearly the nature of communication competence. Research indicates that communication competence is most often understood as achieving a successful balance between effectiveness and appropriateness (Spitzberg & Cupach, 1989). **Effectiveness** refers to the extent to which you achieve your goals in interaction. **Appropriateness** refers to fulfilling social expectations for a particular situation. There are many cases in which a person is effective without being appropriate; consider a job applicant who lies on a resume to get a job for which he or she is unqualified. That person might be very effective in getting the job, but is such deceit appropriate? On the other hand, many times people are appropriate to the point of failing to achieve their goals. For example, a person who doesn't wish to take on an additional task at work, but says nothing because he or she fears causing conflict, might be sacrificing effectiveness for appropriateness. The key is that when faced with communicative decisions, the competent communicator considers how to be both effective and appropriate.

The theories we have discussed in this book provide us clues about appropriateness and effectiveness. In this chapter, we highlight the conclusions we can draw about communication and the influences on communication drawn from the intrapersonal, interpersonal, intercultural, persuasion, leadership, group, organizational, and mass-mediated communication theory.

❖ CONCLUSIONS ABOUT COMMUNICATION

As abstractions, theories don't often provide specific templates with stock phrases for those seeking communication advice. They are not topographical maps that can be followed mindlessly from point A to point B. Instead, theories tend to provide general sorts of directions, relying on practitioners to fill in the details. As an analogy, a theory will not tell you to follow Bethlehem Pike for four lights, make a left on Dager Road at the BMW dealership, and then take the first left onto Houston Road. Rather, a theory will tell you that you should be traveling north; it is up to the driver to use his or her own creativity in figuring out the best way to go north. Nevertheless, in reviewing Chapters 2 through 9, you will note that the theories seem to converge on two general decision points that commonly face communicators: whether communication should be direct or indirect (or some point in between) and whether the communication should be similar to or different from previous communication.

The first decision point is whether communicators ought to assert directly what they are thinking or what they need. Certainly, being direct is likely to be an effective choice because there is less room for misunderstanding (e.g., going "bald on record"). The communication theories discussed in this book suggest, however, that there are numerous influences on whether a direct strategy is also appropriate.

First, as should be clear after reading Chapter 4, different cultures hold different values about clarity and openness. Accordingly, to maximize communication competence, you should recognize and adapt to cultural preferences for directness. Second, there are situational influences on the appropriateness of directness. Politeness theory, for example, suggests that those in power are more likely to be direct, and those with less power tend to use more indirect strategies. There is also a time and place for directness; expectancy violations theory suggests that context plays a role in our expectations for communication. Thus, you might expect a coworker to give a direct answer to a straightforward question during decision making (e.g., "Did the plant finish production last night?"). You might not expect a direct answer during labor negotiations (e.g., "What is the smallest increase you would accept?").

Finally, there are individual preferences for being direct. Recall our discussion of message design logics in Chapter 2. Individuals using an expressive message design logic will value direct communication, whereas those with a conventional message design logic will hold stricter expectations for being appropriate. In sum, to be a competent communicator you need to consider not only whether *you* think being direct might be appropriate behavior, but also what the culture would expect, what the situation demands, and what your conversational partner might prefer.

The second decision point that emerges from reviewing the theories presented in this book is whether a person should communicate in a similar fashion to previous messages, or whether she or he ought to behave differently. This question is at the core of numerous theories. Systems theory makes the general point that patterns of communication can be symmetrical (the same) or complementary (different). Expectancy violations theory (EVT) projects whether a person will reciprocate or compensate based on the reward valence of the communicator and the valence of the violation. Uncertainty reduction theory (URT) predicts that people are more likely to reciprocate during times of high uncertainty. And communication accommodation theory (CAT) suggests that converging (behaving more like the other person) can lead to attraction, whereas diverging (behaving in a different fashion) can be a means of asserting power.

Certainly, these factors will play a role in whether you choose to behave in a similar or different fashion. What if the issue isn't how *you* are going to act, however, but getting *someone else* to act in a particular manner? Beyond the specific advice offered by the theories described here, a wealth of research suggests that there is a strong reciprocity effect (e.g., Burggraf & Sillars, 1987; Sillars, 1980). This means that, over time, people tend to mirror each other's behavior. Therefore, if you want someone to behave in a certain way, you should behave in the fashion you want the other person to behave. Eventually, the other person is likely to reciprocate.

❖ CONCLUSIONS ABOUT INFLUENCES AND EFFECTS

In addition to specific questions that emerge about communication, a review of the theories presented in this book suggests that many variables influence communication and that there are numerous effects of the communication process. Notably, the same variable can be both an influence and an effect. Consider your own values or beliefs. These values can influence how you choose to communicate; being a feminist, for example, might cause you to use gender-neutral language. At the same time, communication can inspire you to change your values or beliefs; someone might persuade you that using the generic "he" is exclusionary, thereby changing your beliefs about the power of language.

Throughout this book, 12 variables emerge as consistent explanations of things that influence or are affected by the communication process. Table 10.1 provides an overview, but we briefly explain each concept and its importance, providing advice along the way.

Cohesion, Connection, and In-Groups. The degree to which individuals are connected with others is a function of the communication experienced by those individuals. For example, symbolic convergence theory suggests that particular communication practices, called fantasy chaining, create group cohesion. Similarly, interaction process analysis suggests

Table 10.1 Concepts Appearing in Multiple Theories

Influence or Effect	*Theories Identifying the Influence or Effect*	
Cohesion/connection/in-Groups	URT (chap. 2) Dialectics (chap. 3) Cultural dimensions (chap. 4) CAT (chap. 4) Face negotiation (chap. 4)	LMX (chap. 6) Interaction process analysis (chap. 7) Groupthink (chap. 7) Symbolic convergence (chap. 7) Organizational identification and control (chap. 8)
Context	Attribution theory (chap. 2) EVT (chap. 2)	Groupthink (chap. 7) Organizing theory (chap. 8)
Expectations	Attribution theory (chap. 2) EVT (chap. 2) SET (chap. 3)	Cultural dimensions (chap. 4) Standpoint theory (chap. 4)
Face/self vs. other orientation	Politeness (chap. 3) Cultural dimensions (chap. 4)	Face negotiation (chap. 4) Transformational leadership (chap. 6)
Individual qualities	Attribution theory (chap. 2) EVT (chap. 2)	Narrative paradigm (chap. 5)
Interest/involvement	Social judgment (chap. 5) ELM (chap. 5) Agenda setting (chap. 9)	Cognitive dissonance (chap. 5) Social learning (chap. 9)
Needs	Politeness (chap. 3) Uses and gratifications (chap. 9)	Functional decision making (chap. 7) Symbolic convergence (chap. 7)
Power/control	Politeness (chap. 3) Cultural dimensions (chap. 4) CAT (chap. 4) Muted group (chap. 4)	Contingency theory (chap. 6) Organizational identification and control (chap. 8) Structuration (chap. 8)
Relationship	EVT (chap. 2) Systems (chap. 3)	Contingency theory (chap. 6)
Rewards	URT (chap. 2) EVT (chap. 2)	SET (chap. 3) Social learning (chap. 9)
Uncertainty	URT (chap. 2) Dialectics (chap. 3)	Cultural dimensions (chap. 4) Agenda setting (chap. 9)
Values/beliefs	MDL (chap. 2) Cultural dimensions (chap. 4) Gender styles (chap. 4) Social judgment (chap. 5) Four systems (chap. 6)	Transformational leadership (chap. 6) Symbolic convergence (chap. 7) Organizational identification and control (chap. 8) Model of culture (chap. 8) Cultivation (chap. 9)

NOTE: CAT = Communication accommodation theory; ELM = elaboration likelihood model; EVT = expectancy violations theory; LMX = leader–member exchange; MDL = message design logic; SET = social exchange theory; URT = uncertainty reduction theory.

that maintenance communication fosters group cohesion. Conversely, many theories focus on the reverse process, suggesting that one's connection to an in-group will influence that individual's communication. URT, for instance, suggests that shared social networks decrease uncertainty, thereby decreasing uncertainty-reducing messages. Leader–member exchange suggests that one's in-group status with a manager might increase supportive communication from that manager. On the other hand, organizational identification and control says that cohesion can function as a means of controlling employees, and groupthink cautions that cohesion can lead to bad decision making. In sum, connection is something that is achieved through communication, but once achieved it can have both positive and negative results.

The practical implication of this recognition is to have an appreciation for when team-building activities are appropriate and when they are not. For example, some amount of team building is often important at the initial stages of group interaction. Team building might be avoided, however, if the group is facing a high-stress decision; such efforts might only lead to groupthink. Moreover, too much cohesion might exacerbate tensions between two groups in a workplace.

Context. Several theories identified contextual influences on communication. EVT, for example, states that context influences your expectations for how interactions will occur. Organizing theory proposes that the central challenge facing organizations is making sense of an equivocal information environment. Similarly, attribution theory posits that one way we can answer the question "why?" is to look to the situation, and thereby make an external attribution. The context, then, can influence not only the nature of our communication, but also our expectations for and understanding of communication. Accordingly, professionals should stop and think about the context in which communication occurs because the same message might be understood very differently in another context. For example, consider how often individuals argue that media stories present them in a negative light because their quotes were taken "out of context."

Expectations. A few theories make special note of individuals' expectations, suggesting that these expectations will play a role in your evaluation of communication events. To illustrate, both Hofstede's theory of cultural dimensions and standpoint theory suggest that one's biological sex is associated with expectations for appropriate behavior. Attribution theory indicates that our expectations for others will influence our attributions—say, for example, when a man behaves in a manner not socially prescribed (and therefore expected). Last, both EVT and social exchange theory suggest that your expectations determine how you evaluate your interactions with others. The practical advice for the professional communicator is to challenge one's own expectations. Knowing why you have certain expectations and making sure to maintain realistic expectations can enhance perceptions of relational and interactional satisfaction.

Face and Self–Other Orientation. Several theories implicitly recognize the importance of sustaining individuals' desired images. Not only is protecting one's own self-needs warranted, theories such as politeness and face negotiation propose that communicators ought to also consider other's face needs in interaction. Such efforts are likely to lead to organizational success; transformational leaders, after all, are those that are skilled at understanding both themselves and others. Accordingly, the advice taken from these theories is to recognize others' needs to protect their image.

Individual Qualities. As indicated earlier, understanding one's self and others is important for effective communication. Three theories explicitly address how qualities of the individual might affect the communication process. For example, EVT suggests that communicator characteristics (age, sex, and the like) influence your expectations for communication. Attribution theory proposes that one of the ways you answer the question "why?" is by looking for stable internal dispositions of the communicator. Finally, the narrative paradigm argues that individuals' character, history, values, and experience determine what they will view as persuasive. The conclusion drawn here is that you cannot presume everyone will respond in the same way to the same message; you need to tailor your communication to match the qualities of the interactants.

Interest and Involvement. Regarding persuasion, several theories posit that individuals must be interested in or involved with the issue at hand if they are to be persuaded. With social judgment theory, a person's ego-involvement determines his or her latitudes of acceptance, rejection, and noncommitment. In the elaboration likelihood model, the central route is used by people who are motivated, or, in other words, by people who are interested and involved. Cognitive dissonance suggests that the more important an issue is perceived to be, the greater the possible dissonance. Turning to mass media theories, agenda-setting theory states that a person's need for orientation, including the information's relevance, determines whether news media set an agenda for that individual. Finally, social learning theory states that the media must first gain audience members' attention if they are to imitate what they see or hear. In short, these theories suggest that to persuade someone to think or behave in a particular way, communicators must make sure that their audience is interested in and involved with the topic. Successful communicators cannot presume that interactional partners or audience members will naturally be engaged in a given topic.

Needs. One way to engage communication partners is to recognize and seek to meet their needs. Politeness theory, for example, suggests that everyone has positive face needs (e.g., the desire to be liked and appreciated) and negative face needs (e.g., the desire to be free from imposition). A different view of needs is proposed by uses and gratifications theory, which states that people select particular media forms to meet particular needs. Symbolic convergence posits that fantasy themes and fantasy chains meet psychological needs of the group. Finally, functional group decision making argues that communication in groups must meet four functions (or achieve four needs) to make effective decisions. Professional communicators, then, ought to match particular messages to the needs of those with whom they are communicating. Note that this is receiver focused; certainly meeting one's own needs is important, but competent communication also recognizes the needs of the receiver.

Power and Control. A recurring theme among the theories discussed in this book is that communication is a central means for exerting power; power influences the types of communication used. The link between communication and power can take a macroscopic focus (big picture) or a microscopic focus (individual interactions). On a large scale, Hofstede's cultural dimensions recognize that some cultures accept large differentials in power, whereas others don't. The extent to which a culture tolerates a large power distance influences the perceived appropriateness of particular communication strategies. Also taking a macroscopic perspective, muted group theory provides more depth to the sorts of assertions made by Hofstede's theory; muted group argues that the experiences of groups with less social power (especially women) are either overlooked or are not easily described because language is literally a "man-made construction."

A slightly different macroscopic view of communication and power are taken by organizational identification and control (OIC) and structuration theory. Both center on the hidden forms of control that exist in organizations. OIC focuses on the role of unobtrusive (shared values) and concertive control (peer pressure) in organizational life. Structuration theory recognizes that structures created by organizational members also subtly constrain behavior, thereby serving as a form of control.

Other theories focus on the role of power in more microscopic settings. Contingency theory asserts that a leader's position power helps to determine the most effective type of leadership for any given situation. Both politeness theory and communication accommodation theory suggest that people are more likely to adjust their behavior if they have less power than their interactional partner. Accordingly, you will likely engage in more politeness or will converge to your partner if you perceive this person as having more power than you have.

At the beginning of this section, we stated that a number of the theories presented in this book suggest that communication is the means by which power is exerted. By now you should recognize that *who* gets to say things, *what* is said, and *how* it is said (or what is *not* said and *why* it is not said) are important questions for uncovering how power is understood and being carried out in any interaction. Competent communicators recognize and are aware of not only obvious examples of power enactment, but also the less obvious examples.

Relationship. Just as different contexts call for differing types of communication, diverse relationships call for varied types of communication. To illustrate, contingency theory suggests that the nature of the relationship a leader has with other group members should determine how leadership is exerted in particular situations. This concept can be explained by expectancy violations theory, which asserts that the relationship you have with interactional partners forms your expectations for how an interaction should proceed. Moreover, outside observers may be just as likely to understand a given relationship as are the relational partners; systems theory suggests that all communication includes a relationship level that provides clues as to the nature of the relationship between communicators. As practical advice, communication professionals should be mindful of existing relationships (whether agreeable or poor) and monitor the relationship levels of messages to gauge how an interaction is proceeding.

Rewards. One way to understand individualistic cultures using Hofstede's cultural dimensions is to recognize that members of individualistic cultures ask "what's in it for me?" Many theories discussed in this text explicitly recognize the power of rewards in making sense of communication interactions. Uncertainty reduction theory, for example, says that the incentive value of an interactional partner can increase your uncertainty about him or her; the more rewarding the person is, the more likely you are to seek to reduce uncertainty. Several other predictions are associated with rewards. EVT suggests that the reward value of the violator will determine in part whether a person will reciprocate or compensate. Social exchange theory predicts that people seek to maximize rewards and minimize costs in relationships; thus, lack of rewards can lead to dissatisfaction or relational termination. Finally, social learning theory argues that people will be more likely to emulate behavior if there are perceived rewards associated with a particular action. Accordingly, people will make choices based on perceived reward power; those who have reward power will be subject to more uncertainty reduction, will have others compensate for perceived negative behaviors, will be perceived as more attractive to relational partners, and will be emulated more often.

Uncertainty. The notion of uncertainty is frequently proposed as a central motivator for human communication. URT proposes that uncertainty is uncomfortable, so we use communication to reduce it. Agenda-setting theory says that a person's need for orientation, which includes his or her uncertainty about an issue, determines the extent to which the agenda-setting effect occurs. On the other hand, several theories propose that the relationship between uncertainty and communication is more complex; dialectics argues that individuals have conflicting desires for certainty and uncertainty (in the form of the predictability and novelty dialectic). Hofstede's cultural dimensions suggest that cultures vary on uncertainty avoidance, with some cultures more tolerant of uncertainty than others. Nevertheless, it seems clear that uncertainty is often perceived as problematic and can drive a person to send or seek specific messages.

Values and Beliefs. Finally, a theme that emerges consistently throughout our presentation of theories is yet another cognitive variable: people's values and beliefs. Suggested earlier in this chapter, values and beliefs are related to communication in a complex fashion. On one hand, a person's values and beliefs lead that individual to communicate in a particular fashion. On the other hand, communication might be the means by which you reinforce, modify, or change your values and beliefs. At least 10 of the theories discussed in this book address values and beliefs. The theories range from those focusing on intrapersonal settings (message design logics posits that people's beliefs about communication influence how they communicate); to interpersonal settings (social judgment theory predicts that the likelihood of one person persuading a coworker is dependent on the coworker's preexisting beliefs on the topic); to group settings (symbolic convergence states that group members construct a rhetorical vision, which is a system of values or beliefs about how the world works); to organizational settings (Schein's model of organizational culture identifies values and assumptions as abstract ways of understanding how to operate within an organization); to mass-mediated settings (cultivation theory says that heavy television viewers are "mainstreamed" into believing television reality). In all cases, the advice to the communication professionals is to understand others' values and beliefs and to recognize the difficulty in asking people to change them.

❖ RETURNING TO COMMUNICATION COMPETENCE

At the beginning of this chapter, we asserted that competent communication requires one to be both effective and appropriate. After reviewing the 12 common concepts we have identified, it should be clear that achieving your goals often means considering what the receiver might view as appropriate. If we were to summarize the single biggest piece of advice culled from all of the theories discussed in this book, it would be that competent communicators are those who take a receiver orientation to communication; in the pursuit of their own goals they consider what others need to hear (and how they might hear it) so that they might accomplish those goals.

According to Spitzberg and Cupach (1984, 1989), the development of communication competence is contingent on three elements: motivation, knowledge, and skill. *Motivation* references your reasons for doing things; knowing what you want is the foundation for being a competent communicator. That you have taken this class and have read this book provides some indication of motivation for improving your communication skill. *Knowledge* refers to knowing how to act. It is not enough to have good intentions, one must also understand *how* to be effective and appropriate in communication. We hope that the theories discussed in this book have served the role of increasing your knowledge in this area.

The final component of competence is skill. *Skill* is the actual behavior. Despite the best of intentions and a wealth of knowledge, we don't always behave competently. As with any skill, however, communication skill can be developed and enhanced. Skill development requires practice, adjustment after evaluation, and being open to constructive criticism. The challenge that you will face as a professional communicator is to use your motivation and knowledge as a foundation for increased skill.

❖ CHAPTER SUMMARY

This chapter provided a synthesis of the theories presented throughout the text. First, we identified two decision points that communicators might face: whether to be direct or indirect and whether to behave in a similar or different manner compared with other communicators. These decisions were framed in the balance of effectiveness and appropriateness that needs to be achieved to be a competent communicator. Then we turned our attention to 12 important variables that influence the communication process. These variables include cohesion and in-groups, context, expectations, face and self–other orientation, individual qualities, interest and involvement, needs, power and control, relationship, rewards, uncertainty, and values and beliefs. Specific pieces of advice for the professional communicator were interspersed throughout the discussion of these variables.

References

Adler, N. J. (1997). *International dimensions of organizational behavior* (3rd ed). Cincinnati, OH: South-Western College.

American Hospital Association. (2001, June). The hospital workforce shortage: Immediate and future. *TrendWatch, 3,* 1.

Andersen, P. A. (1991). When one cannot not communicate: A challenge to Motley's traditional communication postulates. *Communication Studies, 42,* 309–325.

Ashby, W. R. (1962). Principles of the self-organizing system. In H. von Foerster & G. Zopf (Eds.), *Principles of self-organization* (pp. 255–278). New York: Pergamon.

Aylor, B., & Dainton, M. (2004). Biological sex and psychological gender as predictors of routine and strategic relational maintenance. *Sex Roles, 50,* 689–697.

Aylor, B., & Dainton, M. (2001). Antecedents in romantic jealousy experience, expression, and goals. *Western Journal of Communication, 64,* 370–391.

Axley, S. R. (1984). Managerial and organizational communication in terms of the conduit metaphor. *Academy of Management Review, 9,* 428–437.

Bales, R. F. (1953). The equilibrium problem in small groups. In T. Parsons, R. F. Bales, & E. A. Shils (Eds.), *Working papers in the theory of action* (pp. 111–161). Glencoe, IL: Free Press.

Bales, R. F. (1970). *Personality and interpersonal behavior.* New York: Holt, Rinehart, & Winston.

Bales, R. F. (1988). Preface: SYMLOG the present state of applications. In R. B. Polley, A. P. Hare, & P. J. Stone (Eds.), *The SYMLOG practitioner: Applications of small group research* (pp. xiii–xxi). New York: Praeger.

Bales, R. F. (1999). *Social interaction systems theory and measurement.* New Brunswick, NJ: Transaction Books.

Bales, R. F., & Cohen, S. P. (1979). SYMLOG: A system for the multiple level observation of groups. New York: Free Press.

Bandura, A. (1977). *Social learning theory.* Upper Saddle River, NJ: Prentice Hall.

Bandura, A. (1986). *Social foundations of thought and action: A social cognitive theory.* Englewood Cliffs, NJ: Prentice Hall.

Bandura, A., Ross, D., & Ross, S. (1963). Imitations of aggressive film-mediated models. *Journal of Abnormal Psychology, 66,* 3–11.

Barge, J. K. (1994). *Leadership.* New York: St. Martin's Press.

Barker, J. R. (1999). *The discipline of teamwork: Participation and concertive control.* Thousand Oaks, CA: Sage.

Barnes, L. B., Christensen, C. R., & Hansen, A. J. (1994). *Teaching and the case method* (3rd ed). Boston: Harvard Business School Press.

Bass, B. M. (1985). *Leadership and performance beyond expectations.* New York: Free Press.

Bass, B. M. (1997). Does the transactional–transformational leadership paradigm transcend organizational and national boundaries? *American Psychologist, 52,* 130–139.

Bass, B. M. (1998). *Transformational leadership: Industrial, military, and educational impact.* Mahwah, NJ: Lawrence Erlbaum Associates.

Baxter, L. A. (1988). A dialectical perspective on communication strategies in relationship development. In S. Duck (Ed.), *Handbook of personal relationships: Theory, research, and interventions* (pp. 257–273). Chichester, England: Wiley.

Baxter, L. A., & Montgomery, B. M. (1996). *Relating: Dialogues and dialectics.* New York: Guilford Press.

Berger, C. R. (1979). Beyond initial interaction: Uncertainty, understanding, and the development of interpersonal relationships. In H. Giles & R. St. Clair (Eds.), *Language and social psychology* (pp. 122–144). Oxford, England: Blackwell.

Berger, C. R. (1995). Inscrutable goals, uncertain plans, and the production of communicative action. In C. R. Berger & M. Burgoon (Eds.), *Communication and social processes* (pp. 1–28). East Lansing: Michigan State University Press.

Berger, C. R. (1997). *Planning strategic interaction: Attaining goals through communicative action.* Mahwah, NJ: Erlbaum.

Berger, C. R., & Bradac, J. J. (1982). *Language and social knowledge: Uncertainty in interpersonal relations.* London: Arnold.

Berger, C. R., & Calabrese, R. J. (1975). Some explorations in initial interaction and beyond: Toward a developmental theory of interpersonal communication. *Human Communication Research, 1,* 99–112.

Bingham, S., & Burleson, B. (1989). Multiple effects of messages with multiple goals: Some perceived outcomes of responses to sexual harassment. *Human Communication Research, 16,* 184–216.

Bormann, E. G. (1982). The symbolic convergence theory of communication: Applications and implications for teachers and consultants. *Journal of Applied Communication Research, 10,* 50–61.

Bormann, E. G. (1996). Symbolic convergence theory and communication in group decision making. In R. Y. Hirokawa & M. S. Poole (Eds.), *Communication and group decision making* (2nd ed., pp. 81–113). Thousand Oaks, CA: Sage.

Bormann, E. G., Cragan, J. E., & Shields, D. C. (1994). In defense of symbolic convergence theory: A look at the theory and its criticisms after two decades. *Communication Theory, 4,* 259–294.

Brown, P., & Levinson, S. (1978). Universals in language usage: Politeness phenomenon. In E. Goody (Ed.), *Questions and politeness* (pp. 56–89). Cambridge, England: Cambridge University Press.

Brown, P., & Levinson, S. (1987). *Politeness: Some universals in language use.* Cambridge, England: Cambridge University Press.

Bryant, S. E. (2003). The role of transformational and transactional leadership in creating, sharing and exploiting organizational knowledge. *Journal of Leadership and Organizational Studies, 9,* 32–43.

Burgoon, J. K. (1978). A communication model of personal space violations: Explication and an initial test. *Human Communication Research, 4,* 129–142.

Burgoon, J. K. (1994). Nonverbal signals. In M. L. Knapp & G. R. Miller (Eds.), *Handbook of interpersonal communication* (pp. 229–285). Newbury Park, CA: Sage.

Burgraff, C. S., & Sillars, A. L. (1987). A critical examination of sex differences in marriage. *Communication Monographs, 54,* 276–294.

Canary, D. J., & Dindia, K. (1998). Recurring issues in sex differences and similarities in communication. In D. J. Canary & K. Dindia (Eds.), *Sex differences and similarities in communication: Critical essays and empirical investigations of sex and gender in interaction* (pp. 1–17). Mahwah, NJ: Erlbaum.

Canary, D. J., & Hause, K. S. (1993). Is there any reason to research sex differences in communication? *Communication Quarterly, 41,* 129–144.

Canary, D. J., & Zelley, E. D. (2000). Current research programs on relational maintenance behaviors. In M. E. Roloff (Ed.), *Communication Yearbook 23* (pp. 305–339). Newbury Park, CA: Sage.

Canary, D. J., Cody, M. J., & Manusov, V. L. (2003). *Interpersonal communication: A goals-based approach* (3rd ed.). Boston: Bedford.

Canary, D. J., Emmers-Sommer, T. M., & Faulkner, S. (1997). *Sex and gender differences in personal relationships.* New York: Guilford Press.

Child care in Sweden. (1998). *International Journal of Early Childhood, 30,* 20–26.

Children Now. (2001, May). *Fall colors 2000–2001: Prime time diversity report.* Oakland, CA: Author.

Cialdini, R. B. (1993). *Influence: Science and practice* (3rd ed.). New York: HarperCollins.

Cialdini, R. B. (1994). Interpersonal influence. In S. Shavitt & T. C. Brock (Eds.), *Persuasion: Psychological insights and perspectives* (pp. 195–218). Boston: Allyn and Bacon.

Cohen, B. C. (1963). *The press and foreign policy.* Princeton, NJ: Princeton University Press.

Collier, M. J. (1989). Cultural and intercultural communication competence: Current approaches and directions for future research. *International Journal of Intercultural Relations, 13,* 287–302.

Conrad, C., & Poole, M. S. (1998). *Strategic organizational communication into the twenty-first century,* 4th ed. New York: Harcourt Brace College.

Craig, R. T. (1999). Communication theory as a field. *Communication Theory, 9,* 119–161.

Craig, R. T., Tracy, K., & Spisak, F. (1993). The discourse of requests: Assessment of a politeness approach. In S. Petronio, J. K., Alberts, M. L. Hecht, & J. Buley (Eds.), *Contemporary perspectives on interpersonal communication* (pp. 264–283). Madison, WI: Brown & Benchmark.

Crossen, C. (1994). *Tainted truth: The manipulation of fact in America.* New York: Simon & Schuster.

Cupach, W. R., & Canary, D. J. (1997). *Competence in interpersonal conflict.* New York: McGraw-Hill.

Cupach, W. R., & Imahori, T. T. (1993). Identity management theory: Communication competence in intercultural episodes and relationships. In R. L. Wiseman & J. Koester (Eds.), *Intercultural Communication Competence* (pp. 112–131). Newbury Park, CA: Sage.

Cupach, W. R., & Metts, S. (1994). *Facework.* Thousand Oaks, CA: Sage.

Dainton, M., Aylor, B., & Zelley, E. D. (2002, November). *General and relationship-specific social support, willingness to communicate, and loneliness in long-distance versus geographically close friendships.* Paper presented at the National Communication Association annual conference, New Orleans, LA.

Dansereau, F., Graen, G., & Haga, W. J. (1975). A vertical dyad approach to leadership within formal organizations. *Organizational Behavior and Human Performance, 12,* 46–78.

Deetz, S. A. (1994). Future of the discipline: The challenges, the research, and the social contribution. In S. A. Deetz (Ed.), *Communication Yearbook 17* (pp. 565–600). Thousand Oaks, CA: Sage.

Deetz, S. A., Tracy, S. J., & Simpson, J. L. (2000). *Leading organizations through transition.* Thousand Oaks, CA: Sage.

DePaulo, B. M., Stone, J. I., & Lassiter, G. D. (1985). Deceiving and detecting deceit. In B. Schlenker (Ed.), *The self and social life* (pp. 323–370). New York: McGraw-Hill.

Dervin, B. (1993). Verbing communication: Mandate for disciplinary intervention. *Journal of Communication, 43,* 45–54.

DeVito, J. A. (2003). *The interpersonal communication book* (10th ed.). New York: Longman.

Dion, K. K., & Dion, K. L. (1993). Individualistic and collectivistic perspectives on gender and the cultural context of love and intimacy. *Journal of Social Issues, 49,* 53–59.

Dockery, T. M., & Steiner, D. D. (1990). The role of initial interaction in leader–member exchange. *Group and Organizational Studies, 15,* 395–413.

Duarte, N. T., Goodson, J. R., & Klich, N. R. (1993). How do I like thee? Let me appraise the ways. *Journal of Organizational Behavior, 14,* 239–249.

Dyer, W. G. (1987). *Team building: Issues and alternatives* (2nd ed.). Reading, MA: Addison-Wesley.

Eagly, A., H., Karau, S. J., & Makhijani, M. G. (1995). Gender and the effectiveness of leaders: A meta-analysis. *Psychological Bulletin, 117,* 125–145.

Edwards, R. (1981). The social relations of production at the point of production. In M. Zey-Ferrell & M. Aiken (Eds.), *Complex organizations: Critical perspectives* (pp. 156–182). Glenview, IL: Scott Foresman.

Egan, M. D. (1999). Leadership training increases in popularity. *National Underwriter, 103,* 30.

Ellis, D. G. (1999). *Crafting society: Ethnicity, class, and communication theory.* Mahwah, NJ: Erlbaum.

Festinger, L. (1957). *A theory of cognitive dissonance.* Stanford, CA: Stanford University Press.

Festinger, L. (1962). *A theory of cognitive dissonance.* Stanford, CA: Stanford University Press.

Fiedler, F. E. (1967). *A theory of leadership effectiveness.* New York: McGraw-Hill.

Fisher, B. A. (1978). *Perspectives on human communication.* New York: Macmillan.

Fisher, W. R. (1984). Narration as a human communication paradigm: The case of public moral argument. *Communication Monographs, 51,* 1–22.

Fisher, W. R. (1987). *Human communication as narration: Toward a philosophy of reason, value, and action.* Columbia: University of South Carolina Press.

Fitzpatrick, M. A., & Ritchie, D. (1992). Communication theory. In P. Boss, W. Doherty, & S. Steinmetz (Eds.), *Sourcebook of family theories.* New York: Plenum.

Freeman, P. (2002, November 4). Gaps widen in rural health care despite initiatives. *Puget Sound Business Journal.* Retrieved December 2, 2002, from http://seattle.bizjournals.com/seattle/stories/2002/11/04/focus1.html

Frey, L. R., Botan, C. H., & Kreps, G. L. (2002). *Investigating communication: An introduction to research methods* (2nd ed.). Boston: Allyn & Bacon.

Gardner, L., & Stough, C. (2002). Examining the relationship between leadership and emotional intelligence in senior level managers. *Leadership & Organization Development Journal, 23,* 68–78.

Gass, R. H., & Seiter, J. S. (2003). *Persuasion, social influence, and compliance gaining* (2nd ed.). Boston, MA: Allyn and Bacon.

Gerbner, G. (1998). Cultivation analysis: An overview. *Mass Communication & Society, 1,* 175–194.

Gerbner, G., Gross, L., Morgan, M., & Signorelli, N. (1980). The "mainstreaming" of America: Violence profile no. 11. *Journal of Communication, 30,* 10–29.

Giannetti, L. (1982). *Understanding movies* (3rd ed.). Englewood Cliffs, NJ: Prentice Hall.

Giddens, A. (1979). *Central problems in social theory: Action, structure, and contradiction in social analysis.* Berkeley: University of California Press.

Giles, H., & Coupland, N. (1991). *Language: Contexts and consequences.* Pacific Grove, CA: Wadsworth.

Giles, H., Mulac, A., Bradac, J. J., & Johnson, P. (1987). Ethnolinguistic identity theory: A social psychological approach to language maintenance. *International Journal of the Sociology of Language, 68,* 66–99.

Glaser, B. G., & Strauss, A. L. (1967). *The discovery of grounded theory: Strategies for qualitative research.* Chicago: Aldine.

Goffman, E. (1967). *Interaction ritual: Essays on face-to-face behavior.* New York: Pantheon Books.

Goleman, D. (1998). What makes a leader? *Harvard Business Review, 76,* 93–102.

Gouran, D. S., & Hirokawa, R. Y. (1983). The role of communication in decision-making groups: A functional perspective. In M. Mander (Ed.), *Communications in transition* (pp. 168–185). New York: Praeger.

Gouran, D. S., & Hirokawa, R. Y. (1986). Counteractive functions of communication in effective group decision-making. In R. Y. Hirokawa & M. S. Poole (Eds.), *Communication and group decision-making* (pp. 81–92). Beverly Hills, CA: Sage.

Gouran, D. S., & Hirokawa, R. Y. (1996). Functional theory and communication in decision-making and problem-solving groups: An expanded view. In M. S. Poole & R. Y. Hirokawa (Eds.), *Communication and group decision making* (pp. 55–80). Thousand Oaks, CA: Sage.

Graen, G., & Uhl-Bien, M. (1995). Development of leader-member exchange theory of leadership over 25 years: Applying a multilevel perspective. *Leadership Quarterly, 6,* 219–247.

Gray, J. (1992). *Men are from Mars, Women are from Venus: A practical guide to improving communication and getting what you want in your relationships.* New York: HarperCollins.

Griffin, E. (2000). *A first look at communication theory* (4th ed.). New York: McGraw-Hill.

Griffin, E. (2003). *A first look at communication theory* (5th ed.). New York: McGraw-Hill.

Guerrero, L. K., & Burgoon, J. K. (1996). Attachment styles and reactions to nonverbal involvement change in romantic dyads: Patterns of reciprocity and compensation. *Human Communication Research, 22,* 335–336.

Guerrero, L. K., Jones, S. M., & Burgoon, J. K. (2000). Responses to nonverbal intimacy change in romantic dyads: Effects of behavioral valence and degree of behavioral change on nonverbal and verbal reactions. *Communication Monographs, 67,* 325–346.

Hall, E. T. (1976). *Beyond culture.* Garden City, NY: Doubleday.

Hall, A. D., & Fagen, R. E. (1968). Definition of a system. In W. Buckley (Ed.), *Modern systems research for the behavioral scientist* (pp. 81–92). Chicago: Aldine.

Hammonds, D. I. (2003, July 23). Disappearing act; Gains made during robust '90s are evaporating for African Americans. *Pittsburgh Post Gazette,* p. B-9.

Hartsock, N. (1983). The feminist standpoint: Developing the ground for a specifically feminist historical materialism. In S. Harding & M. B. Hintikka (Eds.), *Discovering reality* (pp. 283–310). Boston: Riedel.

Hecht, M. L., Collier, M. J., & Ribeau, S. A. (1993). *African American communication: Ethnic identity and interpretation.* Newbury Park, CA: Sage.

Hegel, G. W. F. (1966). *The phenomenology of mind* (2nd ed., J. B. Braillie, Trans.). New York: Humanities Press. (Original work published 1807)

Heider, F. (1958). *The Psychology of Interpersonal Relations.* New York: Wiley.

Hirokawa, R. Y. (1994). Functional approaches to the study of group discussion: Even good notions have their problems. *Small Group Research, 25,* 542–550.

Hirokawa, R. Y., & Salazar, A. J. (1999). Task-group communication and decision-making performance. In L .R. Frey, D. S. Gouran, & M. S. Poole (Eds.), *The handbook of group communication theory and research* (pp. 167–191). Thousand Oaks, CA: Sage.

Hofstede, G. (1980). *Culture's consequences.* Beverly Hills, CA: Sage.

Hofstede, G. (1986). Cultural differences in teaching and learning. *International Journal of Intercultural Relations, 10,* 301–319.

Hofstede, G. (2001). *Culture's consequences: International differences in work-related values* (2nd ed.). Beverly Hills, CA: Sage.

Hofstede, G., & Bond, M. H. (1984). Hofstede's culture dimensions: An independent validation using Rokeach's value survey. *Journal of Cross Cultural Pscyhology, 15,* 417–433.

Holston, N. (2003, August 10). They're queer. They're here . . . But will mainstream America accept the new wave of gays on TV? *Fanfare,* p. D10.

Huckins, K. (1999). Interest-group influence on the media agenda: A case study. *Journalism and Mass Communication Quarterly, 76,* 76–86.

Huesmann, L. R., Moise-Titus, J., Podolski, C. L., & Eron, L. D. (2003). Longitudinal relations between children's exposure to TV violence and their aggressive and violent behavior in young adulthood 1977–1992. *Developmental Psychology, 39,* 201–221.

Iyengar, S., Peters, M., & Kinder, D. (1982). Experimental demonstrations of the "not-so-minimal" consequences of television news programs. *American Political Science Review, 76,* 848–858.

Jandt, F. E. (2004). *An introduction to intercultural communication: Identities in a global community.* Thousand Oaks, CA: Sage.

Janis, I. L. (1972). *Victims of groupthink: A psychological study of foreign-policy decisions and fiascoes.* Boston: Houghton Mifflin.

Janis, I. L. (1982). *Groupthink: Psychological studies of policy decisions and fiascoes.* Boston: Houghton Mifflin.

Jones, D. S. (2001, February). Just what the doctor ordered. *Real Estate Center at Texas A&M University.* Retrieved December 2, 2002, from http://recenter.tamu.edu/news/42-0201.html

Jones, E. E., & Davis, K. E. (1965). From acts to dispositions: The attribution process in person perception. In L. Berkowitz (Ed.), *Advances in Experimental Social Psychology* (Vol. 2, pp. 220–266). Orlando, FL: Academic Press.

Katz, E., Blumler, J. G., & Gurevitch, M. (1973). Uses and gratifications research. *Public Opinion Quarterly, 37,* 509–523.

Kelley, H. H. (1967). Attribution theory in social psychology. *Nebraska Symposium on Motivation,* 15, 192–238.

Kelley, H. H. (1973). The processes of causal attribution. *American Psychologist, 28,* 107–128.

Kilbourne, J. (1999). *Deadly persuasion: Why women and girls must fight the addictive power of advertising.* New York: Free Press.

Kilmann, R. H., & Thomas, K. W. (1977). Developing a forced-choice measure of conflict-handling behavior. The MODE instrument. *Educational and Psychological Measurement, 37,* 309–325.

Kim, E. Y. (2001). *The yin and the yang of American culture: A paradox.* Yarmouth, ME: Intercultural Press.

Kirk, M. K., & Pill, E. (1987/2003). The overhauling of straight America [electronic version]. Retrieved January 7, 2004, from http://www.sphi.com/the_gay_agenda.htm

Kotter, J. P. (1990). What leaders really do. *Harvard Business Review, 68,* 103–111.

Kramarae, C. (1981). *Women and men speaking: Frameworks for analysis.* Rowley, MA: Newbury House.

Lamke, L. K., Sollie, D. L., Durbin, R. G., & Fitzpatrick, J. A. (1994). Masculinity, femininity, and relationship satisfaction: The mediating role of interpersonal competence. *Journal of Social and Personal Relationships, 11*, 535–554.

Larkey, L. K. (1996). Toward a theory of communicative interactions in culturally diverse workgroups. *Academy of Management Review, 21*, 463–491.

Lewin, K. (1951). *Field theory in social science: Selected theoretical papers.* New York: Harper & Row.

Lewis, R. D. (2000). *When cultures collide: Managing successfully across cultures.* London: Nicholas Brealey.

Light, T. (2002). Thinking ahead about buyer's remorse. *RealEstate ABC.* Retrieved November 20, 2003, from http://content.realestateabc.com/homebuying/remorse.htm

Likert, R. (1961). *New patterns of management.* New York: McGraw-Hill.

Littlejohn, S. W. (1999). *Theories of human communication* (3rd ed.). Belmont, CA: Wadsworth.

Littlejohn, S. W. (2002). *Theories of human communication* (7th ed.). Belmont, CA: Wadsworth.

Littlejohn, S. W., Rogers, R., & Gray, R. (1996). *Faculty desk reference: Theories of Human Communication* (5th ed). New York: Wadsworth.

Maccoby, E. E. (1990). Gender and relationships: A developmental account. American Psychologist, *45*, 513–520.

Mael, F., & Ashforth, B. E. (1992). Alumni and their alma mater: A partial test of the reformulated model of organizational identification. *Journal of Organizational Behavior, 13*, 103–123.

Maltz, D., & Borker, R. (1982). A cultural approach to male-female miscommunication. In J. J. Gumpertz (Ed.), *Language and social identity* (pp. 196–216). Cambridge, England: Cambridge University Press.

Manzoni, J. F., & Barsoux, J. L. (2002). *The set-up-to-fail syndrome: How good managers cause great people to fail.* Cambridge, MA: Harvard Business Press.

McCombs, M., & Bell, T. (1974). The agenda-setting role of mass communication. In M. Salwen & D. Stacks (Eds.), *An integrated approach to communication theory and research* (pp. 100). Hillside, NJ: Erlbaum.

McCombs, M., & Shaw, D. (1972). The agenda-setting function of the mass media. *Public Opinion Quarterly, 36*, 176–187.

McPhee, R. D. (1985). Formal structure and organizational communication. In R. D. McPhee & P. K. Tompkins (Eds.), *Organizational communication: Traditional themes and new directions* (pp. 149–178). Beverly Hills, CA: Sage.

McQuail, D. (1987). *Mass communication theory: An introduction* (2nd ed.). Newbury Park, CA: Sage.

Menon, V. (2003, August 14). Buy-sexual TV getting ridiculous. *The Toronto Star*, p. A30.

Mieder, W. W. (1986). *Encyclopedia of world proverbs: A treasury of wit and wisdom through the ages.* Englewood Cliffs, NJ: Prentice Hall.

Millar, F. E., & Rogers, L. E. (1976). A relational approach to interpersonal communication. In G. R. Miller (Ed.), *Explorations in interpersonal communication* (pp. 87–203). Beverly Hills, CA: Sage.

Miller, G. R. (1978). The current status of theory and research in interpersonal communication. *Human Communication Research, 4,* 164–178.

Miller, K. (2002). *Communication theories: Perspectives, processes, and contexts.* New York: McGraw-Hill.

Miller, K. (2003). *Organizational communication: Approaches and processes* (3rd ed.). Belmont, CA: Wadsworth.

Modaff, D. O., & DeWine, S. (2002). *Organizational communication: Foundations, challenges, misunderstandings.* Los Angeles, CA: Roxbury.

Monge, P. R. (1973). Theory construction in the study of communication: The system paradigm. *Journal of Communication, 23,* 5–16.

Montgomery, B. M. (1993). Relationship maintenance versus relationship change: Dialectical dilemma. *Journal of Social and Personal Relationships, 10,* 205–224.

Morley, D. D., & Shockley-Zalabak, P. (1991). Setting the rules: An examination of organizational founders' values. *Management Communication Quarterly, 4,* 422–449.

Morton, T. D. (1999, October). Understanding organizational culture. *Ideas in Action, a publication of the Child Welfare Institute.* Retrieved July 16, 2003, from http:// www.gocwi.org/pdf/ideas1999october.pdf

Motley, M. T. (1991). How one may not communicate: A reply to Andersen. *Communication Studies, 42,* 326–339.

Mulac, A., Bradac, J. J., & Gibbons, P. (2001). Empirical support for the gender-as-culture hypothesis: An intercultural analysis of male/female language differences. *Human Communication Research, 27,* 121–152.

Nystrom, P. C. (1990). Vertical exchanges and organizational commitments of American business managers. *Group and Organizational Studies, 15,* 296–312.

O'Keefe, B. J. (1988). The logic of message design: Individual differences in reasoning about communication. *Communication Monographs, 55,* 80–103.

O'Keefe, B. J. (1997). Variation, adaptation, and functional explanation in the study of message design. In G. Philipsen, & T. L. Albrecht (Eds.), *Developing communication theories* (pp. 85–118). Albany: State University of New York Press.

O'Keefe, B. J., & Delia, J. G. (1988). Communicative tasks and communicative practices: The development of audience-centered message production. In B. Rafoth & D. Rubin (Eds.), *The social construction of written communication* (pp. 70–98). Norwood, NJ: Ablex.

O'Keefe, B. J., Lambert, B. L., & Lambert, C. A. (1997). Conflict and communication in a research and development unit. In B. D. Sypher (Ed.), *Case studies in organizational communication 2* (pp. 31–52). New York: Guilford Press.

O'Keefe, D. J. (1990). *Persuasion: Theory and research.* Newbury Park, CA: Sage.

Oetzel, J. G., & S. Ting-Toomey. (2003). Face concerns in interpersonal conflict: A cross-cultural empirical test of the face negotiation theory. *Communication Research, 30,* 599–624.

Palmer, B., Walls, M., Burgess, Z., & Stough, C. (2001). Emotional intelligence and effective leadership. *Leadership & Organization Development Journal, 22,* 5–11.

Parkinson, J. R. (2003, March 24). Business advice column. *Milwaukee Journal Sentinel.* Retrieved July 14, 2003, from the LexisNexis database.

Parks, M. R., & Adelman, M. B. (1983). Communication networks and the development of romantic relationships: An expansion of uncertainty reduction theory. *Human Communication Research, 10,* 55–79.

Pattee, H. H. (Ed.). (1973). *Hierarchy theory: The challenge of complex systems.* New York: Braziller.

Peake, J. S. (2001). Presidential agenda setting in foreign policy. *Political Research Quarterly, 54,* 69–86.

Peters, R. S. (1974). Personal understanding and personal relationships. In T. Mischel (Ed.) *Understanding other persons.* Oxford, England: Rowman and Littlefield.

Petty, R. E., & Cacioppo, J. T. (1986). *Communication and persuasion: Central and peripheral routes to attitude change.* New York: Spring-Verlag.

Poole, M. S. (1985). Communication and organizational climates: Review, critique, and a new perspective. In R. D. McPhee & P. K. Tompkins (Eds.), *Organizational communication: Traditional themes and new directions* (pp. 79–108). Beverly Hills, CA: Sage.

Poole, M. S. (1988). *Communication and the structuring of organizations.* Unpublished manuscript, University of Minnesota, Minneapolis.

Poole, M. S. (1999). Group communication theory. In L .R. Frey, D. S. Gouran, & M. S. Poole (Eds.), *The handbook of group communication theory and research* (pp. 37–70). Thousand Oaks, CA: Sage.

Poole, M. S., & McPhee, R. D. (1983). A structurational approach to organizational climate. In L. L. Putnam & M. E. Pacanowsky (Eds.), *Communication and organizations: An interpretive approach* (pp. 195–220). Beverly Hills, CA: Sage.

Poole, M. S., Seibold, D. R., & McPhee, R. D. (1985). Group decision-making as a structurational process. *Quarterly Journal of Speech, 71,* 74–102.

Poole, M. S., Seibold, D. R., & McPhee, R. D. (1986). A structurational approach to theory-building in group decision-making research. In R. Y. Hirokawa & M. S. Poole (Eds.), *Communication and group decision-making* (pp. 237–264). Beverly Hills, CA: Sage.

Poole, O. (2002, October 3). Life turns nasty for TV's Queen of Nice. *The London Daily Telegraph,* 17.

Putnam, L. L., & Conrad, C. R. (1999). Teaching organizational communication. In A. L. Vangelisti, J. A. Daly, & G. W. Friedrich (Eds.), *Teaching communication: Theory, research, and methods* (2nd ed.). Mahwah, NJ: Erlbaum.

Ragins, B. R., Townsend, B., & Mattis, M. (1998). Gender gap in the executive suite: CEOs and female executives report on breaking the glass ceiling. *Academy of Management Executive, 12,* 28–42.

Rahim, M. A. (1986). *Managing conflict in organizations.* New York: Praeger.

Rapoport, A. (1968). The promises and pitfalls of information theory. In W. Buckley (Ed.), *Modern systems research for the behavioral scientist* (pp. 137–142). Chicago: Aldine.

Reinard, J. (1998). *Introduction to communication research,* 2nd ed. New York: McGraw-Hill.

Reynolds, P. D. (1971). *A primer on theory construction.* New York: Bobbs Merrill.

Richmond, V. P., & McCroskey, J. C. (1979). Management communication style, tolerance for disagreement, and innovativeness as predictors of employee satisfaction: A comparison of single-factor, two-factor, and multiple-factor approaches. In D. Nimmo (Ed.), *Communication yearbook 3* (pp. 359–373). New Brunswick, NJ: Transaction Books.

Roeper, R. (2003, August 4). "Gay summer" a big hit, but not at White House, Vatican. *Chicago Sun-Times,* p. 11.

Rothwell, J. D. (1998). *In mixed company: Small group communication* (3rd ed.). New York: Harcourt Brace.

Salant, P., & Dillman, D. A. (1994). *How to conduct your own survey.* New York: Wiley.

Salazar, A. J. (1995). Understanding the synergistic effects of communication in small groups: Making the most out of group member abilities. *Small Group Research, 26,* 169–199.

Schein, E. H. (1985). *Organizational culture and leadership.* San Francisco: Jossey-Bass.

Schein, E. H. (1992). *Organizational culture and leadership* (2nd ed.). San Francisco: Jossey-Bass.

Segrin, C., & Nabi, R. L. (2002). Does television viewing cultivate unrealistic expectations about marriage? *Journal of Communication, 52,* 247–263.

Shanker, A., Elliott, R., & Goulding, C. (2001). *Understanding consumption: Contributions from a narrative perspective.* Retrieved January 7, 2004 from http://www.ex.ac.uk/sobe/Research/DiscussionPapersMan/Man2000/Man0009.pdf

Shockley-Zalabak, P. (2002). *Fundamentals of organizational communication* (5th ed.). Boston: Allyn and Bacon.

Sherif, M., & Hovland, C. I. (1961). *Social judgment.* New Haven, CT: Yale University Press.

Sherif, C. W., Sherif, M., & Nebergall, R. E. (1965). *Attitude and social change.* Philadelphia: Saunders.

Signorelli, N., Gerbner, G., & Morgan, M. (1995). Violence on television: The cultural indicators project. *Journal of Broadcasting and Electronic Media, 39,* 278–283.

Sillars, A. L. (1980). The sequential and distributional structure of conflict interactions as a function of attributions concerning the locus of responsibility and stability of conflicts. In D. Nimmo (Ed.), *Communication yearbook 4* (pp. 217–235). New Brunswick, NJ: Transaction Books.

Simons, H. W. (1976). *Persuasion: Understanding, practice, and analysis.* Reading, MA: Addison-Wesley.

Sivanathan, N., & Fekken, G. C. (2002). Emotional intelligence, moral reasoning, and transformational leadership. *Leadership & Organization Development Journal, 23,* 198–204.

Sparks, G. G. (2002). *Media effects research: A basic overview.* Stamford, CT: Wadsworth.

Spitzberg, B. H., & Cupach, W. R. (1984). *Interpersonal communication competence.* Newbury Park, CA: Sage.

Spitzberg, B. H., & Cupach, W. R. (1989). *Handbook of interpersonal competence research.* New York: Springer-Verlag.

Stop Promoting Homosexuality International. (1999). *The Gay Agenda.* Retrieved August 14, 2003, from http://www.sphi.com/the_gay_agenda. htm

Tannen, D. (1990). *You just don't understand: Women and men in conversation.* New York: Morrow.

Texter, L. A. (1995). Attribution theory. In R. L. Hartman & L. A. Texter (Eds.), *Advanced interpersonal communication* (pp. 53–68). Dubuque, IA: Kendall Hunt.

Thibaut, J. W., & Kelley, H. H. (1959). *The social psychology of groups.* New Brunswick, NJ: Transaction Books.

Thomas, K. W., & Kilmann, R. H. (1974). *Thomas-Kilmann conflict mode instrument.* Tuxedo, NY: Xicom.

Ting-Toomey, S. (1988). Intercultural conflicts: A face-negotiation theory. In Y. Kim & W. Gudykunst (Eds.), *Theories in intercultural communication* (pp. 213–238). Newbury Park, CA: Sage.

Ting-Toomey, S. (1991a). Intimacy expression in three cultures: France, Japan, and the United States. *International Journal of Intercultural Relations, 15,* 29–46.

Ting-Toomey, S. (1991b). Cross-cultural communication: An introduction. In S. Ting-Toomey & F. Korzenny (Eds.), *Cross-cultural interpersonal communication* (pp. 1–7). Newbury Park, CA: Sage.

Ting-Toomey, S. (1992, April). *Cross-cultural face-negotiation: An analytical overview.* Paper presented at the meeting of the Pacific Region Forum on Business and Management Communication, Vancouver, British Columbia.

Ting-Toomey, S. (1994). Managing intercultural conflicts effectively. In L. Samovar & R. Porter (Eds.), *Intercultural communication* (7th ed., pp. 360–372). Belmont, CA: Wadsworth.

Ting-Toomey, S., & Oetzel, J. (2002). Cross-cultural face concerns and conflict styles: Current status and future directions. In W. Gudykunst & B. Mody (Eds.), *Handbook of international and intercultural communication* (2nd ed., pp. 143–164). Thousand Oaks, CA: Sage.

Tompkins, P. K., & Cheney, G. E. (1985). Communication and unobtrusive control in contemporary organizations. In R. D. McPhee & P. K. Tompkins (Eds.), *Organizational communication: Traditional themes and new directions* (pp. 179–210). Beverly Hills, CA: Sage.

Triandis, H. C. (1995). *Individualism and collectivism.* Boulder, CO: Westview Press.

Troemel-Ploetz, S. (1991). Selling the apolitical. *Discourse and Society, 2,* 489–502.

United States Equal Opportunity Employment Commission. (n.d.). *Job patterns for minorities and women in private industry, 2001.* Retrieved August 12, 2003, from http://www.eeoc.gov/stats/jobpat/2001/national.html

Vecchio, R. P., Griffeth, R. W., & Hom, P. W. (1986). The predictive utility of the vertical dyad linkage approach. *Journal of Social Psychology, 126,* 617–625.

Vivero, V. N., & Jenkins, S. R. (1999). Existential hazards of the multicultural individual: Defining and understanding "cultural homelessness." *Cultural Diversity and Ethnic Minority Psychology, 5,* 6–26.

Von Bertalanffy, L. (1968). *General system theory: Foundations, development, applications* (rev. ed.). New York: Braziller.

Von Sternberg, B. (2003, August 10). Climate has changed on gay-rights issues; What seems to be a sudden burst in recent weeks affecting gay-related issues has been long in the making. *Minneapolis Star Tribune,* p. 1A.

Wadsworth, A. J., Patterson, R., Cullers, G., Malcomb, D., Lamirand, L., & Kaid, L. L. (1987). "Masculine" vs. "feminine" strategies in political ads: Implications for female candidates. *Journal of Applied Communication Research, 15,* 77–94.

Watzlawick, P., Bavelas, J. B., & Jackson, D. D. (1967). *Pragmatics of human communication: A study of interactional patterns, pathologies, and paradoxes.* New York: Norton.

Weick, K. E. (1969). *The social psychology of organizing.* Reading, MA: Addison-Wesley.

West, R., & Turner, L. H. (2000). *Introducing communication theory: Analysis and application.* Mountain View, CA: Mayfield.

Women Employed Institute. (2002). *The glass ceiling.* Retrieved October 24, 2003, from http://www.womenemployed.org/facts/glass_ceiling.html

Wood, J. T. (1993). Gender and moral voice: From woman's nature to standpoint theory. *Women's Studies in Communication, 15,* 1–24.

Wood, J. T., & Dindia, K. (1998). What's the difference? A dialogue about differences and similarities between women and men. In D. J. Canary & K. Dindia (Eds.), *Sex differences and similarities in communication: Critical essays and empirical investigations of sex and gender in interaction* (pp. 19–39). Mahwah, NJ: Erlbaum.

Wulff, D. H., & Nyquist, J. D. (1999). Selected tools and methods to engage students in learning. In A. L. Vangelisti, J. A. Daly, & G. W. Friedrich (Eds.), *Teaching communication: Theory, research, and methods* (2nd ed.). Mahwah, NJ: Erlbaum.

Wyatt, N. (1993). Organizing and relating: Feminist critiques of small group communication. In S. P. Bowen & N. Wyatt (Eds.), *Transforming visions: Feminist critiques in communication studies* (pp. 51–86). Cresskill, NJ: Hampton.

Zimbardo, P. G., Ebbesen, E. B., & Maslach, C. (1977). *Influencing attitudes and changing behavior.* New York: Random House.

Zurawick, D. (2003, August 13). Make way for the "metrosexual man": Unlike the old TV staples—the breadwinner, the cop, the doctor—he's getting in touch with his feminine side. *The Baltimore Sun,* p. D5.

Index